LOVEY

Liv Amber Rose

LOVEY

Copyright © 2022 Liv Amber Rose

All rights reserved.

ISBN: 9798843968373

LOVEY

This is for those who feel they have had a part taken from them, which they never allowed for another to take.

For those who use their notes app as free therapy.

For the men who sense no one understands how it can feel to be so complex, in a society that teaches you to remain silent.

For the hearts who have lost someone who they loved more than themselves.

…This is for anyone that needs to feel less alone.

LOVEY

Before you commence into Liv's mind I'd like to say, everything you are about the read is truthful, non-fiction. Every word, every text, every letter, it all happened.

From the beginning, I never wanted to embellish the story. Because if I had, it would never to be able to connect authentically to those who need something real, tangible, in the moments you need it most.

So, the journey you're about to enter is the closest to the truth I could get you, without you having to live it for yourself.

LOVEY

This is for those who feel they have had a part taken from them, which they never allowed for another to take.

For those who use their notes app as free therapy.

For the men who sense no one understands how it can feel to be so complex, in a society that teaches you to remain silent.

For the hearts who have lost someone who they loved more than themselves.

…This is for anyone that needs to feel less alone.

LOVEY

Before you commence into Liv's mind I'd like to say, everything you are about the read is truthful, non-fiction. Every word, every text, every letter, it all happened.

From the beginning, I never wanted to embellish the story. Because if I had, it would never to be able to connect authentically to those who need something real, tangible, in the moments you need it most.

So, the journey you're about to enter is the closest to the truth I could get you, without you having to live it for yourself.

LOVEY

<u>I would like to put a trigger warning before you read any further.</u>

In this book you'll witness,
the act of sexual assault,
the word 'rape',
themes of self-harm,
eating disorders,
suicidal thoughts,
sex,
death,
love and
heart break.

LOVEY

Now, with that in mind,
we shall begin…

LOVEY

Introduction

It's cold. No, it's numb. It's nothing.

It was the 23rd of July 2021, when the twenty-four-year-old, five-foot-four, black-haired Liv, you'll soon meet, lost her life. Not in the sense she is no longer physically existing, but in the understanding her life as she knew it was taken from her. Stolen, after someone decided they had the right to take her body. Take the only part she had left to protect, the part she knew if she ever lost, things would never be the same.

You see, you'll learn Liv is lost but brave, she's hurt but a hopeless romantic, she's numb but, simultaneously, she feels everything and now she no longer exists and is having to rediscover what it all means.

This is the fall out. Aftermath. A journey set in motion after a date, a date you'll witness in the form of reliving with her while we backtrack to explain just how we got *here*. *Here*, being broken, *here* being a floating form of who she knew she was.

I wish I could tell you that this story ends with Liv overcoming her trauma and somehow the universe guiding her back home into the

LOVEY

arms of her person, Rowan, Roe. You'll meet Roe. Where everything works out and they both journey into the sunset, after travelling the world, to build the most incredible life, in spite of all the pain existing has subjected her too. But this is not how this story ends, in fact, it ends quite differently. You'll come face to face with the important players in Liv's life, they each have their story, but you'll find Roe scattered throughout. His and Liv's tale intertwines itself around the year you are about to live and beyond.

There are many important moments which we must visit. But for time's sake, there will be windows we only peek in, doors we push ajar to only poke our heads in, but there will be others where we take a deep breath, turn the handle, walk slowly inside, and sit down. We'll sit and feel how it felt and live these moments for ourselves.

You'll find Liv just before that night and you'll hear her words through these pages, that's if you'll listen. The purpose of this is not to harm or trigger but to soothe, to connect, to feel less alone. There are many books about healing from trauma, sexual abuse, and heartbreak but this isn't one of them. This is, however, where Liv has poured her soul and is hoping you'll be gentle with it.

LOVEY

Chapter One

It was ironic really, she went on these dates to feel *something*, provoke an emotion other than the hollowness, misery that had become her normal. The emptiness that your left with when you lose the only thing in your world that meant anything to you. Not just anything, *but everything.*

After a final point of heart-breaking devastation, she went on the only way she knew how. She made a desperate attempt to fill her void riddled life with new friends, dates, and be kept busy with extra hours at the ethical clothing shop she worked in, located in the lanes of Brighton, all while in the summer break before her final year of university. The shop she worked in, had since 2019, sold bright, colourful clothes. They were famous for their dungarees in particular. She always regarded herself lucky after getting that job. It was a cult brand, famous in Brighton and had a sunny work culture. She had come from working part time in large supermarkets so to have a job she genuinely enjoyed whilst alongside her Neuroscience degree made her feel grateful. Not only were the clothes colourful but so were her colleagues. They all quickly became friends and made every shift feel like that rare concept – *'that work could be fun and joyful'*. She never wore much colour herself, so when new

LOVEY

collections were released, she'd often take the darkest or only black option as uniform. Regardless of the fact that she'd never rock the latest pair of vibrantly printed dungarees, she was often complimented on her muted twist and was always welcomed by the team who admired her stylings of the ethical clothing.

The new friends she had gathered through switching her dating app into *'friend mode'*, became everything she was looking for and would quickly turn into her closest friends. Liv had always been quality over quantity in terms of who she kept in her life but was also extremely talented at isolating herself when need be. It left her starting from scratch. The bonds she started building began translating into fun memories being made and was able to share that common feeling young women get when they are not already part of an established friendship group, going out every weekend, updating each other every day in a WhatsApp chat, with a cute group name composed of an inside joke. She had found girls that wanted to fill that same deprived part of themselves with laughs and cocktails whilst also navigating their dating disasters and quarter life crisis'. The dates she fully booked herself with induced a sense of confidence that was only growing, starting from an already barren point. All these new plans and different characters in her life kept her busy and her part time job kept all these distractions just barely funded. Splitting time between the home she had built in her one-bedroom flat positioned on the seafront of Brighton and Hove and her new friends residing in London, her life was quickly drawing her up to the capital. Life had technically never looked so full, and if we were judging from her Instagram, she looked busy and happy. Consistently sharing her latest outing and her latest gym session, posting the routines that had contributed to the four stone weight loss she had achieved in under six months, quickly requiring the rediscovery of her new physique. She stayed constantly surrounded by friends, seemed the most confident she had ever been, and most certainly miles away from any former self. But *she knew*, all along it felt like *nothing*. She was desperate to feel *something*, but she felt out in the cold, numb. She was walking down an icy dark road, with raw

LOVEY

bitter air running over her skin, turning her numb just to survive. She knew it should have, brought some degree of happiness. Every time she was sat with friends in a bar drinking her favourite alcoholic concoction or sunbathing on Clapham Common during an unusual English heatwave. However, she'd always return home with the same feeling. No matter what she did, where she went, how much she loved her friends, or how drunk she got, she always ended up at the same the door. The door of emptiness. Where you turn the handle, step inside, and sit. You sit down in the empty room, on the only chair positioned in the corner and are confronted with the bareness you feel. No more distractions and just the silent truth of what you are left with after losing the person that used to make that room so full, that used to make that room, *home.* So, you now use the place you used to call home to recover, house your belongings, where you sleep and eat, but it is not home. She could no longer find her way *home.* Trying to outrun what she knew standing still would mean. She began a path of self-destruction in a way that seemed beautiful from the outside and could only take acknowledgment when life took her efforts of distraction and halted her into a place of nothingness. She had promised herself these changes would make her happy, if only she had them. She felt hollow sat on these dates with men she occupied her nights with. The men she always hoped she'd receive attention from. *Perhaps it was temporary?* she thought, and *maybe that it was even a good thing?* She rarely stopped for a moment to truly think of why or what she was doing. Maybe because if she did, she'd realise her motives were driven by Roe's ability to exchange them for meaningless casual interactions with strangers. After he broke her heart, she thought *'if he can do it, so can I'.* And after all, she started to believe, maybe it was preferable she didn't feel too deeply for anyone, *after Roe…*

LOVEY

*

Oscar

Oscar embodied everything she had desired. He ticked every box on paper. He was tall, six-foot-three. Brown wavy haired rugby player who lived in London, and among the few she was spreading her time texting across, after the absence of Roe in her life, it was his name she would hope to see, and it often was. When she started to date, she knew she had nothing to offer these people other than a casual part of her time and self. She made this clear. Before she knew it, she was stood at Clapham North tube station, where she was not long before after her last encounter with Roe, dragging herself away from her one true person. But this time she was stood in a little black strappy top, exposing a little under-boob, her beloved Motel Rocks brown patterned trousers and beige converse which made her just a touch taller. Stood at the entrance, making it through the tube barriers, facing out to the main road and the pub on the opposite corner, she turned left and made her way down the high street. Oscar had asked her to tell him when she was on the tube so he could come meet her when she arrived, but she didn't. She didn't like the idea of him stood waiting for her. The thought intimidated her slightly. She wanted to settle first, make sure her makeup looked fresh and to feel a touch more in control. That evening Oscar had been watching the Euro semi-finals and had bailed on their plans to meet for a drink before, so the plan changed and was now for her to go straight to his which he shared with three other boys. The change didn't bother her like she thought it might. Maybe because she knew the date part didn't mean anything to either of them. She was almost a little proud of the fact that she had grown so much in her confidence that she didn't need to text someone for a long period of time, in this case a week, to just rock up. She had been used too, in the past, building such a repour before the first meet but this was just one of the signs, she knew she had changed. Maybe not for better, just a little numb now. She went into all dates with the mindset of *'I'm way more concerned of if I like you, than if you like me'*

LOVEY

but doubts always creep in. *Always.* She texted him she had arrived to which she followed up with visiting the local Sainsburys while she waited and to look for any cans of gin she could take with her. Finally, after deciding against the gin, her phone lit up with…

29th June 2021. 20:53pm

> Oscar: Oh I was going to come get you!
>
> I'll come over x
>
> Where are you

She left the corner shop and walked the short journey up the road to where Oscar was stood across from her, in his overly casual entre, a loose t-shirt she would later sleep in and jeans. She was a touch disappointed at his lack of effect for the briefest of moments. She looked left and right before making her way across the overly wide road to reach him. This is where the self-doubt set in. They wrapped one arm around the other, half hugging each other and started the short walk to his house. A mixture of nerves and excitement flooded her body. She liked him. In the way she intended. He was gorgeous, in societal standards, being extremely good looking. And also, a little posh and well spoken. He had a strong jaw line and a nice smile with good teeth. He had the type of cheeks that easily flush a rosy colour which she did adore. Her friends described him as extremely good looking but also looking like he could have a trust fund, they giggled over this. Eventually, they got to his bedroom after completing a decent amount of small talk. After climbing multiple flights of stairs, they reached his room. It was filled with stuffy warm air and a window that overlooked the Clapham High Street overground track. Hesitant to let her makeup sweat off from the humidity, she went to change in the one of two bathrooms situated outside his room. She placed her black satin shorts and cropped shirt over her red Loungewear lingerie set which, to her, felt a touch

LOVEY

powerful as it's a bra and thong Roe never saw. She walked back in with a level of internal confidence she had actually never felt before. Nothing loud or obvious from the outside. She sat on the bed with the red wine he had handed her as she lowered herself to his level. She felt happy with the situation she had entered into. Her mind wondered for a moment. She was weirdly conscious over the fact that Roe was probably home, only a two-minute walk away. What were the odds she'd match someone so close to him? He sat beside her on the bed. Intense eye contact told her that, any minute, as she was talking, he would kiss her, so she did what *this* Liv would do, she kissed him first. She thought he was so unbelievably handsome and felt entirely safe. As their kiss intensified, he grabbed her waist and placed her on his lap. Not long after, Oscar stood his tall frame up, wrapping her legs around him manually. This response did not come naturally as she'd never usually let anyone lift her up and hadn't settled into the fact that she weighed a lot less than she used too and was now a small size eight. Whilst still in mid-air, being held by this incredibly strong almost stranger, he placed his well-endowed self inside and a breath was taken away. And even though he was dominate and powerful, she felt in control with clear communication always and a tiny bit of magic mixed in.
As they took breaks from their indulgent evening, he surprised her at every point. His compassion for the environment, awareness of mental health struggles and self-analysis. He confessed his experience with panic attacks, being able to emphasise with Liv. She felt ever so slightly connected to him whilst knowing the situation they were in was nothing special to either of them. But he was a good guy, and she was just happy he was more than she had expected him to be, being the first person she had slept with, since Roe.
All evening and night he continued to be incredibly affectionate with her. Laying down for an exhausted embrace he would grab her, pulling her in, whilst squeezing her tightly, but in an almost loving way. She gave very little affection back though, to the point he affirmed…
"You're not that affectionate, are you?

LOVEY

Little did he know she had been labelled Roe's little backpack due to the love for clinging to him at all times.
Looking out away from him, she internally answered with *"just with the right people."* but outwardly, did not meet his comment with much rebuttal. As the night reached the early hours of the morning, the pair quietly laid in bed as *'All Eyes On Me'* by Bo Burnham played out his laptop whilst they both fell to sleep.

…But as much as Oscar seemed faultless and on paper, was perfect, especially for Liv, he wasn't. No one was… but him, *but Roe*.

This was **not** the date that turned the already empty Liv into, *well*, the Liv that is now what you'd describe as someone who is physically alive but is gone.

She left Oscar's feeling quietly powerful after doing something she had never done before whilst also feeling no emotional attachment towards him. She thought this was growth but maybe it was because that part of her that she used to connect to others was already dying.

Dying from all the heartbreak.

LOVEY

23rd of July 2021

The night Liv survived and then *died* all at once.

LOVEY

*

Yellow handprints

She looked in the mirror, double taking the state her body had been left in, she looked closer at her back, bum, and down her legs. Curving her neck round trying to capture as much as she could of her body. She became fixated on the glowing red handprints that had been tattooed on to her body. Hands so red, the insides of the fingers had gone yellowish from the blood escaping the area. *She knew it hurt.* Adrenaline had not masked the pain her mind tried to escape but seeing the proof… the physical evidence revoked a reaction deep inside her already complex psychology. She stayed in the locked, hospital-like bathroom with the cold harsh white light beaming above her, as long as she could, staring at the vessel she no longer recognised, till she knew she had to re-emerge. She contemplated her options. Couldn't leave, it was the middle of the night, nowhere to go. She was in pain and scared. *The damage was already done*, she concluded in her mind. Her own consciousness trapped her, but only with intentions to survive, keep Liv alive. Lifting the safety handle anti-clockwise which in turn unlocked the door, she made her way back, purposefully laying each foot down softly on the laminate floor, trying to remain silent. Finally reaching the bed, she slipped herself under the duvet. Taking her battery pack out of her handbag, she plugged in her phone, curled up as far away as the width of the bed would allow and passed away to sleep. The next she woke it was nearly eight, being the time she had set her alarm, catching it before the man could be woken. Disorientation hit like a tonne of bricks, only being accelerated by the lack of sunlight as a result of the absence of windows in the hotel room. It felt like she had stepped into her own personal prison. There was something about that room from the moment she stepped foot inside. The type of room you'd put any living organism in, and it would die. Plants immediately become brown and limp, animals curl up in the corner like they couldn't bear to exist there. It was as though she could feel

LOVEY

something would change once engulfed behind the locked door. Like all her bubbly energy drained away. The essence of her, *stolen.*

She finally left that room, that hotel. The minute she woke she gently slid out of the bed, doing her best not to disturb him. Back in the bathroom, although this time she was on a mission. She clothed herself in last night's entre and brushed her hair over the sink. It felt like she had served a prison sentence and today was her release day. She had no idea what would now lay out there, in the world, but it had to be better than this small claustrophobic room where life goes to die. Gathering all her belongings, she quietly unlatched the room door, made her way down the halls, past the front desk and suddenly she had surfaced into the morning sun. Hastily walking to Old Street tube station, she demanded her little legs to carry her as far away as they could, as quickly as possible. It had already begun. She found herself starting to bargain with her internal fears. Trying to make sense of it whilst remaining detached. Putting the whole night down to *'bad sex'* and him being into sexual preferences she was not. *Not sexually compatible,* she deemed it, whatever that weak reasoning meant to her at the time. But that bargaining that had begun was the same survival mechanism which had allowed her to survive the night without unlocking that bathroom door, making her way to the busy streets of Shoreditch and jumping in front of a tube or bus. Because she knew, she knew stood in front of that full length bathroom mirror that she had just changed *forever.* Something had just happened to her person which would change the trajectory of her life. *She'd lost everything.* But whatever mechanism that numbed her just enough to protect her, was the same one that haven't worn off yet, but it would soon start…

LOVEY

*

Control

Control has always been a struggle for her. Not in the way we all search for but in the sense of constantly needing to have power over her own mind and pain others inflict upon her. This could be believed to be a side effect of her damaged past, resulting from others, the people that were there to protect, but instead exacting pain on her in ways she could not influence. I mean, how many people listen to a child? See the pain, fear, in their eyes? She learnt very early it is better to remain silent. She physically and mentally suffered first-hand, *yes*, but she also witnessed too much for her little brain to process. She felt protectiveness over people she loved and physically could not defend, thus creating the person she was today. From as far back as she could remember, she always tried to absorb the pain within others like a sponge whilst keeping her own agony from seeping out. This trait would later be taken advantage of. Nevertheless, she has always used her judgement to save her. Her form of protection was and always had been, escape. She was never a fighter, never angry but upset, she'd cry and run. She'd hide under her duvet praying to a God she wasn't sure she believed in, to be spared at least one night. Growing up she became the first to leave a situation at any moment of uncertainty or '*gut feeling*'. She used this as her guiding light however some now may call this anxiety.

Regardless, the Liv we are now getting to know, did not leave this night.

*

Lynn

Lynn said something interesting to Liv a week following the assault. She was in such admiration at the certainty in which Liv loved Roe and always had. Lynn was a counsellor who Liv had met in her first

LOVEY

year of university after falling into the deepest depression she had known yet, but their interactions would span beyond this and last her duration of university and Lynn ended up being less of a counsellor and more of a comforting auntie figure. Her days back then involved drinking a whole bottle of wine she had retrieved from the local Co-Op located on campus. She'd sit in her university halls, drawing deep lines down her arms which cried red till she passed out from the cheap wine, desperately wanting to sleep forever. Lynn reiterated a conversation Liv and her had after Roe had entered the then twenty-one-year-olds life. She brought back how happy she was, she reminded the lost soul that it was real, and she had witnessed it, even if it was in a brief setting. I guess the intention was to remind Liv that happiness does exist and lives within her somewhere and there was a day she met someone who brought it out, even at a time she believed she'd never feel happiness again. Lynn also added an understanding note that, it's hard to live with that knowing you no longer have that person and in turn, that feeling. But she persisted to say, *"It's so rare...so many people are riddled with doubt about love,"* and there's Liv, *"you have absolute certainty."*

*

The way she loves

To understand the way she falls,
we must understand the way she loves.

She tried to love with everything she had, even if it reached the point that it took all the love away from herself. Maybe upon reflection this was because she felt it was only thing she could offer. She was so painfully aware she was damaged and had to work ten times harder just to function some days. Not being able to recall a time in your childhood that didn't encompass physical and mental abuse evokes an existence that feels broken before you got the chance to begin. You'll feel undeserving of the most basic human experiences. She

LOVEY

just wanted to be normal, but she wasn't, she never was, never got the chance to be. She knew how it felt to feel alone, had felt it all her life, she was determined to never let someone know that emptiness she was so familiar with, as long as she had something to do with it. *'No one needs to feel alone, if they've got me'*, little Liv held in her mind always. In her eyes, the worth she held herself at, there was no way she was worthy of deep lasting love. She wanted to prove that it is possible however, to have someone love you and never stop. Never leave. And I guess indirectly, she silently hoped she'd receive the same in return.

*

Second-hand suicide

In the days that followed the assault, *'second-hand suicide'* was all Liv started to think about, *that* and just ordinary suicide. Let me explain, second-hand is simply wanting to die but not wanting it to be at your own hand. This is so people won't feel that desperate responsibility or guilt, feeling they could have done something differently or that they'll hate her for not being strong enough. She wanted it to be external. Bus, tube, accident, disease... going against her very strong existing health anxiety.

Suicide was always a tendency her mind liked to visit. It was a road that had been paved so early in life. First serious wonders down this dark path being twelve, then fourteen. It was the ultimate act of control when life was unbearably uncontrollable. She needed to feel she had some say, some reign over what happened to her. That and just life simply be agonizing from the moment you wake to the moment your conscious let's go and allows you to rest.

LOVEY

*

Thread

She was on a thread. A soft cotton thread which she knew was vulnerable. One strong yank and she knew she was over. She still tried though, even after Roe betrayed her in ways she had always been most afraid of and *utterly convinced he wasn't capable to commit.*

LOVEY

⟨ Notes

Nothing matters now. There's a type of power that comes with being suicidal. When something makes you feel awful or something happens, it suddenly doesn't matter because you won't be here much longer. And if anything, it just strengthens your existing desire. Desire to never feel anything else in this overwhelmingly painful world. I believe some people have the most wonderful life. This doesn't mean they don't experience the most horrible ways the world can work, but the good out weighs it. It's that balance we are all trying to keep. I was always okay with things happening, just as long as there was always something to live for, love, Australia, graduating. They have to be heavy. Sometimes really heavy to keep you grounded to earth and not float up into heaven. But when these things become weightless… what's holding you down? Fear of destroying your family and family for me only means Flum and Flannie. It can only pull you down for so long because if there's anything I have learnt it's that at the end of every night, you need your own reason to get up and do the next day.

I'm not scared to die anymore.

If it was a switch, I wouldn't be here now.

LOVEY

*

Looking at him, looking at me

To understand where we are now, the journey with Roe, how him and Liv's relationship led her where she is, we must travel back a little first.

January 18th, 2020.

She could feel it in her bones, in the pit of her stomach, he was *gone*.

She sat in the grey hard uncomfortable chair that were organised in rows, containing other students also sitting their end of term Neuroscience and Behaviour exam, she could barely write. Barely think of all the revision she had done prior. All the nights she had sat in her tiny studio, Kitchen Nightmares playing from YouTube in the background, as Roe quizzed her with the cue cards they had made. After the exam was over, which she knew she had failed, she sat on the bus and was consumed by how quickly everything could be taken away. I think anyone in Liv's life at the time of Roe entering it, would say her happiness was radiating. Life was far from perfect but suddenly, she glowed. In the space of two days he had completely changed, the way he text, barely spoke, all his adoring energy was seeming to vanish every hour that went by. That night, on the phone to Roe, in one last desperate plea to prevent what she knew was impending, although Roe never said, but sometimes you can just feel when someone is leaving, even when they are still there. *"I will fight for us, I love you too much."* sat on her thick carpet that laid beneath her where she'd often sit on the floor to do her makeup, verbally noting she could feel his rapid withdrawal. She needed to say it, she hoped she'd catch his heart before it *left for good.* He was silent, then said, "I'll see you tomorrow, night bub." and put down the phone.

She broke down. She'd lost him.

LOVEY

In the days that led up, it was never said but it was something you could sense. His heart was quickly disappearing, and she knew the next time she saw him, which being the following night, would be the last.

Letting himself in as he pushed the heavy fire door against her thick grey carpet, into the tiny studio he grew to spend most nights in, but only this time, the Roe she loved never arrived. In his place, someone cold and distant did. He stood awkwardly in his new vintage rugby shirt he had gotten from Depop after asking Liv for her approval. There in the new white, red, and navy colour-blocked top and black cargos, he lowered himself onto her bed. Liv immediately noticing he had no bag with him this time. He knew he wasn't there to stay. She didn't try to fight for him, he was already *gone.* As he explained the reasons as to why he believed their lives should no longer intertwine, she moved her gaze from his eyes, down to his lap, then up to the large white mirror that was hung to her right, on the opposite wall. She looked at his reflection, looking across to her. She took in his being. Absorbed his side profile, everything about him, everything she'd miss. She ran through all their memories like it was a cliché from a movie, flashing before her eyes.

> Roe: We are gonna be so happy forever!!
>
> Roe: I'm so excited for when we live together, have a family with a dog and never be apart!
>
> Roe: No because that's not how we do things, we talk and work them out. I'm the one who doesn't deserve you, don't ever think you don't deserve me. I will literally do anything for you. You're the one for me I have told you this
>
> Roe: Literally you're my world. You mean so much to me! Literally make me get out of bed everyday
>
> Roe: I will never let you be without me

LOVEY

> Roe: I promise bub I'll be with you forever!!!
>
> Roe: You will forever be mine bub!! You will never be able to get rid of me
>
> Roe: You will never have to live without me

This would be *goodbye*.

She sat in silence and took his heart-breaking reasoning with no comment. Fighting desperately would have made it worse. *It wouldn't bring him back, change his mind,* she thought. He had made his decision, *he was done.*
"I'm surprised you're not more upset." he said with tears falling from his eyes, looking deep into hers.
"There's nothing to say. I understand." she answered calmly and quietly.

All words had been said and now all that was left was to say goodbye.

As he departed, he seemed so incredibly tall as he lowered his frame to embrace her tightly. That's when she cried. She couldn't cope with this being the very last time she'd hug him, be in the only arms that ever made her feel safe. She wanted to stay buried in his chest forever. They reluctantly made their way out the studio and onto the communal landing, hugging one more time before his departure. She collapsed on her stairs outside her front door as she watched him leave through the window as he walked out the main entrance, to his car. He turned back peeking through the same window to see her still sitting on the stairs, sobbing to herself. He started to gesture for her to go back inside as he wiped tears from his eyes.

He left.

LOVEY

She reluctantly carried herself back inside and walked over to the window they had sat out on so many times. She waited and watched his car drive round the corner and up the road. She immediately walked a couple of steps out her kitchen and collapsed onto her carpet, sobbing till she exhausted herself to sleep.

The days that followed were strange.

She didn't eat. Dipping a teaspoon into a jar of peanut butter for any moments she felt she would faint. She'd spend hours and hours at the gym every morning before university, to pass time as she could barely sleep. She'd lay there, motionless, in bed from 4am, waiting for civilisation to awake. She barely cried too. She felt numb but also the worst she'd ever felt, but in a totally new way.

*

23rd January, her birthday.

She was flooded with texts celebrating her 22nd birthday. Friend after friend, wishing her a happy day, she wondered if Roe would do the same. Before she could speculate too long, a WhatsApp message lit up her phone in the early hours of the morning.

> Roe: Hey, I know you probably don't want to speak to me but I wanted to say Happy Birthday!
>
> Liv: Thank you!

She replied to his text, believing he always wanted to remain polite.

> Roe: So, I was wondering if you would be ok with meeting up next week on Monday or Tuesday? I want to talk about everything that's kinda happened now it's been a few days, and also would like to know how you're feeling. Not sure if you're going to Paris or not, but if you are I could do another day

LOVEY

> Liv: Yeah okay, I'm going to Paris so can't do Monday and I'm late at uni Friday
>
> Roe: Shall we do Tuesday then? I'll come down when you're back. I can give you a lift from Gatwick if you need?
>
> Or I can do Friday after you're done at uni I don't mind
>
> Or today whatever
>
> Liv: Do you mean meet today?
>
> Roe: Or next week? Was just giving options
>
> Liv: I can tonight.

Even though it could very possibly ruin her birthday, it was already ruined, and she didn't want to spend her entire time in Paris wondering what he was going to say. She wanted it over with, as soon as possible.

> Roe: I'll come after work?

He walked inside the same flat he had left a heartbroken Liv in. She opened the door and walked straight over to the kitchen, grabbing two glasses out of the cupboard. He stood in the door frame with a bouquet of flowers.
"Don't worry, they are for your birthday." he said, handing them to her. She was taken a little back then placed them in the sink. As she turned her back to him, he sat himself on the bed. She joined him but at a distance, putting an invisible wall between them, needing to protect herself after the days of starvation, and feeling nerves she had never felt before. He wanted her to initiate in telling him how she had been felling however, she insisted he must as he was the reason they were now sat in front of each other once again and wanted to know what his intentions were.

LOVEY

"I've made notes," he said as he opened up his phone to his notes app.
"I've hardly done any work today." he confessed as he pulled an innocently timid face, seemingly nervous before beginning his prepared speech.
…How annoyingly sweet.
He went on to explain his reasoning as to why he thought he had made such a rash decision and how it had very little to do with the actual duo. She internally knew that. They were, quite honestly, a pretty great team, and had both always counted themselves lucky for having found it so young.
"That video you made just kept replaying in my head. I made a mistake." him referring to the video she had made of a little compilation of them and all their memories.
As the words she spoke remained past tense, she could see his blood drain out of his body the more she chose terminology such as, *'used to feel', 'before this'*. His fear that he had made an irreparable mistake and now she was done made his heart visibly sink. Liv wasn't sure either, whether she *should* be with him now. He had shown her he could just leave. With no warning. Break her heart like it was nothing. Then, after a few days, want it all back.
In the moment she made her decision. One side of the internal battle had won. She took a moment and looked at the face she had fallen so deeply in love with and was honest with herself. She explained how much she truly wanted their future but how things had to be different going forward. The relief overcame him like a wave. They embraced and consummated their reunion.

He came back.

She realises now, she never fully trusted him after that. The way he could decide in a matter of days and just end their entire relationship. She would later be proven right.

LOVEY

"I know it will take time for you to trust me again, but I'm here, I love you and I'll never let you go."

*

Paris

They had originally planned a birthday trip for Liv to Paris. She had contacted her tattoo artist that was based just off a beautiful Parisian street in central. She had already seen her once before, getting a linework tattoo on her right forearm, almost a year ago to the day. She wanted to incorporate getting another tattoo with the weekend away that had originally been planned to celebrate Liv's birthday whilst also acting as the couple's first adventure out the UK.
The tickets were booked, hotel reserved. They were both excited. Planning outfits and restaurants and all the sights they wanted to see.

Liv from the beginning noticed how Roe had always been very heavily influenced by his family, particularly his older sister Lexi and his dad. Before Roe had spooked himself and ended their relationship, in the days leading up to the trip, Roe was reminded by Lexi that it was that weekend he was in Paris that was also their dad's 60th birthday party. Roe had double booked. Liv overheard a conversation between the siblings as Lexi was unaware Roe's phone laid on his desk and was connecting Liv to their discussion. Lexi proceeded to make Roe feel incredibly awful for missing their dad's birthday party, *"Family comes first"*. He came back on the phone a different person and that's where he started to tumble, it all started coming away at the seams. He was never the same after that phone call. Liv soon realised into their relationship that Lexi had a unique power over Roe. She often had times of speaking down to him, like she didn't respect the man he was becoming or his opinion and often replaced with her own. Liv couldn't help but wonder whether it was one of the reasons he ended the relationship. Did it contribute to his rash spiral?

LOVEY

Even though they got back together by the time Paris had come around, Roe still attended his dad's birthday and Liv changed the name on the flight to her mums.

*

Fliv and Flum in Paris

Liv persisted to go to Paris, now going with Flum to get her tattoo and celebrate her birthday. On the day of her tattoo, sat in cosy café, her mum (aka Flum) handed her a small card with a woman on the front, wearing a black and white striped top, with a red beret hat, holding a wine glass.

> Happy tattoo day!
> in Paris
> (with Me, haha)
>
> So exciting, ♡
> I Love you fliv
> Puff, big hugs
>
> FLUM
> xxx

LOVEY

The pair had the most incredible time, eating hummus and bread out of their 20th floor balcony in the centre of Paris. The décor of the hotel room was laced with navy and gold and was stunning. The view out their double doors lit up their room with the beautifully busy streets of Paris. They spent this spontaneous trip together exploring the city and having yet another adventure with one another.

...And even though the trip wasn't how she pictured it to be, she was so incredibly grateful for Flum and the best friend she was.

LOVEY

*

Valentine's Day 2020

To My Bubba Dear

I love you so much, I wish I could express it better sometimes and wish i was better on days like today, were I just don't think about how to make you feel special.

I know when I left you I made a huge mistake and it will take time for you to fully feel comfortable with me again, but just know i will always be here for you!

LOVEY

I can't wait to spend the rest of our lives together I will love you forever!!!

*

Out of order

19th October 2020. 01:37am

> Roe: This might be really out of order but do you want to have sex?

Yes. This is, word for word, what the text said.

After everything they had been through, all which you'll learn, this is what lit up her phone in the middle of the night, under the name she cherished so deeply, a month since he left, for good this time.

Every other time they had parted ways Liv made it her mission to keep *'no contact'*. Any heartbroken girl will know what this is but if you don't, you'll find thousands of videos and TikTok's explaining but simply, you absolutely, under **no** circumstances, contact your ex. You give them exactly what they want, what they have chosen by leaving, you give them your total absence. Liv did this every time. For her own sake, as much as his. She made sure, no matter how much she wanted to speak to him, she'd find strength in silence. The final, official break up however, she felt a little differently. She knew there was no coming back this time and hated how it had been left, so a week following, she texted him asking if they could speak. Roe agreed and took the call out of his family home, on a walk. He told her he was glad she called. She wanted to express the things she had thought since they both had distance and time. They had a pleasant

LOVEY

conversation, but Liv ended it on, *"I still believe it's us, it doesn't have to be now, but I believe it's us."* They both gushed a little over their relationship and he sweetly replied, "It would make a great story." Liv smiled down the phone and left each other's lives in a sweet peaceful way with no nothing but love between them.

> If she had one wish, this would be it.
> If she had to change one thing,
> she would have left them here.
> This should have been the end.

*

The Scrapbook

'I know you didn't want the book but it's yours and I feel its rightful home is with you, do what you like with it'.

She wrote on a piece of paper, sliding that and the scrapbook she had spent days, weeks making for their anniversary, inside the postage bag.

'Our first date'
'Night in London'
'Christmas'
'Lockdown'
'Texts'
'This is my favourite picture of us'
'One day, we will see the world'

The scrapbook contained all their highlights, best bits. First page *'Where is began…'* featured printed screenshots of their first dating app conversation she saved before deleting the app when they met. A hand drawn Spyro for the page highlighting a cosy day spent playing PlayStation. Next pages revealed pictures from a special date Roe had planned, ending in the drunken pair finding themselves in M&M

LOVEY

world buying overly expensive mugs. This spanning from an evening in The Comedy Club for their first night in London as the pair were falling in love. This night, alongside their yellow and orange mugs that were overly priced and shaped as M&M's, Roe also bought Liv a keychain. It was a gold bar with red M&M's engraved on it. She placed it on her keys the moment they bought it. Not that it was her aesthetic, at all in fact, but it was, in her opinion, the best thing she owned.

This night packing up the book, she took off the key chain she never thought she'd remove. She placed it in her memory box as that's all they'd become. The bounded scrapbook burst with differently themed pages, days at the Zoo, dinners they had cooked together, homemade pizzas, mushroom risotto, award ceremonies for him after he had achieved an incredibly high score after his accountancy exam, Natural History Museum, camping on the beach in late summer, walking through Bedgebury forest, scattering Bud's ashes one year on, Boundary festival, screenshots of texts from both of them. The elaborate pages went on and on. London Dungeons, Sea Life centre and Wagamama's, Halloween matching gangster clown costumes, NYE at his friend Georges, Facetime montages.
It all ended with pictures of beautiful places in different countries, *'One day, we will see the world'*, Liv titled the page, truly believing all her adventures would be with him. And in the back of the book, before sending it back off to him, she wrote, *'I will never stop loving you'*. She returned his anniversary present back to its rightful owner.

*

The promise

After the breakup they entered into an *'agreement'* to sleep together. She knew logically it would have one ending and that would heartbroken, but she deemed it later Liv's grief to face. She didn't want to lose him, not fully. She'd do anything to delay a life

LOVEY

completely without him. Maybe he just needed some time where there wasn't any pressure and he'd feel everything again, like he did before… and maybe more.

A routine quickly formed, seeing each other roughly every two to three weeks during the winter lockdown. What Roe was unaware of was that she was starving herself to the point she struggled to walk to her own bathroom in her flat. Seeing stars for minutes as she stood. She had quite quickly developed an eating disorder.

Roe came down to Brighton the following day after sending that text late the night before. He came in. Into the flat he knew so well, this being her new, bigger flat in Hove, to see Liv, something else he knew so well, but instead, this time, he was here for something else. They put a movie on. It was surprisingly not awkward. They had a lot of wine. And then they had sex. The next day she had no idea where she stood. *Was this a one-time thing? Do we go right back to broken up and not talking?*

A few days past, and Liv trying to get his attention, sent him a mirror picture of her in a baby pink bra and thong. He came down again. And thus, I'm sure you can see how they fell into what turned out to be seven months of seeing Roe, but knowing just because he looked like him, and sounded like him, didn't mean he was him. She didn't recognise the person he became.

Liv had one rule, one condition, no one else. No one else can be involved. He agreed, *he promised.*

LOVEY

*

Queue the sex montage

So, this would be the part of the movie where a stream of collated sex scenes of Liv and Roe would play on the screen.

It was a strange time. They were aware there was no way you could *'get over'* someone you still were incredibly in love with, all while still seeing them every couple of weeks and texting nearly every day. She was trapped between letting him go and saying to herself *'one more time'*. In his absence she'd often give herself deadlines to which she'd promise yourself she would end whatever it was they were doing. *She never did.* Their sex life was never lacking in their relationship but since their interactions turned to purely what it was about, the emphasis turned to various fantasises and fun they could have. They'd sext all week, describing in minute detail as to what they would do to each other once reunited. One occasion she turned her high-ceilinged flat into one big giant fort using white nets she had ordered from Amazon. She secured them to the walls using command hooks, creating the ultimate den. The foundation inside was composed of her cream sofa cushions. She took all the blankets she owned and laid them down on top of her duvet, to further cushion out with more pillows. She lit candles and put Roe's favourite flavour Pringles in bowls inside on the small black coffee table which was also being used to prop the laptop on. Before Roe walked in on this particular occasion, she changed into her latest expensive lingerie set she had ordered and placed a black satin pyjama short set on top. After hearing his motorbike engine outside, she ran out her flat and peaked through the front door to confirm, she quickly bounced back in feeling that sense of impending excitement. Moments later he walked in with his big heavy leather jacket and helmet on. She slid to the side of him as she closed the door behind him. Before he moved through the flat she instructed him to take off his motorbike helmet and close his eyes. He was taken off guard but seemed excited for the surprise. She took his

LOVEY

hands in hers and slowly guided him into the main room and to the entry of the fort where she had clicked the net doors open with hair claw clips. She let go of his hands and gently moved him in front of the entrance by placing each of her hands on the sides of his arms to position him in place. She let go and stood back.

"Open!" Liv excitedly waiting for his reaction.

"Oh my god." he laughed, not believing she sheer amount of effort the whole creation must have taken. He was amazed at her handiwork. *I wonder if he ever felt bad.* Bad knowing that he was letting her slip right back into girlfriend mode, where she'd cram her brain of ideas, trying to make every time they saw each other special, knowing he felt nothing and was purely there for sex.

Using sex dice, they sat on the sofa cushions, Roe in shorts and Liv in a red lingerie set covered by an oversized black satin shirt. They took turns between sexual favours which were determined by the two dice. One gave location and one decided the act. Rolling the dice, one landing on pillows next to them. *Lick.* That was the instruction. Next, she rolled the body part. *Finger.* She took his hand and placed his finger deep down her throat and sucked, maintaining unbroken eye contact.

Their sexting turned to their next encounter. The masseuse roleplay began to light up conversations.

> Roe: Ahhhhh fuckkkkk that'll be such a fucking tease. I'll just be thinking the whole time you're only here for a massage, she's so fucking fit and I want it but you don't... I'll be imagining seducing you which will make me hard and you won't be able to resist

Roe laid stomach down on the cushioned floor Liv built again in the cosy lounge of her flat. She began in character, covering his broad body with baby oil as she massaged it in with her soft hands. She moved the slick oil and glided it over his back and bum and down between his thick thighs, letting it drip onto his balls. In and around deep between the upper parts of his thighs she massaged.

LOVEY

"Turn over please." she voiced quietly, in a professional tone. He rolled his tall frame over to lay on his back and revealed his extremely erect self.

"Close your eyes." she whispered.

She began rubbing more oil over his torso and down his legs, making sure he was well covered. After massaging his arms and down to his hands she began to gently rub and tease around his crotch. Intensifying his erection but never touching it.

He started stroking her leg as she knelt beside him, but she responded by gently picking up his hand from her thigh and placing it by his side, keeping it professional. After watching his cock twitch as the blood rush intensified with every minute that went by, she moved from besides him to behind his head, deeply massaging his shoulder. After reaching a breaking point of arousal she positioned herself forward onto his face and moved her red thong to the side where he enthusiastically began oral.

"Finally" he moaned.

Her legs started to shake uncontrollably and after a few minutes she climaxed. Sliding herself down and turning her body around she sat on his cock and began to straddle him, only being helped by the oil as they thrust into each other's bodies.

Some nights, when they weren't in an extensively built cosy fort, or elaborate masseuse roleplay, they'd be simply cuddling up watching Avatar whilst they took turns stroking each other's hair. They'd have pizza making night with large amounts of wine. They'd judge each other's toppings to then be interrupted by Roe lifting Liv on to her kitchen counter. He'd hold up her legs, wrapping them around his waist, moving her thin pink thong to the side and would place himself inside, all whilst the pizzas cooked. They had always, throughout their relationship and beyond, matched each other's high sex drive.

This all might sound a little like dating, in the sense that it could be cute, cosy evenings where they'd catch up on their lives. Roe would

LOVEY

talk about his new promotion at work which the pair had both believed to be well overdue, and would therefore, celebrate. Liv would show him her latest t-shirts she had designed. He was always her number one fan and cheerleader. He always hyped her up into thinking she could truly do *anything*. They'd talk about everything apart from what they were doing. What it meant. Why it was no good for either of them. But also, why Roe couldn't stop and let them both more on.
"You look different every time I see you." Roe referring to the dynamically quick weight loss Liv had been starving herself for. "You've got a sharper jaw line than mine now." he added, half joking, half serious, with a hint of concern.

Finally, he noticed.

One night, sat on the floor, swaddled in blankets by the large open windows, he began to speak about soon moving out of his parents' house and up to London. He had viewed a couple of flats via SpareRoom. Liv only thought this could be a good thing. If he was independent, he could start his real life, maybe they'd be so glad they were still in each other's lives and go back to being together. But in a new way, put all the lockdowns behind them, find what they had before the world was turned upside down, whilst both being adults and being able to shape their lives the way they wanted. No more Brighton-Guildford distance. No more parents overcrowding his mental space. She had always planned to move to London as well, could be perfect she thought. Liv was always an optimist and to be fair to her, he had always come back. He had never wanted to live long without her in his life since the moment they met.
"Will I see your flat in Clapham?" she asked timidly.
"Of course you will!" he said as though he was surprised it was a question. *So, he still pictures me in his life*, she thought, *even in a few months, when everything changes for him, for the good.* She settled into the idea moving to London and finally out of his parents' house might give him enough space in his mind to straighten everything

LOVEY

out and Liv would never have to feel she made a huge mistake in what they had been doing for months, and staying right where she's always been, *in love*.
She had spent months of her life being used for sex.
She had spent months trying to give him everything he wanted so he didn't look elsewhere.
She had spent months starving herself so somehow, she'd be worth something more.

Her entire life revolved around the next time they'd see each other and was anxiously aware he could call it off at any minute.
She was exhausted and absolutely mentally fucking shattered into tiny fucking pieces but calling it a day? No, it just wasn't an option. She wanted it to be. *So badly*. But she could never love herself enough to truly believe she deserved better than what he was giving her. In all honestly, it was disgusting how much he became a stranger to her. How he spoke, acted, how it all changed. How sex was the only thing he cared about and wanted from her. She was clear on what it was but *really?*
You loved someone so fucking much, to then, use them for months and months and months, fully knowing she still loves you. Hopes you'll *'come back'*. Liv realised much later on that the *'before and after'* Roe's, how they were different people in her mind, were actually the same person, all along.

*

Don't open the draw

She was too scared to ask. Too scared to face what any answer would mean. After he had moved into a house share with two other boys, just off the Clapham high street, she wondered what that would now mean for them. Whether they'd keep seeing each other or Roe would cut it off as he'd soon have other girls to sleep with. To her surprise, they continued to see one another but his Instagram

LOVEY

number began to grow. And all full of young women with 'London' in their bio.
"No apps, *right?*" she asked the back of his head the next morning as he sat at his desk.
"No." he said.
"Have you?" he immediately bounced the question back.
"No." Liv answered truthfully.
After he went out of his bedroom and into the bathroom, Liv lent across the black framed bedstead the room had come furnished with and opened the top draw in his unit.
Condoms.
New packet.
Open.
She was almost sick.
From that moment, every time she saw the pink Durex box with the yellow lips on, in shops, it provoked a sick, disgusting, sinking feeling. Maybe they were from when they used them at the start of their relationship and had simply packed his room and moved them up. She knew this was not true. But she'd do anything to not imagine him with someone else.
The next time she was in that bed, she slowly opened the draw which could either prove his loyalty and innocence or guilt and betrayal. Her heart sank. Broke. Died. Sick felt like it rose to her mouth. Her adrenaline fuelled eyes saw not only many missing from the pink packet but also a whole new box. After he returned to his bedroom in a t-shirt and black Adidas shorts, she looked at him. Just simply upon him. The man she believed would always look out for her, look after her, even if they weren't together. "You okay?" he asked concerned at her gaze. She stayed silent for a moment, realising she was suddenly with a stranger. She did not know this man that would hurt her so deeply. All her loyalties had always remained with him. The loyalties he did not deserve.

LOVEY

*

Her fault

It was all her fault, right? Roe not loving her. Being unable to feel anything other than pain? Not going home that night. Going back to that hotel? She tried so hard to know what the right thing to do was. She was always led with her gut and heart, always. She honestly thought how wrong can I go following my heart? Turns out, very. Especially when others are being led by something else.

> It felt like I was there to be tortured for someone's pleasure. Hit so hard that I had to brace myself each time knowing it was only getting more painful. It's like I didn't exist. So aggressive so quickly then didn't stop. Don't know the place I went in my head when I knew it wasn't going to end. Maybe that's when I died. Just didn't know I was dead yet.
>
> Lynn said I was in shock.

*

Moments to survive

She could smell him for days. His scent was powerful. She thought this in the moment they met. But it wasn't cologne, it seemed to be an offensive laundry detergent that lingered unpleasantly in his clothes. The power of smell would months later be the catalyst to a trigger.

Tucked away on the lowest shelf in her black Ikea storage rack located in her bathroom, she sprayed her vanilla Christmas cookie

LOVEY

room spray throughout the halls. As she walked out in her little black satin shorts and an oversized t-shirt. The scent hit her nose. Her heart immediately started to palpitate. It felt as though her mind hadn't caught up, whilst her body had already entered an immediate panic attack. She barely got two steps in front when she suddenly collapsed to the floor in the instantaneous fit of panic. For those who don't know, a trigger is a psychological stimulus that revokes an involuntary recollection of a traumatic event. They can be touch, sight, sound, taste, scent, any of the senses but they induce a type of PTSD response that provokes a truly disturbing reaction.

These are the small moments which are invisible to the outside world.

These are the reasons why they are called survivors. It's all these moments that need surviving. The long, ongoing, lasting effect assault has, it loudly reintroduces itself back in, unannounced.

*

The week that followed

The week that followed the rape was the quickest yet slowest week of her life. Flashbacks became this real phenomenon that started happening. YouTube adverts sparked trauma responses to her nervous system, reminding her of a conversation they had engaged in on the date while she thought this experience *wouldn't ruin her life.* Of course, she wanted to say,

FUCK HIM.

HONESTLY FUCK HIM AND EVERYONE.

Then, she gets up and goes to live her life and not let this be what takes her.

What finally drowns her.

LOVEY

But it feels like rocks.

No…

Not rocks…

…Huge boulders which are unmoveable, tied to her ankles at the bottom of the ocean where it's dark, cold, and terrifying. And there's people around her, telling her, shouting, she can move them, not only move them, but swim to the very top of the ocean with them. *Impossible.* That's why she's at the bottom of the seabed, peacefully floating waiting to die because she knows no one is coming. Not the person she needs to cut the ties or move the rocks. Because like I explained earlier, it has to be really heavy to keep her here.

*

Get me back to Brighton

24th July 2021.

In a rush, she left that hotel in Shoreditch, travelling back down to Brighton to meet her start time at work. She sat tucked away into the window of a Thameslink train. Her sole concern was to make it to work on time. It was less of a worry as the shop was located around a five-minute walk from the train station. Walking down the bricked road, under a small tunnel which led into the Brighton lanes. She made it just in time. She put the events of the early hours of the morning to the back of her mind and focused on work, the one thing that was consistent and she knew how to do. After an hour of the shop opening, she had made repeated visits to the vibrantly painted stockroom however, on one particular trip she caught a quick glance of herself as she passed the large brightly painted mirror tucked away in the basement of her shop. She stopped and took a double take at what she couldn't immediately comprehend. The self-reflection revealed the physical devastation of what would

LOVEY

internally slowly start to cripple her. She looked down and held her leg. Over the entirety of her back-left thigh was where his right hand had disbursed his strength. Not just her thighs but her arms, stomach, chest, back, face. She ran her fingers over the deepening bruises to prove them as a reality. Quickly, she pulled out her phone from her skirt pocket, switching it to camera to prove they were really there, she took a photo and stared at it, for minutes. Again, just bad sex, *right*? Just stuff she's not into, *right*? She randomly got a message from Oscar which was out the blue as she had left a few messages from him on read. He sent her a photo of his quite frankly, rock hard tensed abdomen. When she first met him, she couldn't quite believe how firm his abs had been and how strong this man was. Not in a scary way, just attractive. She replied to provide herself with an immediate distraction and a conversation started which led to a loose plan being made to see each other again. She felt everything will be fine, forget last night just go back to what you know. She actually believed she could replace the memory of last night with a situation she knew she had control and felt safe. She soon realised there was no number of times which would restore this belief. Her large blood bruises were only getting darker and starting to deeply ache. She went upstairs to join her manager. She knew she had been on a date and asked how it went. Liv started quite innocently briefly touching on the events that occurred the night before, however, the more she spoke the more she was met with a mix of shock and concern. Her manager asked,
"Are you… okay?"
Liv promptly said "Yeah!"
She hadn't quite gotten there yet but it was all starting to add together and come crashing down. Her manager growing with concern, "Can you be here? Do you need to go home?"
Liv again, very reassuringly, "No! I'm fine, honestly."
It's as though everyone around her was processing what had just happened ten times faster than she was. Then one moment she was left alone to stare out to the front of the shop from behind the bench, which was used as a till and a flashback, a phenomenon she

LOVEY

didn't realise was about to become a reoccurrence, from the night before, replaying like watching a movie scene of him grabbing her chin, pulling it straight to face him, looking her dead in the eyes to which he then slapped across the face, once and then another.
She fell.
"I think I need to go home."
"Yeah, I think you do, go home, be safe."

*

Liv²

Liv squared are two best friends. It's quite self-explanatory if I'm honest. Made up of two Olivia's who are absolutely each other's missing piece, twin flame, yin and yang. Spiritually separated somewhere along the way in universe terms but brought back together in time to cause trouble and be each other's loves and saviours. Liv squared were a relatively new double act but when somethings meant to be, it feels like it was there *always*.

*

The suffocating Brighton lanes

Our Liv left work and desperately grabbed her bulky iPhone eight plus with its extra girth being added by a black card holding case. She started typing to Liv asking if she was free to talk. Hastily dodging the crowd of people through the busy Brighton lanes, the sun beaming down on her screen making it hard to see. She was unsure if what she had typed had made any sense but all she knew was that she needed to get home as quickly as possible. Liv had already filled Liv² in on the night before using voice notes for the duration it took to get to the tube station from hotel. Telling her it was just bad sex and was not going to see him again. The Liv's agreed to move on and put it down to a bad night. At this point other Liv did not realise what had actually happened, hence the *'we move on'*.

LOVEY

Other Liv is good for Liv's brain. She keeps the devils away. She reminds her not to get in her own head and let it spiral but it was too late. On the bus, all she could contemplate was moment by moment survival. Frantically fixated on what she needed to do to get home, get through the busy Brighton lanes which suffocated you on Saturday's, get on the bus, count the minutes, breathe, then walk home, run from the bus stop to the black and white wide checkerboard stairs which led to her apartment which had originally, when built, been a part of a grand large townhouse on the Brighton and Hove seafront. She ran against the clock till the tower came tumbling down. Desperately wanting to avoid the crash.

She made it just in time.

Safe haven.

She's in her safe haven. So much time had been put into making her Hove flat the home she dreamt about. The old high ceilings with historic mouldings engraved on the walls made it feel grand, the cream rustic shabby chic matching furniture found through Facebook marketplace spread throughout, fairy lights hung over the cream plush sofa. Her art and designs hung from the walls. She could have never anticipated that leaving her home the day before, that her return would be an empty shell of the girl she walked out being. There was a sense of relief that flooded her being ever so slightly as she reached the only place she felt safe, her flat. She walked in with the knowledge she should use the extra time from leaving work early to get all dolled-up ready as she has always had plans to go back out in London that night but, before she knew it, she found herself in a ball on the top of her cream shabby chic French bed, crying till her body shook. The penny had officially dropped. The world and reality of last night had completely collapsed in on her.

LOVEY

*

Fast forward a month

We're back at Clapham North, where life likes to bring Liv back too. First night out the house since **that** night. Liv's mum had been staying on her sofa. Everyone agreed that her thoughts were swinging so low she shouldn't be left alone for long and for Liv, who has always been fiercely independent, this was just shy of suffocating.

*

Flum

Let's meet Liv's mum. They made up nickname's years ago. The origin had gotten lost in time, but it takes your first name, takes away your first letter and adds '*Fl*' in front. So mum was Flum, Liv was Fliv, Roe became Floe. You get it. Fliv and Flum were inseparable. They were best friends from day one. Liv had always been able to tell her mum stuff you'd never normally be able to divulge to a parent but, in the ways she lacked as a traditional mother, she made up for in being Liv's number one, always on her side, and forever being able to make each other wee with laughter along the way. Flum has an incredible story of her own to tell and throughout this book we'll learn what we need too but a small glimpse starts with her own abuse, enduring seven years of sexual assault starting at the age of just nine too then being twenty-three, leaving for America to where she'd nanny for a wealthy family, falling then into a brief spout of modelling for Playboy followed by countless adventures leading her back home and into the eye line of who would soon be Liv's father.

Flum is a special soul which made her a special mum. She's a lost soul searching through life, but her lack of convenutal parenting led to her creative and fun energy. Growing up, they'd dance and sing, putting on a pair of her mum's high heels, both in leotards, in her

LOVEY

very early teens, they'd play Beyonce music videos and dance in Flum's bedroom or play on her mum's DJ decs she had after Flum got with her DJ boyfriend, who Liv adored. They'd go for night time drives when one or the other needed a peaceful escape. They'd watch lifetime movies on snow days from school, cuddled on the sofa. They'd go makeup shopping in Brighton and Tunbridge Wells, finding products they had seen on YouTube or Pinterest. Then once Liv could drive, they'd nip through winding lanes in Liv's Mini listening to *'We are the people'* by Empire Of The Sun blasting out the car speakers with the windows which sat all the way down. They were always more equals than mother and daughter and it worked. For them, it meant they both got what they needed, so it seemed, Liv felt seen and heard and in control and Flum got a best friend.

Liv from a young age started to notice that her mum lived in a dream world, and in turn, so did Liv. That's where her escape into scenarios in her own mind would come from.
The older Liv got the more she realised Flum had relied on her ability to mentally walk into other worlds because that's how she survived. Her childhood was broken, violating and painful and she created a place to live in her mind that was safe and somewhere she could create magic. Regardless of how painful her stepdad made her world, the bond she had with her mum, Liv's Nannie, was unbreakable. "I was best friends with my mum, I knew it was always going to be the same with us." Flum softly telling Liv that being friends, sharing the bond they did, was why they had glittery, sparkling magic between them.

*

I'm fine, I'm fine, I swear

A little halter top made up of her brown and gold monogram satin scarf, a black satin midi skirt which she had pinned into a mini skirt the night before, preparing her outfit, all ready for the quick change, a low black heel which she knew would leave her in pain after an

LOVEY

hour like they always did, her cropped black denim jacket for some warmth she knew she'd need later in the night and she was ready. Her bruises were deepening but they were tucked away around the back of her thigh and up her back, hoping her mini skirt would cover most of the evidence. She placed her earphones in and shuffled her playlist that was full of songs which were upbeat and powerful. She stepped out her front door in the early evening, feeling it was touch early to be dressed how she was, but she knew she'd feel confident and more appropriate later.

Again, she's stood at Clapham North station, knowing Oscar was in Cornwall and Roe, well Roe not wanting to see her and probably out with a girl, turns out, she later found out he was back home in Guildford with Covid. She walked up Clapham high street, past Roe's road which she always turned her head to look upon, eventually making it to the bar where she met her friends plus a large group of people she had never met before. Any other former versions of Liv probably would have bailed but this Liv walked straight in, stood over the table with all the chairs full and no space in sight, she still didn't bolt. She was trying to remain the girl she knew she had become and was gripping to tightly to remain. Keep the power she had spent so much time tiresomely building. The girls made quickly shuffled their seats and made space for another and began introductions to all those Liv did not know.
"Oh my god Liv!"
"What are they from??"
The group of girls who Liv would eventually class as close friends clocked the intense purple bruises that were only growing darker by the hour. It hurt to bend her leg. They were painful to the touch.
"Are you okay?" all the girls growing in concern.
"I'm fine, I'm fine, I swear."

She stayed as long as she could but found herself around midnight suddenly escaping the night out. What she'd usually deem as a good thing, men looking at her, staring, making advances, the typical

LOVEY

attention she started to receive but suddenly she was confronted with the reality that she desperately did her best not to face. She had made a mistake in pretending that life could just carry on as normal. She had changed. She had been damaged. It was time to go home and face what came next. She ran in her little heels back to Clapham North, away from the group to then arrive at London Bridge station as quickly as possible.
Get me back home

<u>This would be the last time she'd leave the house in weeks.</u>

*

Let's get back to that night

Shoreditch, mini golf, the bar, cheap hotel. The destinations. Let's separate the night. Liv had met him at the lobby of his hotel.
"Want to leave your bag here?"
He seemed insistent but she stuck to what she knew was best to do and carried her bag out with her. He was based on the outskirts of London as he had moved out of central in preparation of his plans to move away to China and teach English. All he was waiting for was a visa which were tricky to get since Covid-19. His work was still hybrid in the office so this meant he'd often book cheap last minute hotel rooms for when he had to work in person. Liv enjoyed the fact he wanted to travel whilst being jealous he had imminent plans to do so. This would be why he referred to Liv later in the night saying, "it's annoying when you meet someone you think could be right."
"No, it's fine, I'll carry it." she insisted as leaving it would have meant she was trapped into having to come back to that hotel.
After making their way down the main streets that ran from Old Street tube station to Box Park, she held out her black card all while he was downloading and making a profile to gain entry. Once inside they sat at the side of one of the walkways on a set of stalls. He ordered the first round of gin and tonics. She was her usual sarcastic

LOVEY

self which sometimes went over his head. It felt as though it was hit then a miss. She'd cringe when her sarcasm got miss interpreted but nevertheless, they were getting along, and they were both making each other laugh. After another round of gins which Liv collected from the bar, they went to the pre-booked mini golf which he had arranged. She was excited as it had been a place Liv had followed on Instagram and wanted to go for a while. She wouldn't be able to anticipate that she'd never want to go back again or even walk pass. They completed the course with a couple of overly sweet cocktails which were an un-natural blue colour, topped with sweets, in hand. They eventually sat down at a table after completing the course and Liv's triumph.

After making their way out of the mini golf and to a bar round the corner, she left, nipping to the toilet.

    Date: Are you alive?

Walking out of the pink toilets that laid underneath the bar, she found a girl crouching on the ground to which she fell and laid on the bathroom floor.

Everyone… just… stepped over her.

It was actually kind of awful.

Liv kneeled next her and lifted her head as the girl blurted out, "I'm going to be sick."

Liv quickly helped her closer to the toilet, as, she was right, she **was** going to be sick.

"Where are your friends?"

"Let's get you can Uber."

Liv took her phone and opened the Uber app as the stranger that was this girl continued to throw up.

"What's your address?"

She didn't seem to know, and *'Home'* wasn't stored in her phone. Liv sat and persisted to try and get her details, eventually being able to order a taxi.

"It's two minutes away, let's get you upstairs."

LOVEY

Liv lifted the intoxicated girl to her feet and helped her up the long flight of stairs.
Stood outside Liv clocked the reg and started to run after the black car. The taxi was on the cusp of driving away as the driver seemed confused over where in pick up point was and had been waiting a few minutes. She stopped the car and went back and got the girl. She put her safely inside, double checking the post code with the driver.
"What's your Instagram?" the girl slurred as she handed her phone to Liv once more.
Liv giggled and typed in her name.
"Get home safe."

"Where did you get to?" the date said after she had been gone a good ten minutes.
"I had to help a girl get home, she wasn't well."

The irony was not lost that it would be Liv in fact that would later need saving.

*

Timing is everything

Throughout these pages, Roe has and will become an enigma. Someone Liv loved dearly and broke her heart. But before any of that, as you can imagine, they shared an entire life, love, filled with exploding stars between them.

Let's start from the beginning and maybe we will understand where her certainty comes from. The pair met at an important time in our Liv's life. She had always kept track of any plans through a countdown app instead of using the typical calendar, it would show the number of days till that event. At the time, in her first year of university, Liv had reached a point in her depression where she had picked a date and was committed to giving it till then for life to become worth it or just slightly bearable or she was done. She knew

LOVEY

what it would take to end it all after reading a PubMed document of an overdose using a specific ingredient in a sleep aid medication and had spent the last few months collecting enough of these tablets. She needed life to just be ever so slightly less painful and by giving it this time, no one can say she didn't try. This date was the 31st of July. This will be important soon. When Liv and Roe met, well, it was everything people say love is, to the point it is almost overwhelming to break a part and explain. It was love and for Liv, it was soulmate type of love. From the moment she truly knew him, he was it. The only one she saw. The only one that mattered. After a few months of dating, Roe asked Liv to be his girlfriend, a truly defining moment for Liv because not only was he everything she had ever wanted in a person, but he just so happened to ask on the 31st of July. She had forgotten in the whirlwind of falling in love that *'The end'* date was still in her countdown. She picked up her phone and erased *'The end'* and replaced it with *'BOYFRIEND AND GIRLFRIEND'*. I believe in today's society we don't like to rely on others, especially for our happiness and it is greatly frowned upon but sometimes it takes something heavy, right? Something heavy to keep us from floating. I think life is truly about human connection. *People need people.* Life had done exactly what it needed too and more, to keep her here. It felt more meant to be than she could have ever hoped. The very date she had given the universe to save her from her absolute loss and misery, she gained her soulmate and a future. *Finally,* she thought, *she wanted a future.* We'll learn more about their relationship but for now we must get back to that night.

LOVEY

*

The assault (Trigger warning Sexual Assault)

Lying in the rigid bed, encased within four claustrophobic walls, they began watching a YouTuber on Liv's phone, they spoke of earlier in the night. She knew the sex was expected to start soon but she carried on clicking new videos, delaying the process. She then, after a few more, indicated she had grown tired and wanted to sleep. She reached across to her bedside light and pressed the switch. Suddenly, her shirt was ripped open, followed by her shorts and thong being yanked off. Any decency had landed on the floor. It was rushed and forceful. His body seemed large in the dark room. At this moment she regretted the fact her type was typically tall, strong, rugby players or gym goers. As she laid being pushed onto her back, her thighs bent upwards, she was so vividly aware she didn't want this but in less than a few moments it began. The first hit. More painful than she had ever had but maybe it was a fluke. The second. Even harder than the first. The next she knew she had to brace for. She tensed up in some form of protection mechanism. Harder and harder. More and more painful as if his strength and violating aggression was only growing. The type of pain Liv could only relate with the intention of hurting someone to damage them. Something had turned dark. Before she was able to take note of all areas he was violating, he took his hand, yanked her chin straight to him and slapped her, covering nearly the entirety of her face. He then repeated this act again and once more, each with brutally increasing force. The tone didn't feel sexual, it felt angry, felt evil. She did everything not to cry in pain. He looked down over her body whilst inflicting different areas of hurt, seeming to enjoy the more pain he could inflict. His actions moved all too quickly for her to gather her thoughts. She was gone by this point. The point where it turned from non-consensual sex combined with a beating. He had already proven to her he could hurt her, with a shock inducing amount of force but also, she was alone. In a windowless hotel. In the middle of the night.

LOVEY

On that night she saw someone she hadn't heard from in a long while. She looked like her, only younger, much younger. She sounded like her too, only quieter.

Shhh.
Just survive.
Just get through it.
It'll be over soon.
Then you'll be home.
Safe.

Her childhood brain had been bound by fear and physical abuse her entire life and it had taught her that staying silent could be the key. The key to living. Any fight she had ever witnessed only ended it a worsened ending. She felt scared and that meant one thing in the girl that could only hear her child-self cry.

<u>I'd like to remind men reading – Silence is not consent.</u>

Her body went into shock. He sloppily interrupted his own actions by saying he was too exceedingly drunk to climax. No end in sight.

All hope was lost.

She laid back as all the bargaining she had done with herself, buying time with the assumption it surely could not continue much longer, *had gone.* Her eyes glazed over, soul sunk into the hard mattress and she accepted her fate quietly. After what seemed like a painful eternity, he stopped to leave the vessel he had just created, reaching across the bed for the bottle of water he had placed on her side. She was lulled into a false sense of security believing it was over. He had taken all she had to offer, *now empty.* She was hollow and in pain, naked curled up into a ball on the furthest side of the bed. Before she settled into this belief fully, he grabbed her, with the hands she hoped would never touch her body again, turned her over and

LOVEY

forcefully repeated his actions, inflicting pain at a new level of force.

Please, not again, her soul cried.

> ‹ Notes
>
> I was just jolted back and forth. I was a vessel.
>
> 31st July
> Today is mine and Roe's two year anniversary. Actually, I suppose I should really say it would have been mine and Roe's two year anniversary.
>
> I feel ill today.

*

Anniversary

It got to the week anniversary of the date. Liv was haunted by a memory from that night which suddenly dawned on her mind.
"When do I get to see you again?" he shouted down into her ear over the predictable pop music that played loud enough to drown out most thoughts.
"I don't know, up to you." Liv shouted optimistically into his ear on her tippy toes with a warm feeling that is given to you when someone makes you feel special.
"I have a date Friday, but I'll cancel it for you."
The warm feeling grew. She had spent most of the evening feeling relatively happy, or a lukewarm version of that word, but regardless, she had laughed a lot and felt as though she was doing exactly what she wanted too.
"You won't cancel it." Liv insisted.

LOVEY

The entire conversation they engaged in previously clearly setting boundaries started to seem blurry with a continuation leading to him saying "It's annoying when you met someone you think could be right, when you know your moving away soon." Because it was true. They really did get on. They had things in common and it felt as though something nice could have been shared between them. Liv still felt distant, no matter what. She knew where her heart lied, and she quietly knew no one was ever going to compare and that would never change.

The date. The date he was going to cancel. A few days after the assault, Liv blocked him. This was after receiving multiple texts of him getting angry for her lack of reply. He probably went on that other date. She felt riddled with guilt. *Was she meant to stop him? Was she meant to say something? She should be stronger and report him.* These thoughts acted as an undetectable tsunami in her already trauma riddled mind.

Please notice, I refuse to give the date a name. That's how he'll remain throughout these pages. This is not out of fear, but out of the fact that people who have names in Liv's life are all players. They all play their part and, well, his part will not be graced with a name. With an identity. He's already scorned his role on her body and mind, *enough.*

LOVEY

Chapter Two

Winter 2019.

Gazing up at the large square window encased by a diamond pattern over the exterior. Her window into the world that peaked over the underwhelming coffee shop that Liv lived over. Late one autumn evening, Liv had left work at the local supermarket. Walking the five-minute journey home in the brisk evening, she looked up at the light coming from her window. It was always a symbol of hope as it implied she was nearly there, and after the long shift of retail was over, it was always a welcomed sight. As she grew closer on this particular evening, she was suddenly overcome with an unfamiliar feeling, *content.* Absolute contentment for everything in her life. In the window she spied her Roe cooking in the kitchen. She knew she'd be greeted with lit up eyes and a loving welcome. He had let himself in with the set of keys she had given him not long before, excited to share everything she had with him. The kitchen was practically situated in the bed, but she didn't mind for a long while as it was the first time, she fully had her own space. Her own home after being in university halls. She couldn't wait to see his face light up as she came in for him to follow up with the excitement of what concoction he had put together for their dinner. However, Liv found herself merely standing outside, looking up and gazing at him standing over the oven and then grabbing plates out of the one and

LOVEY

only cardboard to which he laid down on her tiny one-person table ready to dish up. She could not wait for that moment when she forcefully pushed her heavy fire door open against the resistance of the thick carpet which lay within her tiny studio flat which somehow fit her, six-foot-two, love of her life, in. She took a deep breath and thought that *right now… I've got everything and more.* Everything she had ever wished for.

This is something we'll learn about Liv. She didn't ask for much. Just love… and to feel safe. *Everything she never had.*

*

Balcony

The world stood still on that balcony. In the late summer, entering the fall season, they'd lay all the blankets and duvet on the small balcony that you'd climb out of her wide window to get too. This would be the window Roe would later climb through after Liv had locked her keys inside on one evening after they had been out for dinner. The balcony sat on top of the run-down coffee shop. They'd play music out of his portable speaker, take snacks out, they'd cuddle and confide their most random thoughts. They'd giggle and kiss. It was a tiny spot on this earth where she had everything she ever needed.

*

OT bop

Most couples have romantic songs which they deem as '*their song*' but Liv and Roe both loved a particular DJ set by Solomon and OT bop, sharing a love for rap, R&B and afrobeat.

One weekend leading up to Christmas, the pair drove down for a party of one of Liv's friends before they departed down to Cornwall for Christmas with his family. Walking into the top floor penthouse flat, they were greeted by a group of her friends. After a few drinks, OT bop started to blare out the speakers. Liv and Roe, stood facing

LOVEY

one another in the open plan kitchen on the wood laminated floor began to swing their arms in unison, mimicking the dance in the music video.
Roe always called them *'The Dynamic duo'*. Liv later put this as an Instagram caption. Always referring to the fact they so effortlessly were each other's perfect other half.
"You stole my caption!" Roe jokingly contested as Liv had put up a picture of the couple first and used his suggestion.
"You can put it too!" Liv laughed.
They posted matching pictures with the matching caption. Liv felt they were impenetrable. She had never felt like such a team, in her entire life.

*

Lewis

Now don't get me wrong, Liv had other partners in the past. Lewis was another player in Liv's life we're about to meet. He was the most stable, consistent, and reliable thing she had ever had and to this day this remains true, and at the time of their relationship, he was exactly what she needed. They shared a charming love, filled with lots of laughs. They were best friends for a while. But unfortunately, that's almost all it was. They met when Liv was sixteen, Lewis nineteen. Both deeming each other as one another's first loves. This would be a fact Liv re-evaluated as nothing ever seemed to match or even come close to Roe. It later made her question if she ever was really in love with Lewis, but she was, it was just different. A lesson she later learnt was, every love you have will feel unlike the one before but that doesn't mean love wasn't shared. After all, it's about finding the one you want to last in, forever. Regardless, after six quick months they moved in together and as a result of Liv's persistent persuading, not long after, Lewis bought them a dog, a puppy, a pug puppy. In Liv's eyes she had gone from an unstable, reckless, painful family, but that no longer mattered as she finally had her own. She depended on Lewis to create the family she never had. They shared a

LOVEY

life together for four and a half years, watching each other turn from the baby ages of sixteen and nineteen too still, the young ages of twenty and twenty-five. For a lot of that time together they were happy. They went through more than most for a young couple. Every test that your usually faced with when you're with someone into your early twenties. However, one defining day would change everything.

Only a baby, *Buddha*, their pug developed reoccurring seizures which featured as a symptom of her underlying, rare neurological disease. The couple suddenly turned from their innocent life of the normality to relapses of their Bud-pudding. Rapidly, Lewis' savings had disintegrated keeping Bud alive. Liv working as much as possible whilst keeping up her college to enable her to reach university. The place she thought she'd finally be happy. We know she was wrong, but she didn't yet and in fact, that goal was the only thing that got her through most of this time. Lewis' long shifts as a police officer kept the couple apart and when they were together, they were exhausted.

Liv always had a voice which whispered for more. As she grew, she went through many different phases and a lot were the opposite to Lewis' unchanging stubbornness. Nevertheless, they both never wavered, not till near the end. Lewis stood back and not just let Liv grow in any which way she needed too but he supported her at every turn. The frustration grew, nevertheless. *"Why don't you want to travel? See the world? There's so much for than this?"* Liv referring to the little life of just buying a property in the town where they had both grown up in, referring to Lewis' biggest aspiration. This was a relentlessly reoccurring conversation. He just had no desire. For that and plenty of other things. He was content. Liv knew she couldn't spend her life with Lewis, she knew eventually she'd have to leave, but not yet. Liv received her acceptance letters from her university choices in winter 2018. She had gotten accepted everywhere she wanted to go for Neuroscience. It was suddenly between

LOVEY

Nottingham and Sussex. She knew really, she didn't actually have a choice where she went. Nottingham was hours away and Sussex, well, Sussex was an hour at the very most and she had a baby in the form of a sick pug and a partner all at home.

The University of Sussex open day was disaster. Liv, Lewis, and her mum sat in Lewis' mini.
"I don't like it." Liv insisted.
I think the whole day had overwhelmed her. Here was this place she had worked so hard to get too and she hated it. It felt cold and she couldn't imagine herself happy here. Nevertheless, no choice, remember? …and in the September 2018 Liv started her degree in Neuroscience at the University of Sussex and there she would fall so deep it would take a miracle to save her.

*

NME

As this is not a Neuroscience textbook, I will not ponder on the ins and outs too long but, NME stands for Necrotizing Meningoencephalitis. It is a fatal inflammatory brain disorder which commonly effects Pugs, but in itself, is a rare disease. Put simply, it is inflammation of the brain, typically one side. The symptoms include seizures, blindness, circling, difficulty walking and more. The medication suppressed most of these effects, most of the time. If you googled *'Meningoencephalitis life expectancy'*, it'll tell you the disease has poor prognosis and survival times typically range from eight to thirty days. You may be able to now see why Bud was special. She was Liv's pride and joy and was the longest living dog, having battled the disease for four years. She was happy too. A lot of that time she was sleeping or eating or licking her mum and dad to death or bouncing round parks or excitedly spinning after her parents got in from work. Nothing compared to walking in late from work and having her baby Bud run to the door and start spinning with excitement. Liv always said when trying to explain how she loved

LOVEY

her, she didn't have a baby, a human one, so Bud was the closest thing she knew to how much she could love another living thing.

Liv would always be thankful for Bud for so many reasons but one being she led her to her love of neuroscience.

*

Neuroscience

Yes, the real decision to study neuroscience came from Bud whilst doing her biology, chemistry, and physics A-levels but the spark first began a lot earlier.

Standing in a school science room, science being her favourite subject, and maths, a herd of her fellow pupils surrounded a human brain which had been brought in for a science experiment. They wanted to dissect it, work out the structures and *yes*, so did Liv but she was overcome by how this was once an entire person. Every thought they had. Every word they said. Action they made. All the love they felt. All took place and now laid in front of her. That's what made her a little different, science can be very cut and dry. Factual, as it should be. You'll find a lot of scientists lack the emotive approach. But she never lost her touch to human connection. She could never fully detach herself.

*

Harry

Now I've left Harry's introduction for a little while as his and Liv's friendship has been nothing shy of complicated. Speaking in present day, they are best friends. He has been an undeniable rock in Liv's life. I really don't think there is anything he or her wouldn't do for the another. They have a unique connection which has seen the test of time and pain. They somehow have remained so incredibly

LOVEY

strong, through the worst of times, and still are able to sit and make each other cry with laughter.

From day one, they just *got* each other. And in the moments, they didn't or couldn't, they'd *try* and that meant the absolute most. Their beginning was a little complicated and rocky to say the least but eventually they'd find a way of being exactly what the other needed them to be. From the start, and an outside perspective, he was Lewis' best friend from secondary school and has remained that way up until their mid-twenties. So, as I guess you can presume, Liv and Harry were around each other quite a lot over Liv and Lewis' four and a half relationship. However, it was only towards the very end of the relationship they really started to really *see* each other for who they really were. *For Liv, it started with a phone call…*
Liv had rung Harry to see if he was going to be popping round the flat which Liv and Lewis shared. This was not unusual as Lewis was awful at making plans with friends and was normally left for Liv to arrange. He just seemed off. He just seemed sad. But the type of sad which you use all your energy to hide. The type of sad that only someone who knew that pain, could detect.
"Are you okay?"
"Yeah, I'm fine."
Liv took a pause.
"Are you *really* ok?"

Harry *broke.*

Maybe it was the question he needed, maybe from the person it needed to come from, maybe the right time, we don't know but it was the beginning. Harry was a typical young man, extremely talented at hiding how he truly felt. This is a terrifying truth in men and their mental health which sparked Liv's passion for wanting to break this cycle. He started unravelling at the seams, but Liv was a safe place. Harry knew Liv was quite open about her struggles and had confidence when talking about it. No shame. They slowly

LOVEY

became the exact people they needed for each other. Liv was scared to leave Lewis even though she knew it's what she wanted, and Harry had broken up with his own long-term girlfriend and was about to move to Australia. *Devastated.* Harry sat across from Liv and Lewis revealing he was quitting his job and moving to the other side of the world. The place Liv had always yearned to be. However, she was stuck and about to start university. The pair had taken a day out not long before, doing something alone for the first time. Their partners at the time thought it was strange but accepted the plan. A moment after they had gotten back and were sat in Liv's Mini waiting to pick up Harry's girlfriend from her work, Liv confessed she *just wanted to leave.* She wanted to pack up and move to Melbourne, Australia. We only know now that Harry had booked his flight to this precise place to which Liv would later find out. Finally, she found someone who '*got her*'. Lewis never seemed to understand the complexity of her mind, but it seemed Harry could, maybe, one day.

Harry and Liv became close as they bonded ever more over how painful life could be. In Liv's eyes Harry had always been one of those men that was more '*lad-ish*'. He was constantly in the gym. Eating chicken and rice six-million times a day it felt. They always got on, he always took an interest in things Liv was doing and her studies. Often sitting with her at the dining table of their friends flat as the rest of the friendship group played PlayStation as Liv tried to fit in her assignments whilst remaining sociable. She would have never anticipated the depth that laid beyond the surface of this man. The more Liv dived into Harry's mind, she learnt he was as deep as the ocean. After sustaining a gym injury in his arm and up his neck, which in time turned into chronic pain that possessed him to feel trapped in his immensely agony riddled body, she'd soon learn how truly desperate he was and lengths he'd go to escape.

Abandoned. The one person she grew to need for that feeling of being seen after so long of not having it and he was leaving. The last

LOVEY

time they saw each other was around their entire friendship group, she was left feeling cheated as they could never fully be themselves when around the others which resulted in a goodbye that felt surface level and fake as the rest of group had a quietly disapproving attitude towards the two and their growing friendship. Liv stood over the large window of one of their friends flat, that overlooked the resident car park, she took a picture of his van before he drove away.

> Do you ever just need someone to believe that the monster you see, you sense, you fear... is real. I think the more someone denies the thing that's so real, it grows stronger. It's there, laughing, knowing that it can haunt you, hurt you and no one is coming to save you.

*

Men's mental health

Liv learnt quite early on that mental illness can present quite differently in men compared to women, but regardless, is no less real. According to mind.org 43% of men had said they have suffered from regular low mood for a period of time. Quite high right? Now imagine all the men that never say a word. Never speak up to be a part of statistic. Now imagine that figure a lot higher. *Scarily higher.* 100% of the men Liv had ever met suffered in some way with their mental health, and more, each one of these men believed themselves to *"never be someone who will suffer mentally."* I think some people think they are immune but if you have a brain, just like you do a body, it can become ill, in ways you can't foresee or out run. Most importantly, *it's okay...* you are allowed to become a little unwell mentally, but just like when you are physically ill, you must

LOVEY

rest, medicate sometimes, recoup, but most of all, acknowledge you don't feel quite right and allow yourself to feel and then, in turn, get better.

> You are not weak.
> You are still a 'Man'.
> You are <u>human.</u>

Now, I won't ever pretend to know what it feels like from a male perceptive, as that would be impossible and ingenuine, but I do know someone that can…

> …*Hi, it's Harry.*
>
> *It's temporary Harry. It's temporary.* That's what I'd tell myself. It was always hard to try and take on people's advice along with implementing it, especially when I know that even the perfect string of words, taken in the right way (which is hard enough in itself), would not change the physical element of my struggles. My thoughts would always quickly wonder past the point of constructive or helpful at all. I'd find over time that more thoughts would rush through my head, trying my best to rationalize the situation and say myself that if things had to stay, then that would be okay…Deep down, I knew I couldn't continue on like this, something had to change whether for the better or worse. Unfortunately, the latter was quickly becoming the more likely.
>
> *What the fuck is going on?*
> *Why won't it stop?*
> *I've tried everything.*
> *Why me?*
> *I must have done something to deserve this.*
> *Nobody understands.*

LOVEY

I know how to make it stop.

Mental health clearly affects and manifests itself in different ways based on each individual and their situations. A therapist I once had explained depression and how it differs from person to person in a way that stuck with me. Imagine a bucket and everybody starts with their buckets filled up to different levels and some people are more susceptible to chronic depression and anxiety along with other mental health conditions than others. Sometimes it may not take much for your bucket to become full and overflow, compared to others. I would think about this often when in pain and struggling with in a particular moment and start comparing myself to people (which is rarely a productive task at the best of times) as the saying goes, *comparison is the thief of joy*, and I certainly had no joy to steal. I would find people who were also suffering of pain who also had sustained permanent lifelong injuries due to number of circumstances, who were pushing through, trying to make the most of their lives by trying to turn a negative into a positive. *How! How are they doing this?* Life had dealt these people a bad hand one way or another and their tendency is to fight against it, not let it destroy them. I was well aware that things are never as black and white as they seem. I'm sure these people were hurting deep down too but they had found a way to channel it or accept it at least.

What drove me here? Was it my ego? Selfishness? Or something else?

Perhaps this is where I hoped therapy would help maybe if I try to learn about myself and behaviours. In turn it would help me deal with this situation in a different way and come to terms with it…

LOVEY

"Come to terms." I left there thinking why should I listen to this person telling me to *'come to terms'* with something they can't even feel? I did appreciate the fact my therapist was trying to help, and she did but it's easy to just say words when you are experiencing a totally different reality. I always left my sessions not knowing how to feel and moreover, feeling frustrated. I don't know what I was expecting from these meetings. I guess just talking about things helped in some kind of way as talking about how I felt never seemed like an option to anyone close to me, partly because talking in itself couldn't take my issues away, only action could.

Your brain will mask it and do a great job at locking it away in a box when things are better. *But it's always there.* And at the most unexpected moments, it will loosen the lid every now and then. It's crazy how things could spiral out of control. I used to sit in my work van on Brighton seafront at different times of the night, due to my job, lay down on the seats and go to *that place.* Shortly after I'd start too cry. I'd think of my family. Picture life for them after they found me. Found that my mind had taken me. But I concluded life goes on, what else can it do. Even if people *did* care, they can't do anything for me, and I knew that. Part of me always wished that someone would just see me in there and knock on the window. Ask if I was okay and tell me everything would be alright. Get me out of the van and make me go with them. *To not worry about the job, it's not important and we're going to do whatever we need to sort this* and walk off to the sunrise, but I knew life didn't work like that, only in movies. Instead, I would lay there screaming into my coat, wanting it to stop until I was tired enough to fall asleep. Wait for my phone to jingle from dispatch, giving me a job, and then sit up and pretend that

LOVEY

it all never happened, wipe the tears from my face, take a deep breath and go back to my reality.
I guess I should explain how me and Liv came into it. Now, mine and Liv's relationship has been complicated to say the least. Not only due to the fact we met through my best friend at the time, *Lewis*, which I'm sure you've heard all about, but it was funny, because Liv had been with Lewis for a number of years before we ever *really* spoke in length. For some reason whenever we were around each other we would just resort to insulting one another, almost like when you were a kid, and you met that friend you were very similar too and you would just start teasing each other. Me and my partner at the time used to go round to Liv and Lewis' place quite a bit. Order some food, maybe watch a film or sit and play PlayStation. You know, normal things friends do. Funnily enough, talking at length about anything interesting was never a staple of these evenings which was something that I was clearly lacking, and I had a sense Liv felt the same. I remember one of the first times we did interact like adults, Lewis and Amy were both out in the kitchen whilst we were on the sofa. We had a short conversation, that's all it was, and was the deepest we had ever communicated up until that point. Even though we said very little, on the way back home, I sat there thinking how I had really enjoyed that interaction and couldn't stop thinking about how it made me feel. *She has a way about her.* One where you can feel she knows exactly what you're feeling, without having to say it. The desire grew and I began to just want an excuse to talk to Liv more. This is where in my own head at least, I started to create problems.

I can't be friends with my best friend's girlfriend, that's weird.

Why can't me and Lewis talk like that?

LOVEY

What if Amy finds out that we are talking, in any capacity.

This and plenty more ran through my mind. Even though it was Liv's place, due to her and Lewis living in a flat her grandad rented out to them, I always felt I needed to *'okay it'* with Lewis for me to come over. I didn't want to make it seem like I was more interested in seeing Liv than him, which was the truth, of course.

The next part happened quite quickly from there. I handed in my notice as a gas engineer, a role I hated. I split up with my partner, which should have happened long before it did. Then I bought a one-way ticket to Melbourne, Australia. Before I made the decision to end my relationship, me and Liv decided to go to Brighton together for a day out. It felt a little weird to me as I was being questioned by my girlfriend *'why are you going to Brighton with Liv?' 'What for?'* As if I should have had another reason other than we've become friends and enjoy each other's company. I was determined to not let that put me off. The first thing I always asked Liv, when doing something, I'd ask if it was okay with Lewis. I got the sense that she didn't like me asking about him, like she needed permission which, of course, she didn't. But for me at least Liv was still my friend's girlfriend at that stage, and it took a while for that to change.

When I moved to Australia, Liv helped me a lot. We didn't speak everyday but when we did, I would voice things that were happening, and she would just listen. She wouldn't say *'make sure you do this'* or *'don't do that'*. Sometimes she wouldn't suggest anything, and she'd just sit and listen and try and help in any way she could. This was a part of our friendship that was unique to me at least. There was no judgement or undertone of expectation which I felt with

LOVEY

other people, just saying words for the sake of it. This can be dangerous in itself. It can be dangerous to someone listening. Sometimes, being silent is okay. After a long chat one day or evening, depending on what side of the world we were on, I was still in a lot of pain and made the decision to book a flight home after four months of being in Oz, making a short stop in Bali. Liv and Lewis arranged to pick me up from the airport. I remember having mixed emotions, being disappointed and confused. But in a small way I was happy to be somewhere familiar. Liv greeted me with a hug at the arrivals part of Heathrow airport. The hug was quite unremarkable due to my lack of affection. Looking back now, it must have been difficult for Liv as I definitely acted so differently when Lewis was there which was stopping our friendship from being as good as it could have been at the time. I knew she needed to leave Lewis if she wanted to move on and experience different things, the differences between them became even more evident the closer I got to Liv.

As the months went on in our lives we were always in contact. We would go through stages of being on the phone for hours a day. Even after our relationship grew and I felt comfortable talking to Liv about most things in my life, there were times that even though I knew she was there and would answer the phone if I called or needed her, I wouldn't pick up the phone. I feel like when men are in a position of complete despair, even if there *is* someone to talk to, it just doesn't matter. And this is where self-sabotage comes in, and it's a slippery slope from there. It's easy to look at it from being out of that mindset or in a third person perspective and think when you're in that moment to just make contact but sometimes you can have all the help you require but still feel completely alone. These were the moments I used to question, *there must be*

LOVEY

something wrong with my brain. I called Liv one night out of the blue in the early hours of the morning. She was with Roe at the time, which was something I could always tell right away. Her voice was different, but in a good way, a happy way. It wasn't often that I'd call in the middle of the night, one saving grace for me is that I rarely had trouble sleeping. At one point, it was my favourite thing to do. I'd make any excuse to go to bed as I couldn't feel any pain there. But this night I just couldn't sleep. I tried everything and the longer I was up, in my room alone, the worse things got. Part of me wanted her to not answer. What I came to realise as time went on is that, what is said sometimes is irrelevant. It's only when the moments become easier to handle, that the cloud starts to lift. If you can fill the painful moments with something, *anything*, that is better than nothing. On this night she *did* answer, and it filled a desperate moment is with *something*, the something I needed.

Liv really helped me transform as a person over the next few years. There were a lot of behaviours and mindsets that I had and were only made apparent to me in certain situations. Because I trusted Liv and would let my guard down, I found myself taking moments out on her. I used to react and say things I'm not proud of and on multiple occasions consciously made wrong decisions because I'd want to avoid any emotional discomfort.

"Just because you're in pain doesn't mean you can treat me like that!"
This one hit home.

I used to bottle everything up so much and as I was in a customer facing job, having to smile multiple times a day, every day, when the last thing I wanted to do was smile. It

LOVEY

all became harder and harder. I would usually take this out on myself in one way or another when home, and occasionally would snap at Liv. I remember this being her response one day when I did. I think about that often. It was the first time she ever said anything back.

Why and how have I done this to myself? and maybe this is how things are meant to be for me. That was a constant thought. Being a skinny teen fresh out of school with no real life experience or confidence to being surrounded by a bunch of trades men on building sites was a disaster waiting to happen. I got picked on *a lot* for being slim which wasn't something I was really used to up till then. School was a good experience for me luckily. But after it became a reoccurring theme at work, I started to understand what it felt like to be that boy at school that was always being bullied for the way they looked. I always felt sorry for them but never knew what to do. Well, that was me now and yeah, it's awful. So, I got myself down to the gym, like a lot of lads do in their late teens, and after a period of a few months, I had started to become a lot more confident with my image which ironically only became a problem to me when other people said it was. So, I ended up spending most of my free time, five days a week, at the gym. This is where confidence can turn into ego and vanity. Especially at a young age. When your testosterone is increasing by the day, and to me at the time, I was happy finding this side of me, although I can look back now and see an emotionally immature boy with a growing ego. At the time I just remember thinking *'just keep working out and things will get better'*, but you know how the saying goes, *'ignorance is bliss'* and I found that out the hard way.

I saw how different Liv was when with Roe. I'd never seen her like it since knowing her. Just content. Pure

LOVEY

contentment. A lot of things that I knew worried Liv in the past were barely topics of conversation anymore, which was great. I'd only met Roe a handful of times and every time we got on really well. Humour was always a constant between me and Liv, always being able to make each other properly hackle and go weak with laughter, and I could tell right away it was no different with them. To say I was happy for anything at that time would be a lie but seeing them together and the way Liv's voice was just *different* when talking about him, made me feel good. Relieved in a strange sense, relieved that as long as she was with him, she was in a safe place. It's really difficult going through change but ultimately necessary and my relationship throughout the years with Liv is the perfect example of that. I only realise now how patient Liv was in those moments of frustration where I just wanted her to feel what I felt. There were moments my frustration would boil over, but all Liv saw was a good person who was just hurting and didn't know what to do about it. She never wavered from my side. No matter what I did or said. At the time I was confused, *why are you still doing this for me? Why do you care? You can't change my situation as soon as I get out this car and leave you, I'm in pain! It doesn't stop for me!* We have both experienced our own separate reality and we'll always struggle with the fact that neither of us will fully ever be able to sympathise but, the fact we **understand** is what makes our connection so strong. I am so grateful for everything Liv has done for me, especially when it comes to making me question my own views, because I wouldn't be the person I am proud to be today, without her. She has said thing to me over the years, sometimes just the simplest of things but I think about them all the time and they help me in my life.

LOVEY

I always think about that Black Mirror episode on Netflix where a doctor designs this mesh hat with sensors which he puts on and he can feel what the other person are feeling. I wanted one of these with me at all times so I could just put it on people and go, *yes, I'm working, I'm smiling and putting on a brave face, but this is what I'm dealing with! So, give me a fucking break!*

Now things didn't just go from bad to better to good in a nice straight line. The last four to five years has been a huge rollercoaster and not a particularly fun one. Being in physical pain every day is awful, going to bed just hoping you can wake up and it's gone, and you have dreams about waking pain free so vivid you swear you lived it and then BOOM! Your eyes open and of course, it is still there and that was in fact, just a dream HARRY.

Over all these years and many, many different therapies, the pain *is* better, something I thought I'd never say but it is and to be honest there is nothing that scares me more than being back in that place, and I make sure I show gratitude that I am no longer there, every day.

One very vital thing I have learnt was how important it is to have at least one good person around who is willing to listen and help if need be. This can be a much more difficult thing for a lot of men to admit that we need. But regardless of sex, **'People need people'** to share the best times and be there for each other in the worst because circumstances can change in a blink of an eye. The fact that suicide is the highest cause of death in young men in this country is truly awful and should highlight just how bad things are can get for every young man out there.

LOVEY

I know it is beyond hard but find someone willing stay and someone that makes you feel less alone. Because it is ***those people*** who you want in your worst moments, not just the best.

*

SOS

"Your phone keeps ringing. I think it's Harry." Roe slurring his words whilst nudging Liv to wake in the early hours of the morning. She turned her phone over and revealed a lit-up screen filled to capacity with missed calls. It was Harry. *Her stomach dropped.* Adrenaline instantly released into her blood stream. She knew, she knew something was so incredibly wrong. She called him instantly back. He answered. *Thank God.* His sobbing poured down the phone. "I can't do this anymore." Liv barely deciphering his words through his tears. She knew he wasn't well mentally. But she also knew how bad he must have been to call her like this. *A cry for help.* Panic coursed through her body. She was in Brighton and Harry lived an hour away, she couldn't get to him. Roe quickly realising something was deeply wrong, he sat up with Liv in bed, trying to comfort her as he put his arm around her waist and pulled her in slightly, a way of saying *'you're okay, I've got you'*. She looked down at him whilst holding the phone to her ear and placed her hand on his thigh. Harry had a past of suicidal thoughts. He once told Liv a plan he had, and he had put it in motion, but had managed to stop himself. *One more day,* he told himself. She talked him down. Talked till he fell asleep. It was a terrifying night for everyone. Roe held her extra tight that night.

*

"Promise me I'll be okay?"
"I promise." Harry said with conviction.

Liv ended her relationship with Lewis.

LOVEY

*

It's the end

16th of October 2018 Liv and Lewis' relationship ended.
16th of November 2018, Buddha died.

Timings were strange. Liv always felt in tune with the world around her. Her and Lewis had broken up, but he was still in process of moving out of their shared home whilst Liv occupied her university halls as much as possible, whilst still maintaining a balance of seeing her Bud, who she hated being apart from. Last minute on one random weekday evening, "I'm staying at the flat tonight." Liv rang Lewis whilst on the train back down to home. She had stood in her university room with the strongest sense *she should go home.* "That's fine, I'm not there, I'm away, your mums looking after Bud." Lewis informing Liv he had gone away with friends, including Harry. Later that evening, tucked up in bed, Liv sent Lewis a picture of Bud sleeping, cuddled up with a hot water bottle as she had bedded her and Bud down. After four years, Liv had become incredibly sensitive to waking up to Bud's seizures the second they started. It became a reflex.
"What's wrong?" Flum catching Liv running down the stairs.
"Bud's relapsing." she informed Flum as she climbed down the steps to find the Mycophenolate, Phenoleptil and Levetiracetam.

> Mycophenolate: An immunosuppressant. Weakens the body's immune system, decreasing the ability to fight infection.
>
> Phenoleptil: Medication for the prevention of seizures for generalised epilepsy in dogs.
>
> Levetiracetam: An anticonvulsant used to treat seizures and epilepsy.

LOVEY

By this point Liv knew the procedure, what do to when this happened. Knew the medication and how much to give her out of Bud's extensive medicine bag. This relapse was different this time and she knew what it symbolized. Her and Lewis had agreed after her last deterioration, the next one was it, the one where they'd say goodbye. Buddha had outlived the life expectancy by four years, this usually being a month from symptom onset and had given her neurologist a sense of achievement. She was the longest living dog with her disease, Liv always taking pride in this. Going back upstairs with the medication squished into some dog treats, Bud had already come out of one seizure and into another. She took her earliest opportunity to get the medication into her system. At the point her tablets would normally suppress her symptoms, she was instead, in and out of non-stop seizures. The medication was having no effect which meant one thing to Liv, her relapse had reached past a salvageable point.
"We need to drive to Fitzpatrick," Liv pronouncing through to Flum, "she's really not good mum."

They packed up her medication, her blanket and a toy. Fitzpatrick referrals was two hours away which always added an element of urgency. The couple were always made aware she could pass from a seizure in the time it took to arrive, but the added difficulty of her disease is that there are only two vets in the UK which are equip with treating it. So, in the emergencies, it was a race. Climbing into Liv's black Mini, they powered up to Guildford as the time verged on midnight, whilst Bud rested in Flum's lap. On the journey Liv thought as she drove on the baren motorway, *what would have happened if she hadn't randomly come down to stay?* Flum didn't know what medication to give her, she wouldn't have been able to drive to Guildford alone with Bud seizing. There were no trains from Brighton so Liv would have been stuck, Lewis was hours away.

It felt meant to be… *in the saddest way.*

LOVEY

Tens of calls later, no answer.
She called Lewis.
She called Harry.
She called the other friend she knew they were away with.
Nothing.

> Liv: We're at Fitzpatrick, buds relapsed, this is it now Lewis, we're just waiting for you

Liv text fearfully imagining Bud slipping away before her dad gets to say goodbye.
Finally, in the early hours of the morning, he answered and had departed. A couple of hours later he arrived at Fitzpatrick Referrals. They had managed to stabilize Bud on an IV, this being the only contribution as to what was keeping her out of a seizure.
The look Lewis and Liv shared as he walked into the waiting room, was palpable. The baby they both shared and loved so much was about to no longer exist.
 "I had a weird feeling when you sent that picture of her last night, felt like I knew." he said after they both hugged and prepared themselves as much as they could.
As much as it was difficult having Bud, the pair would have never changed it. She was a hub of happiness and made them into a family. A lot of others would have received her diagnosis and put her down there and then and avoided the thousands of pounds in vet bills and emotional torture it was, but it was never a question in their mind. You do what you've got to do. Liv made a deal with Buddha on the day she was diagnosed. As long she was strong and happy, majority of the time, then she'd do everything she could to give her as many happy days filled with food, cuddles, walks and sleep, as she could. They both held up their deal and she could not have been prouder of her furry child.
"I'll leave you to say goodbye." the kind female vet left the room.
The three took turns holding her, cuddling her. Flum was drowning in tears, Lewis was maintaining a dry exterior, Liv sobbed. She

LOVEY

sobbed into the top of her baby's head. Buddha was truly Liv's child. She was her baby, but not just her baby, her ill baby who needed constant care and had been what her life revolved around for the last four years.

"Who will be holding her during?" the vet had re-entered.

"I will." Liv stated strongly, looking down into baby Bud's eyes.

It was so incredibly important for Liv to do. Going back to her very first seizure, she started to fit whilst on Liv's lap to which she begged Lewis to move her off, unable to cope with how traumatic it is to feel so helpless over something you love so much. She had grown so much, so strongly over the past four years that she'd prove she could do this. She was her mum. She deserved her mum holding her till she slept forever.

"Are we ready?" the vet had placed a puppy pad on to Liv's lap and wrapped Buddha into a blanket.

In the seconds leading to the end Liv lowered her head into Buds and said…

"Mummy loves you. Mummy loves you Bud Bud, so much." she whispered into her soft black tipped ears as tears fell down onto her soft fawn fur, holding her tightly into her chest, nuzzling her neck. Instantaneously, as the needle entered the IV, Lewis broke. Broke down into a stream of tears. Suddenly, there was all his emotion. Liv had often wondered where it all was, he could be so cold. All the built-up pain had finally released, he had shattered into a million different pieces.

There it was. The moment she had dreaded since her diagnosis. Her worst fear. She handed her furry baby back to the vet after showering her with her last kisses and left the clinical room.

Walking out in a despairing daze, holding her baby blanket they had swaddled her up in when they picked her up in as a puppy, she sat back in the driver's seat of her Mini, feeling as though she had a limb missing. Who was she now? She felt. Bud had been her purpose, her compelling force so many times. Her and Flum drove home in silence.

LOVEY

*

Back to university Liv went

Her only anchors in this world had disappeared. Died. And she was left with nothing.

> You take away the things that ground you and what are you left with?

*

Spreadsheets

Spreadsheets were a love language of Roe's. Liv sat on the edge of Roe's bed in Clapham while he played with numbers, showing her the potential of compound interest, and investing, she loved when he got excited over his nerdy but well-worth it hobbies. He really found his calling in becoming an accountant. Suddenly, she was warped back to time, to being back in her first tiny flat. She was suddenly in the memory, both laying down on the bed that took up most of the square footage of her studio, on their stomachs, the paired liked to call *'Tummy time'* as it became an on-going joke that Roe liked to lay on his stomach in the way babies to do. In the memory, Roe was creating a spreadsheet of the incomings and outgoings of living together using a specific flat they had both fallen in love with as the reference. They would never end up needing this spreadsheet, but Liv never deleted it. It reminded her of a time when Roe was so committed to her and their life that he wanted to start one, in a home they shared. She quickly shook herself back too into the room however, the lingering feel of the past tugging her back never left, but nevertheless she stayed present and acknowledged quietly to herself how everything went so incredibly differently to how she had imagined.

LOVEY

The night before, laying in his bed, tracing words onto his back she knew she could never say but was maybe hoping somehow, they'd sink into his skin and then maybe his heart…

*

Starred messages

Roe: My beautiful snuggle bum

*

Roe: Bub it's ok, I'm here for you

*

Roe: You're beautiful

*

Roe: I do really appreciate you ya know

*

Roe: I still need time but wanted you to know that I'm not going anywhere

*

Roe: You should tell me when you feel anxious, I'm here for you rememberrrrr

*

Roe: Let's keep getting through this

*

Roe: N'night my bubbie love youuuuuu

LOVEY

*

Roe: Morning my gorgeous bubba! I'm so sorry about last night, I was grumpy and shouldn't have treated you like that. I agree with everything you said, and I hope you believe me when I say I will be better 🩶

*

Roe: I honestly had the best weekend, you did that. Even though I have been feeling down you pulled it off

Liv: My bubs 🩶 I didn't do it bubba, we did it together... we're magic when we're together, let's try to not forget and carry on having millions of special moments

*

Roe: I'm so luckyyyyyyyy

*

Roe: My little bubba bearrrrr

*

Roe: I love you forever

Forever and everrrrrrr

*

Roe: Forever

Liv: Forever

*

Roe: Hang tight I'll be back as soon as I can

LOVEY

*

Roe: I want this forever

*

Roe: I want you at the end of this so if there's something I can do so that's there I will

*

Roe: I will always love you, you'll forever be a part of me

*

Roe: That's love right there

*

Roe: Just remember I love you so much and I'm not going anywhere

*

Roe: I wanna give you the biggest cuddle

*

Roe: Look, I look back at times like this when I need to remember and it gets me through. That's all you need to know. I hope it's not the end, but I understand if you need to look out for yourself. You don't make my days worse, you make them better. Just remember that

Roe: You're helping me more than you know and are the opposite of the problem

*

Roe: Morning my gorgeous sausage

LOVEY

*

Roe: Are we ok? I'm so sorryyyyy

*

Roe: How are you even meant to help me? Like I don't even know what's wrong

Liv: Roe we will get you through this I promise, you have to learn to talk to me, I know it's hard but trust me it's only when you let yourself think about it and talk nonsense that you start to figure out but you have to try. I love you and I'm not going anywhere

Roe: You deserve someone so much better

*

Roe: Thank you for making me stay with you bubba you have been so great to me the last few days, I really do appreciate it

Liv: Aww bubba I am too. You just need a little support and love and I'm never going to let you down. Let's focus on you bubba and getting you through, I'm by your side always and just remember I'm here for when we're laughing so much and can't stop but also in the moments where you feel like crying and just rubbish. I am here. I am all yours.

Roe: I love you

Liv: I love you

*

Roe: I fucking love you so much bub! You're not just another thing on my to do list. I do want you! I am finding it hard at the moment and I'm not sure why, I think I'm just trying to get out of the rut I was in at the start of the year. I still have hope we can get through this!

LOVEY

*

Roe: I will literally do anything for you

*

Roe: Well no because that's not how we do things

We talk and work them out

*

Roe: I'm the one who doesn't deserve you, don't ever think you don't deserve me

*

Roe: I want you to be always with me

*

Roe: Was looking at this last night like how cute is my bubba

*

Roe: You will forever be mine bub!! You will never be able to get rid of me

*

Roe: I miss your beautiful eyes

*

Roe: We will be so strong after

*

Roe: I'm gonna become such a better person after all this bub

LOVEY

It's funny. Roe's one of those guys that is *just* the absolute *sweetest*. He's the one you'd say could never hurt a fly. He'd be the last you'd expect to cheat or betray you. His sweetness was almost childlike. He had an innocence about him that made you feel so incredibly safe. He's the guy you're cuddled up with on the sofa, looking over at you, catching you off guard with saying a funny thing in his baby voice or how much he loves you. Liv missed this person. *Her person. She always knew she needed someone sweet like that, after everything.*

*

"Don't I get a kiss then?"

Coming back from the bathroom, climbing straight into the bed residing in Clapham and turning over to the outside. She thought it was so strange. He was never affectionate anymore. She rolled back over, on to her stomach and reached her lips out to meet his.

Weird, again she thought.

We know now. He knew. Knew he had betrayed her. Knew he'd probably just given her chlamydia. Knew he'd fully lose her. The guilt was finding its way to his heart.

*

The cabin

It surprised her. Roe had suggested after one of his visits during the time their interactions were only labelled as casual. It surprised her the fact that Roe wanted to escalate from their usual encounters from being mostly at Liv's flat in Brighton to an intimate weekend away together. She found a remote cabin with a hot tub in Sussex. They booked it. She was convinced it wouldn't happen, something would come up, ruin it.

LOVEY

How was this just sex? She asked herself. A whole weekend away, a holiday they never went on whilst together.

> Liv: Got the invoice for the cabin, £137 each but not due till the 27th so no rush
>
> Roe: Sweet! Remind me like a day or two before?
>
> Liv: Sweet will do

*

> Roe: I need to tell you something

The one who usually saved her from her panic attacks was suddenly inducing one. Stood on the shop floor of the clothing shop, she looked down at her phone. His name and a very long paragraph lit up her screen as she pulled it out her pocket. Her eyes went blurry as adrenaline instantly released throughout her entire body whilst it simultaneously provoked a powerful sick, fearful feeling in her stomach, only being able to absorb a few of the jumbled words.

> Chlamydia.
> I'm sorry.
> Drunk.
> Slept.
> Someone.

She always wondered what the moment would be. The moment she finally blocked him and *why.* She had always believed that moment would be the hardest thing she'd ever have to do. She excused herself off of shop floor and carried her palpitating body upstairs to where her manager and close friend, all in one, was working.
A full panic attack.
Over and over.
Re-reading the message.
Something clicked.
It felt so unbelievably done.

LOVEY

Finished.
She blocked him,
even on Depop.

*

Euro Finals 2021

Liv and Roe kept bumping into each other's worlds for a while. After he had revealed his betrayal and STI, she removed him from her life with no word. There were no words left. She felt it was the only option to retrieve any power that was left. Her silence would change after a drunken night following the Euro Finals in the summer of 2021, finding herself unavoidably back in his bedroom.
"I have to call Roe. I'm so annoyed I have to call Roe." stood outside Waterloo tube station, which was proceeding to shut as the last tube had run, she called Flum.
"I can't get hold of any friends. Liv's not answering. I can't just stand here all night. There's no trains. No one I can go too."
"You'll have to call Roe." Flum in agreement.

"What do you want?" he answered.
How dare he answer the phone like that after everything.
"I'm stuck at Waterloo and have nowhere to go. Trust me I don't want to see you."
"Come to mine, I'm nearly home."
"Are you sure?"
 "Yeah."

As she walked slowly into his bedroom which she knew too well, laying her bag on his bed, she looked up at him.
"I hate you, you know."
He looked at her from across the room, "I know." hanging his head.
"I don't want to be here… but I had to." she continued.
"I know." he repeated, in a defected tone, barely being able to look at her.

LOVEY

Roe pulled out his draw and gave her a T-shirt. It was one he had bought together in Urban Outfitters when they were a couple. She undressed and placed the oversized tee over her body.
The pair tucked themselves into bed.
She turned over and laid on her stomach with her arms resting on his chest. She looked at him. She couldn't not see all that he was. Someone sweet, who she loved so incredibly. The world knew he was the one person she could never hold a grudge with. His kind green eyes which felt like a window to his soul, told her he was sorry.

That same undeniable magnetism which exists between them, draw them in, again.

Liv sat straddling on top, Roe whispered in the heat of the moment "I thought you'd be at the cabin."
Roe must have not realised the weekend the pair had booked the cabin was the same as the Euro Finals, if he had known, he probably would have chosen a different day as he was a football fan and even paid to watch the final at Wembley. Liv had cancelled the cabin as soon as she received Roe's revelation of his sexually transmitted disease. Instead, she had spent the weekend with friends, in a pub, celebrating the final whilst very intoxicated.
"I wouldn't go without you." she said as she paused looking down into his eyes whilst resting their foreheads to one another, both being held in this intimate moment. After a few seconds of holding each other's gaze he thrusted up into her from underneath, his passion intensified.

Girls will understand how you can be obsessed over the most random parts of a guy's body. For Liv, it was a few, well everything about Roe, but she had a thing for his arms and hands.
"Your hands are huge!" Harry said in amazement whilst sat in restaurant after Liv had introduced Harry and Roe for the first time.

LOVEY

She always loved how they got on so well. He did have big hands, and you know what they say about big hands, and they were right. *But his arms.* During sex, Roe would reach his strong arm over her, holding onto the bedstead. It became a *thing* after Roe learnt how much she loved it. In response, she'd grab his upper arm that was stretched over her head, the arm giving him leverage with each thrust. "Kiss me." she whispered, looking up into Roe's eyes. He looked deep back down into hers with contemplation. Trying to keep hold of any emotional distance he could whilst sleeping with someone who meant so much. I think Roe was always doing his best to detach from her, then he'd see her… and be back to square one. Liv sometimes thought, if they both had to try so hard not to love each other, maybe they weren't meant to. "If I mean more than the others, you'll kiss me." she added. He held her gaze, a second past, he lowered his head, meeting her lips with the passion he was trying to keep at bay. He reached his arm up and smiled, she gripped to it tightly.

The next morning was strange. They ordered breakfast. They sat and watched YouTubers they both had always bonded over. It was a fleeting moment of the normality she used to live in and knew so well. There's not much the pair ever often disagreed on. It had always seemed 99% of their personalities fitted like a glove. They always had this undeniable ability to going right back to being ***them.*** Give them five minutes, no matter what had happened or how long it's been, and they fall right back together, like puzzle pieces. Right back into place. It felt right. It always felt, no matter what life did to try and part them, their bond would be stronger than, *greater than any effort or whim of the world.*

She woke up to Instagram story replies and messages from Oscar after putting up a drunken story of her England flag nipple covers. These made an appearance as England would score which she'd flash the pub in excitement. *I'm not sure what the pub full of men were more excited about, football or boobs.*

LOVEY

"You did give me Chlamydia." she blurted out as he now sat with his back to her, in his desk chair that overlooked his windows. He turned around and looked at her as he remained silent. She could feel the sorrow that ran through his veins as she confronted him with the consequences of his outer character decisions.

*

Clinic

"In cases like these Liv, we have to do a full sexual health screening." the nurse explained softly, taking extra care over her word choice as she believed they are trained to do with sexual assault survivors.
"Of course."
"Did he use protection?"
"No."
The nurse's eyes lit up for a split second, continuing to complete her notes.
"What ethnicity was he? Born in the UK?
"White, yes."
"Okay lovely, take the swab in the loo and insert it, swirl it around and then pop it in the hatch in the door you came past."
"I had chlamydia two months ago, my ex gave it to me. He cheated," Liv trying to almost defend her character… "will that make a difference?"

You can feel when people's hearts break for others. The nurse was *lovely.* Waiting in the empty consultation room after the nurse had stepped out for a moment, her mind went back to wondering *when,* what was the moment, the exact second her soft sweet Roe became this person. When had Roe changed from being the chest she found salvation in, to being a part of the pain she was trying to escape.

LOVEY

*

Back to the morning of the Euro's

Roe's phone buzzed all morning. He was being secretive, something he never normally was. Taking it with him any moment he left the room. He revealed he had started speaking to someone after Liv had probed a little, she met his declaration with a moment of silence. A few minutes past.
"I hate that you're speaking to someone." she said softly, interrupting the quiet air that had been created. She always found the strength in her vulnerability and spoke what she truly felt.
"I hate you are too." he confessed.
She was confused. *Why are we doing this then?* she thought.
"Those people don't mean anything compared to you." she admitted.
"More than one?" Roe seeming concerned and broken, all at once. She uncomfortably sustained eye contact and then lowered her head, remaining silent.

They would leave it there. She collected her belongings and thanked him for saving her again, another moment she needed him, and he was there. They said goodbye and she walked through the torrential rain that was falling over London, making her hair into instant ringlet curls, soaking her entire outfit. She made her way home very damp, and very heart broken.

> It would be twelve days later
> that she would be raped.

She left their encounter with so many things she wished she had said, had she of known she was going to see him. It felt unfinished. In the days that followed she was overwhelmed by the need to finally say it all. Everything she had felt, for months, years.
Sat on a wooden bench along the quiet Hove seafront, watching the large waves crash up against the shore, she broke into tears. She

LOVEY

lifted her hood and covered her eyes with sunglasses as she inhaled deep breaths of the sea air in through her nose. She was overcome with all that her heart held for him. It had been *the* hardest journey with him, and she truly, wholeheartedly believed it would end differently but he couldn't choose her, hadn't in so long, so she had to say goodbye. She had to say everything she wished she had the day she left. She sat and quietly cried as she drafted her message in her notes. Once she had reached the end of all she had to say. She had sat on that bench for over an hour. She wanted to leave it all there. Say all she needed to say and walk home having left him in the past with the knowledge of her heart. She pressed send and lifted her head up to the sky, then back down the sea. She looked out upon the peacefulness it had become. *Calm. Quiet.*

LOVEY

Her goodbye message…

19th July 2021.

Liv: Hey, I doubt you'll read this but it's here if you do. Just had stuff on my mind that I guess I wanted to say even though I'm not sure how to. I know you don't think about us and shut a lot out and that's fair, but I've tried to process a lot of what's happened and some stuff I'll never be able to figure out or make sense of but you dating and starting with someone else says so much. I know I said I'd hope one day you'll find your way back, back to yourself, when life is a little quieter, that you'll feel it… everything you did before and maybe feel even more than ever but I know you won't and maybe you never did. I always knew ya know, always better out there, always more experiences. I honestly believed we came together when we both needed each other, like the world said, here's your soulmate… you need to meet now but you'll need to part at some point for a while and do other things, become better people but you'll find your way back, the magic and bond that's between you both will always bring you back, somehow. But I need you to say it. I know it's hard, the hardest… but it's the only thing I'd ever ask of you and without that, I guess it's all not true. You may have been my person Roe, but that doesn't mean I was yours and I guess I wasn't. I really thought it, us were it, I didn't care we weren't together now, always knew it would take a journey but I didn't understand how we could have everything we do and not be what people search for. Again, I guess I was wrong. Please always stay safe roe, can't imagine a world where you're not ok and please don't be scared to be vulnerable, you're so strong, stronger than you know. And in spite of all your flaws (which we all have) I know you… like fully know you and I'm so proud of you and you honestly deserve the world bub. Maybe you think I see you through rose tinted glasses because you don't hold yourself that highly, but I don't. I just know ya know, it's a feeling. Like coming home but an amazing adventure all at once. Easiest thing I've ever done was love you. I wanted to say a thank you I never got a chance to say. Thank you for loving me exactly how I wanted and needed because while you focus

LOVEY

on how we fucked it, I think about the millions of times you've made me laugh or smile or safe or happy, or brightened a bad day. Moments where I could be an absolute weirdo and fully myself. Times of running down Brighton high street having a sword fight with wrapping paper, skipping through Sainsbury's laughing so loud old couples would stare, spooning you in bed playing with your hair, times when you ran into the kitchen with a note telling me I'm a superstar and you believe in me (while I'm burning the cookies). (I still have this note). Those moments Roe and a million more. I promise the good screams over the bad, over the mental health, Covid, insecurities, mistakes... because yes, you've hurt me. Worst pain I've ever felt. But I see, under it all, for me was a soulmate, not quite ready to love his. Thank you for showing me a life with someone doesn't have to be boring but you can also feel safe and insanely loved all at once. You showed me what a life with your person feels like. You became my safe person. To the point that because you used to put your forehead against mine when I'd be crouched over having a panic attack, I now put the back of my hand to my forehead and imagine you saying I'm safe and to breathe. You did that. Don't focus on ways we've fucked up, focus on how strong and happy we both made each other. Good luck with everything and go have the best life.

And also... I forgive you Roe. For all of it. I hope you forgive my mistakes too.

She knew he'd punish himself more than she ever could.

...His silence was deafening.

LOVEY

*

The days that followed

Being thankful that she was in summer break from university and her manager at work was also a close friend, she was able to give a more in-depth insight into why she'd be taking a little time off.

The days that followed the rape involved a lot of colouring. Filling in a colourless drawing of a home interior from Pinterest on her iPad. It was nice, the only thing she had to worry about was what colour was she going to make the walls or how to decorate the armchair. She barely moved. Barely had the energy to make it to the bathroom to wee.
"What would help?" Flum asked as she sat on the end of her bed. She couldn't speak for a moment. She couldn't bring her body to express the words that clouded her mind. Her body still aching and bruised, she was *exhausted*.
"Nothing this time." her broken voice whispered as she tucked her face back into her duvet.

27th July 2021.

> Roe: Hey, your mum text me saying something happened on the weekend. Please let me know if you want to talk or anything I can do… forget anything about us I just don't want you to have to deal with this alone and happy to help anyway I can. Just let me know anytime

A couple of minutes later…

> Liv: I don't know if I can get better this time

Flum reached a worryingly desperate point with her daughter's mental health. She needed help. She knew there was one person in this world that could save her.

LOVEY

> Roe: You will, it's just going to take a while and be a long journey
>
> You got this
>
> It's gonna be a lot of small steps

"Roe just messaged me." she squeezed a murmur through her blankets covering her mouth.
"Oh good." Flum with a slight amount of relief in her voice.

> And from then, Roe would call and text, every day.

Liv sent the pictures of her deepening purple, green and blue bruises that spread over her legs and elsewhere.

> Roe: Fuck
>
> Does anyone else know?

He seemed determined to make sure Liv wasn't going to do this alone. It surprised her, he felt like *him* again. It was the only glimmer of joy she had during this time. He tasked her with writing post it notes every day and sticking them to her large gold grand mirror. Things she couldn't do the day before like eat, wash her hair, or go outside. The thought of walking out there, in the world, outside her flat, felt equally disturbing. Made her body feel like it was burning whilst having crawling ants over her skin. It felt disgusting when anyone looked at her. She covered up, wore baggy jumpers but it didn't help. She felt violated by a single glance.

> Roe: We will get you outside soon
>
> Will be one of our little steps
>
> Liv: Wish I could see you

LOVEY

> Roe: Would be giving you a big hug and make you know you can be safe again
>
> You'll get through this
>
> Just don't rush it
>
> Liv: Only your hugs make me believe that
>
> I think it's all too fucked this time
>
> I feel like a shell, never felt so weak

She laid in bed being numb to everything but him. These days were filled with lots of little things and lots of nothing.

> Roe: What's the post it for today?

"Roe asked me for my post it today."
"That's good! What are you going to put?" Flum asked sat on her sofa. Liv was practically on suicide watch. It was justified in hindsight as most times she was left due to Flum or Harry's inability to be there, she'd sink right back down, draw lines on her legs with the sharpest knife she could find. It was her coping mechanism, to not let that be the night she floated up into heaven and away from her agony. That may not make a lot of sense to those who don't know but sometimes hurting herself, stopped her from ending herself. Flum was always grateful to Roe. He came back when he had no obligation to. But he wanted, needed, her on this Earth too.

What would her suicide do to him?

How would not having Liv in this world make him feel?

LOVEY

> Roe: I'm out tonight but will call you before I go out
>
> Roe: I'm getting on the tube now, but I can call on the other side

Liv sat in her oversized t-shirt on her kitchen top with her legs tucked into her chest, she looked out of her tall kitchen window waiting for her phone to light up even though no part of her genuinely believed she'd hear from him again that evening.

"Hey!"

She did.

"Just walking to The Prince for someone's birthday. What's today been like? Did you speak to the doctor?"

He lived up to his word, kept his promise, for the first time in a while, all whilst navigating his newly busy schedule since moving to London. He'd call her when he said he would. He was there when she found herself desperately close to a place her mind liked to visit.

> Roe: You can do this
>
> Liv: Don't hate me if I don't make it
>
> Roe: I will never hate you
>
> Liv: I'm just sorry ☹
>
> Roe: What are you sorry about?! You have don't absolutely nothing wrong
>
> Liv: That we met...
>
> I always ruin things for you
>
> Roe: Don't be stupid

LOVEY

You do not ruin anything

None of this is your fault

Remember by 21:00 I want your post-it note of the day

She had a deal. She sent a picture of her pink post-it note through on iMessage. They'd often be about him. This day was…

> *'I had a shower and Roe called me.*
> *Managed to wash my hair and have*
> *some ice cream'*

He'd always respond with, *"Well done"* after she sent it, *"that's a really good post it!"*, *"Baby steps"* he'd say.

But no matter how many small steps she was seeming to conquer, at the end, middle and start of every day, she desperately didn't want to live.

…But the need to not let him down was just a touch stronger.

And that's why she's here.

Because the whole time she couldn't live for herself,

she'd live for *him*.

LOVEY

> I found salvation in your presence. His voice. When he isn't breaking my heart or telling me words that haunt me, he saves me sometimes. Sometimes he's an oxygen tank while I'm drowning. It's never permanent and it always hurts in the end but in some moments it's just enough to keep me alive.
>
> Roe just called.
>
> I haven't cried very much at all. It's strange, crying is normally something I do a lot. Maybe it's the numbness or emptiness.

*

You're my bridge

It's raining outside, and it's loud as the water crashes onto the concrete. It's raining so heavily it feels like you could drown. It's all consuming, suffocating. Your clothes are as wet as if you'd stood in the shower. Then, as you're walking along the wet pavement, trying to achieve shelter from the storm. Suddenly, you step underneath a bridge to take cover. You stop still in your dripping clothes and watch the rain as it falls around you. You can still hear it, still knowing you need to, at some point, face it out there again. But the bridge shields you for a moment. It allows you catch your breath.

Ya know…

The moment you're in the car, and it's raining heavily, and it's crashing down on the windscreen. Then suddenly you drive underneath a bridge, and for a moment it stops. It all stops. Silent.

LOVEY

The rain hasn't, but for a moment in time it stops for you, all that loud, heavy rain now being shielded by the bridge.

You were my bridge.

*

Panic attack

Knelt down on the cold wooden floor of Roe's bedroom in his family home in Guildford, he placed his forehead up against hers.
"Breathe,"
"In through your nose and out through your mouth."
He gently held her hands to stop her from tugging at her scalp, something she never realised she was doing till it was over. Hyperventilating. Liv was never quite sure why her panic attacks happened. Sometimes there would be a trigger and other times they would be random. Random ones were worse. When there is no seeming cause, there's nothing obvious to change, so you have to sit there and ride this wave of absolute torture. Roe breathing deeply for Liv to copy, staying close whilst maintaining contact through their foreheads as she leant over the bed with her head hanging between her legs, saliva dripping out her mouth, heart pounding, short sharp breaths. It must have scared Roe. He had no idea how to manage moments like this but in Liv's eyes he was perfect. More than anything, panic attacks frightened Liv. And even though she had suffered from them since she was fourteen, her first being, the fear never leaves. You can't *'get used'* to them or how they feel. They are 100% terrible, every time. But with Roe, it was the only time that they didn't scare her, even though she or him couldn't stop them, they rode the wave together. Finally, Liv's adrenaline was running out which enabled her to start copying Roe's deep breaths he had maintained doing throughout.

LOVEY

*

She wore her heart on her cheek ♡

As she began to go out the house more, beginning to find a new way of living, she started drawing a small heart on her cheek with brown eyeliner. It laid just below her eye. It was a tiny way of doing her makeup for *her,* not men. It became a tiny symbol of self-empowerment.

She drew it on her face when she needed it most. She drew it till she no longer *needed* it.

*

First time

The first time you have sex after you've been raped is strange. Of course, people's experience will be different, but this was Liv's…

"Are you okay?" Roe pulling away for a moment.
"Yes." as she continued to kiss him.
"Are you sure?" Roe wanting more confirmation.
She pulled her face back to be able to look him in his eyes.
"I'm sure… It's you…it's different."

Sex is **the** most difficult thing in the world after you've been raped and that continues to be the case, but her brain knew, her body knew, *she was safe with him.*

It turned out to be a blessing that he was the first person she slept with since. It helped in getting her to feel normal, even for a moment. It was enjoyable, and almost felt like, for a split second, nothing bad had happen.

LOVEY

*

London Bridge train station

Roe. Who the fuck cares? Who cares where he is or what he's doing, who he's with or how he feels about them. Nothing matters anymore. Literally nothing.

How scary right?

Floating. I'm just floating my way home. I thought I felt sort of normal. I thought I was getting better. I feel warped back to an empty shell of nothing. I just want to be happy. Why is that so fucking hard?? I feel gone. I have nothing left to give.

LOVEY

*

Destiny, fate, and everything in between

Roe: How's it going??

Liv: Yeah I think I'm gunna leave

Hope you're having a good night

Roe: Ahhhh did you get home ok?

Liv: Just getting tube and train now

Roe: How you feeling??

Liv: Shit

Roe: Ahhh fuck it

Made it till the actual night

Where are you going back to?

Liv: Yeah true

Home

Roe: was it good??

Are you alone??

Ahhh I would say mine but still out and probably will be a while

Liv: It wasn't the best tbh

Yeah

When do you think you'd be home?

LOVEY

A part of her wished for him to say, 'I'll leave now, let's go to mine and chill, make you feel better, be safe'. But he didn't.

>Roe: Probably not till 2/3am

>Liv: Ahh fairs

>Roe: Yeeee

Liv wondered how it was her fate to have all these moments happen. Not in a feeling sorry for herself way, but in a, *what the fuck can all this shit lead too?* She was a void, a vessel that now seemed to walk this earth with nothing left to give herself, let alone anyone else. Here she sat on the cold concrete floor on platform four at London Bridge station waiting for her train back to Brighton, back to safety. She really thought she could do it. Could go out with her closest friends and enjoy an event which they had already planned prior to her entire world changing. Be around people, *men*. She wondered if she'd ever be able to get back to her version of normal. She no longer cared about the things that she clung to even in that toughest times. She'd normally find a way of ending up at Roe's, after all he was the thing that gave her safety, but she had even gone beyond that point of caring, and that was now dangerous. Liv wrote her numbness in her notes on her phone. As you'll notice, she does this a lot. Visualising the words out of her head always seemed to validate them in a strange sense. There're real. Thirteen minutes till she's on the train home. She put on her oversized, overly expensive Represent t-shirt that she kept in her bag for warmth over her tiny outfit of a black satin mini skirt and a bikini top she had tied as a cross over halter to give it more of a *going out* feel.

LOVEY

> It's moments like this that pull you right back down to earth. To the lowest point of your own mind. Do I just do it? Do I just wait for a train and jump in front? Stop talking about it and just leave everything and everyone. Flum. How could I destroy her? How could I destroy everyone that cares for me? Does anyone really care for me?...

Ten minutes. She sat shivering, praying she had the strength to just get home. A full force tornado of a panic attack was brewing, and she used all the hope she had left for it to remain dormant.

> I just want to scream, then cry, then curl up in a ball on my bed and pretend none of this happening, just for a moment I haven't got it in me to love anymore. Nothing feels like anything.
>
> It's like they can feel it. Men. Every single time I go out I get unwanted harassing attention from men. It's almost as though they can sense my vulnerability I now have.

LOVEY

*

Little beautiful moments

Liv saw the loveliness in the smallest of things. Other people's happiness filled her soul in way that was unique, and few people possessed. She once was doing her usual walk in the winter lockdown, along the Hove lawns in Brighton and saw within the band stand that stood overlooking the ocean was a couple. The man knelt down on one knee, looked straight into her eyes, a few moments past and he was met with a huge embrace and floods of tears. She stood from the pavement looking in and a thought overwhelmed her which brought her to tears. She knew that she had just witnessed one of the best days in their lives and their happiness was radiating. Even though she stood there and knew that's nothing more she'd want than to have that moment with her own person, instead she felt so overwhelming happy for them that for that day, it was enough to fill her soul even just for a moment.

*

The last time she truly saw him

19th August 2021.

Liv: Saturday, house party in Balham

Roe: Ahh nice I think I'm out

Liv: Ahh nice yeah think we're going out after

Roe: Ahhh well not sure where I'm going so maybe could link up

Am quite horny

I think you should come up tomorrow... I'm in Crawley for work so can meet and have an evening no?

LOVEY

> Liv: Yeah sounds good
>
> Roe: I'll text you when I'm leaving work, hop on a train to London?
>
> And then I fuck you all night

Wearing her House of CB burgundy corset and blue mom jeans, she made her way up to London. Roe's reenrolment into her life after the assault helped. The post it notes helped. The phone calls helped, the texts. She was slowly wondering down a path back to herself, being lit up by guideposts in the form of him. She started conquering the small moments, washing her hair, bearing to be looked at by strangers, managing to, one day, get dressed and dolled up to venture her way to London for dinner with a friend she was determined not to cancel. The only way she bargained with herself though was after Roe had agreed she would go round upon finishing dinner. It made it manageable, a safety net. If she panicked and it became too much, she knew she'd soon be on the northern line, back to where the world didn't hurt so much, where his arms protected her from the pain. The pair slowly fell back into their old ways and he eventually invited her up without any prompt. The texts turned back to flirty and Liv resumed her place right back into wanting any piece of him and his life.

> Liv: Here

His eyes almost lit up for a split second the moment he saw her in dinner and drinks outfit, to which he quickly clicked himself back out of, as they both made their way upstairs into the flat. Laying on his bed, it takes them about, zero point two five seconds to fall right back into them being *'them'*.
"Do you like my top?" Liv looking for a small amount of approval.
"Didn't I say you looked good." Roe questioning her and himself.
"No." she laughed.

LOVEY

"Oh, well I must have just thought it. I swear I said it." Roe still slightly confused.
It felt amazing. Roe was never great at compliments but when they did come, they made Liv glow. All because they came from *him*.

*

The morning

"I wish I could read your mind." she searched for the answers in his silence.
"You basically can," Roe revealed quietly, hanging his head, standing by his window in his bedroom in Clapham.
"You know me better than anyone." bringing his eyes to look straight into hers as they filled with a feeling, she couldn't quite put her finger on.

I can't believe he acknowledged it, finally, she thought.

He had been so shut off, so cold the entire time they were in *'their agreement'*, after they finally called the fight off for their relationship, he sometimes, a lot of the time, didn't even feel like him.
But here he was…she was finally stood in front of the man she had searched months for.

…she had waited so long for him to come back,

she thought he might never find his way.

"I hate this Roe." Liv's quiet voice escaping her lips, feeling she could now be brutally vulnerable as she was suddenly with her old best friend and not the stranger he spent months being.
"I need time." he paused.
"We want very similar things in life, and we'll find our way back to each other, give me, like, a year," he proceeded to promise.

LOVEY

He continued… "I'll be twenty-six, twenty-seven, and thinking about settling down…"
"I know you're my person and I have to live with that," Liv confronting him, finally, with her heart.
A few silent moments past.
"Can I get one year in writing?" Liv quietly joked as they both exhaled with a small amount of laughter.

*

The night before…

"We can't do this anymore." suddenly emerging from his lips. Roe had started to panic. Shake. Very unlike him. He started to freak out. After they had spent the evening drinking red wine, eating Pringles with red pepper hummus and watched a few YouTube videos of a YouTuber they both liked and had finished sleeping together, he started to shake and stood his tall frame from the bed.
"What's wrong?" Liv asked concerned.
"It's just hit me… everything I've done to you."
*What? What do you mean? It's **just** hitting you now?* she thought but did not say out loud. He had been so numb up till now, was probably what allowed him to do everything he had done with no apology or remorse.
"What do you mean?" Liv's stomach dropped. Again, we're here. Roe freaking out. She matched his panic not understanding the origin of where the penny had come from to suddenly drop.
"I can't keep hurting you,"
"I can barely look at you." he whispered.
They moved and sat in silence on the edge of Roe's bed. Liv took a few quiet moments and started to straighten out a few thoughts in her head…

   1. He started this… the stupid fucking agreement knowing I still loved him and would continue to as long as I saw him.
   2. He gave me Chlamydia and still even then, didn't say sorry.

LOVEY

3. Then we're here and he's been the one asking me to come up, to quote *"I think you should come up. I'm quite horny."*

And now he's done? Now he's so incredibly ashamed of how much he's done to hurt me?

The next words that came out her mouth were calm, controlled and broke his heart.

"I wish we never met."

He lifted his hanging head from his lap and looked up to meet her eyes.
She hadn't seen his eyes break like that… *ever…*
"Do you mean that?" he timidly asked with the heaviest heart that ran through his voice.
She left them remaining in silence, the room still with what she had just said. After a minute, she got up in her little black satin shorts and bra and walked out his bedroom. She made her way down the hallway to the bathroom, past both his flatmates' rooms.
Did she mean it? She sat on the edge of the bath, hands grabbing the porcelain on each side, hanging her head low between her legs, she walked through how they had ended up where they found themselves. How had they grown to have so much hurt between them? She stood up and walked over to the sink and looked in the small bathroom cabinet mirror. She knew she didn't. Mean it that is. She loved him too much to wish all their past away, she did, however, hate how it had gotten to this point.

She walked back in and climbed into bed next to him. He knew she didn't mean her comment, but he also understood a part of her needed to say it. She never retaliated, had always taken his action and words with no reaction nor rebuttal so maybe she needed to, for a moment, be someone who could outwardly wish for better, to have avoided all the pain knowing and loving him had inflicted. She

LOVEY

proceeded to nuzzle into him close, he met her affection with lifting his arm and wrapping it around her small frame and pulling her in close and tight.

Liv was back in the only place she felt like she belonged, Roe's arms.

"We'll figure it out." he said optimistically.

"Do you really think?" she said with equal parts of surprise and sadness.

"I really do,"

"We're like magnets," Roe protested trying to comfort her.

"We'll always come back."

"But if magnets are pulled too far apart, they won't come back." Liv added a contradiction whilst nuzzled into his chest, as slow, silent tears fell from your chocolate brown eyes. The eyes Roe first complimented when they met. *"Can't ever have those eyes walking away from me."* he was recalled having gushed.

"Ok, we're like water, it's evaporates into the sky, goes away for a while and rains back down." Roe finding another one of his incredibly random analogies he was famous for.

"But what if you rain back down in someone else's sea!" Liv met with worry.

He laughed softly and hugged her even tighter.

"Please don't say all this if you don't mean it, just too…"

"… make you feel better." Roe finishing her sentence.

"I'm not," he continued, "I think we will find our way back."

She remained silent for a minute.

"Even after everything? You think? Even after the…"

Liv paused for a moment. This entire time she had never said the word. She had said *'assault'*, or *'incident'* but she could never say…

"… after the rape." she repeated almost more back to herself than him.

LOVEY

He looked at her, she could actually see in real time his heart break once again in his widening pupils. He couldn't say it either. He remained silent.
"I haven't said that out loud yet." she added quietly, propped up, sitting more in front of him now, in his bed with the half-drunk red wine still sitting on the bedside tables.
"I know you haven't," matching her quiet volume.
"Look, we'll figure it out," he paused again.
"I can't right now, I just think we have to live our own lives for a bit."
…Even though she felt he was abandoning her again, knowing she wasn't done needing her post-it note prompting life jacket, she knew. She felt with every atom of her body the timing wasn't there for them, but it was almost nice pretending for one more night that the universe would work its magic for the pair that never could quite leave each other behind.

"Can we skip this bit? she said softly with heartbreak running through her voice.
"What, like a year? Roe asked.
"Yeah." she replied, feeling defeated and knowing what he'd say next.
"It doesn't work like that." he said sadly.

              She knew this.

*

Morning

"Why don't you care?" Liv annoyed the next day as she cried knowing she'd be leaving soon, to never return to that bedroom situated in Clapham North, ever again.
"Look if I think about it, I'll cry. So, I'm not going to. Trust me, this will hit me at 2am on a random Wednesday."

LOVEY

*

"You'll be like Zimba"

There are two things in this world that could reduce Roe to tears. Zimba and Liv, it turns out. Roe is a master of distraction. He is extremely talented at avoiding his emotions, escaping their grip. But this talent had exceptions. Zimba, beautiful Zimba who Liv was only lucky enough to see in pictures. He was a big handsome German Shepard Roe had grown up with. Pictures Liv treasured of baby Roe laying on down on Zimba, nuzzling against his head with his blonde curls which were yet to turn brown. Liv could relate as this was one of the things their childhood had in common, her big, beautiful German Shepard that always made her feel safe and family whole, being called *Louie*.

*

"You'll be like Zimba." he said pulling the face Liv knew he had when he was trying not to cry, as his lip shook.
"You'll be something I don't think about. Something I *can't* think about."

She didn't want him not to think of her.

She felt slightly validated that it wasn't only her that felt that their parting would destroy her in a way, but he always seemed to get off easy most of the time, of course she knew this wasn't true. Men just feel things *differently*.

"What did you think of that text I sent?" wanting to know what ran through his mind after she had sat for an hour on Hove seafront, translating her soul into the English language and sent it through as an iMessage. She wondered if he ever read it, and if he had, just once? Did he skim it? Did he look at it late at night? Did he do his best to erase it from his memory?
"I had to read it a couple times," he said timidly.

LOVEY

"It was a lot. It was hard to read." he added then grew quiet.

She got her answer.

A few moments past, Roe wanted to do his best by breaking the silence with something slightly unrelated but light-hearted, she chuckled at his effort.
"Look see, I can still make you laugh." he said softly proud taking hold of a sweet moment.
"You'll always be able to make me laugh." Liv's comment adding to the tension that was pulsing around the room, both feeling how there was so much between them and knowing it was all about to be forgotten. She knew Roe did he best to suppress how he felt but unfortunately, he wouldn't always be able to escape. This brought her no joy.
"You'll never see me again!"
"...how are you okay with that?" her voice began to quieten mid-sentence.
He stood staring at her while being cemented to the carpet placed beneath him by his windows, whilst the bed separated
them. Suddenly, his feet became unglued from the floor. He walked over from across the room and was now mounted in front of her, he waited for less than a second and embraced her deeply. Hugging her so tight she could almost feel everything he couldn't bear to say. They did always have a power of communicating without having to say a word. She always felt she could read his mind like a book. Locked in their embrace, they both lowered themselves on the bed next to each other, sat looking intensely into each other's' eyes, then each other's lips, their faces yearned closer, they lingered over each other's lips for longer than you'd expect without touching, waiting for the other to make the last move. The moment was palpable. Then, almost simultaneously, they both met each other's lips with nothing but love, passion and heartbreak. Confusion cast into the air like a fog, but it also felt incredibly right. Amongst gazing into his green eyes, all she wanted to say was...

LOVEY

'When I look at you, all I need to do is look at you, and… and I'm home.'

…But life knew she needed to find what it meant to stand in front of the mirror and find the same feeling within herself. Only then could she be full.
She said goodbye. She walked out his front door and looked back once down the road and up into his bedroom. She dragged herself away from him for the last time. She cried all the way home.

A couple months later Roe and Mollie went Instagram official.

⟨ Notes

I guess it wasn't a year he needed

*

We all have a lockdown story.

For many of us, the summer of 2020 was difficult. It was something we'll tell the later generations what happened and how it felt. Being locked in our homes. Wearing masks to leave the house. Queueing an hour to get into Tesco for there to be no pasta or bread. However, it was also a time of life slowing down, personal development, banana bread and for a lot, it had the soundtrack of viral TikTok trends. Sat on Roe's lap, she gathered all his curls into a little bun on the top of his head.
"I put it in a bun." she sang.
"I put it in a bun." he sang back.

As Liv had her own flat, Roe spent a lot of time there. Before lockdown, they'd often share time between his, his being his parents, and Liv's. They had more privacy at hers, but she could tell he didn't like being away from home for too long. Lockdown was the biggest test for the couple. However, they also made some of the best

LOVEY

memories through this time. BBQ's every day after work, on the beach facing Liv's front door, cooking jackfruit Thai green curry with red wine, movie projector nights, and facetime quizzes. Liv entertained herself through furlough by trying to bake vegan goods which never went too well. After many baking fails, one evening Roe had finished work and started to play PlayStation, he surprised her by running into her small kitchen as she hoped this batch would turn out well and be their dessert. He ran in, dropping a piece of paper to her and ran away. She picked up the note that had landed on the floor of the kitchen and *smiled.* It was always his small, sweet, soft moments that made her feel so incredibly loved.
I guess this is the person she hoped would come back.

> You can do it
> My Superstar!!
> ★

They dealt with the distance well. They had a little routine, when apart, a way of feeling closer, especially in the extended period in the beginning when leaving our homes was forbidden. On FaceTime, Roe would prop his phone up on this desk and leave Liv whilst he played PlayStation all while she watched YouTube videos or completed for university work. Every so often they'd get each other's attention by doing their *'little thing'*. I don't think I've mentioned

LOVEY

this yet, but they had a way of saying '*I love you*' without having to actually say it. They'd pinch their fingers and thumb together and open and shut them quickly. Almost making a little beak out of their hands.
"I love that's our little thing." Roe gushed as he distracted Liv from filming a makeup tutorial.
"Me too."
"Cause it's like we're saying I love you, without saying it," he continued in his baby voice.
"…Like I can be on PlayStation and do it."
This was a moment Liv treasured. It was caught on camera as she had started spending her furlough filming makeup and fashion videos. She'd re-watch this video often in the times she missed him.

Roe: Wanna FaceTime whilst I play my game in a bit??

It was her absolute favourite. She felt safe just knowing he was there, less lonely. Living alone through lockdown created a type of loneliness Liv was desperate to escape. She loved the fact she had a whole flat to herself but even more she adored sharing it with him. Before lockdown they had viewed a few flats in Brighton and Hove, not taking one in particular that they fell in love with due to Liv being unable to leave her tenancy early. Looking back, it was a blessing in disguise. Or maybe it wasn't. The depression Roe began to struggle with in lockdown, the one they both realised had been brewing for a while after his last accountancy exams, may have been different had they lived in their shared flat with their open plan kitchen and garden. Or the flat that overlooked the popular Brighton lanes which had a little balcony and a very '*Airbnb*' feel to it, in the best way. He was always so good at overthinking and *freaking himself out*, which led Liv to always feeling she had to be the adult for the both of them. When he did have flashes of maturity, he was ecstatic for their future. He couldn't wait for the normality of coming home each night to his best friend, cook dinner together, eventually get their own little German Shepard puppy and allow themselves to be

LOVEY

happy. Maybe he struggled because somewhere, deep down, he knew he had found someone special, the person you do life with, but all too soon. Maybe somewhere inside told him he had other things to do, experience, before you *'do life with your best friend'*. And that's where they differed. She could feel he truly he wanted too. It was only when you left him too long with his thoughts or his sister had said just a little too much and suddenly his entire desires changed. It was unnerving the way he could always just take their future away, at the drop of a hat. Roe was always quite impulsive but even with their lives, her feelings. This trait never stopped. In regard to progressing their future, she was ready. Everything she still wanted to do in life could only be made better with him by her side, she thought. And most of the time, he made her feel he felt the same.

Liv was lonely. Lockdown was a lonely place. *I wonder if Roe ever truly thought about how alone she really was, while he went back to his family home.* A lot of people moved home for the pandemic but that wasn't an option for Liv, not that she would have chosen that anyway, but it was isolating. And that meant relying so heavily on Roe to be everything. Undoubtably it was pressure for him. Liv didn't have the number of friends she did now, she had very few in fact. That was down to a few things. 1. As we know, the beginning of university of difficult and she barely existed, let alone made any friends, 2. She had isolated herself and by the time life was good again, they were in a pandemic. She had friends from home, but all being awful at keeping in communication and to be honest with you, she felt she got everything she needed from Roe. She knows now how unhealthy this dynamic is, knowing she couldn't live without her multiple friendship groups now and her radiating independence, but at the time, Roe was her whole little world, and she loved living there.

Roe spent a lot of time on RuneScape, going back and forth between the game and his spreadsheets for work.
"How do you play?"

LOVEY

"You want to play?" he asked in amazement.
"Yeah! Show me how."
I can't say Liv became a wizard at the game, but she did enjoy collecting the chickens with her bow and arrow, building her strength level, which Roe always found funny in contradiction due to her vegan lifestyle in reality.
"They aren't real chickens, it's okay." she giggled.

But as time went on, these soft, sweet, easy moments became less and less and she could feel him starting to slip away, like sand falling through her fingertips. The harder she gripped, the faster he fell.

*

Will you be my bee?
I forever will bee

From when Liv met Roe, he was always a fan of Reddit. He followed many pages filled with funny and informative content. He'd often screenshot story time's and send them to her while he was at work. A screenshot came through of two pictures. One of a group of bees huddling around one another and next to it was the same picture but zoomed out, being able to see the huddling bees in the centre of a flower, sleeping. The caption read, 'Did you know that bees sleep between 5-8hours a day, sometimes in flowers? Also, they like to sleep with other bees and hold each other's feet'.

> Liv: Omg
>
> Are you my bee and will hold my feet while I sleep?
>
> Roe: Yeah of course I ammmm
>
> Are you my bee?
>
> Liv: I will forever be your bee
>
> Roe: Forever will bee

LOVEY

*

Therapist directory

She was desperate to save what she believed to be worth saving. His moods had hit a new low during the summer lockdown. Liv could feel how painful it was, to have the confusion of why he felt like how he did… she tried her hardest to save him. She had always been the one in the relationship to struggle mentally and now Roe needed help. She did everything she could to even make his day just 1% better. Reaching a point, as Roe was staying down at Liv's by the sea like usual, a rare argument turned into an unravelling…
"I don't want to be together."
"I want to sleep with other people."
"I don't love you."
…And as much as this felt like taking physical bullets to which she started to bleed out from in agony, she knew what this was. He was doing his very best to push her away. She's done this before, so she knew the signs and she knew the only way to prove that, no matter what, she'd be there, his ride or die, was to swallow what he had just said like glass shards and reply…
"I love you and I'm not going nowhere", "if you truly don't love me, tell me when you're calm and when you've felt like this longer than a moment or a day."
Him still protesting, he left. The heavy door of Liv's flat slammed shut. She sat on the edge of her sofa for a moment, not knowing the right thing, respecting his decision, opinion, but knowing her heart told her *'go get him'*. She went out after him. She caught up to him halfway down her road, nearly reaching the sea.
"I don't want this and I don't think you do either." Liv expressed softly but confidently.
"It doesn't matter now! Can't take back everything I've just said to you." frustration in his voice at his own actions.
"Roe… if it means forgetting this moment and having a lifetime with you, I can do that, I know I can…"

LOVEY

After a few moments of staring at each other, they both walked slowly back to the flat, not really knowing what their next move would be or how'd they would recover this time.
"Play your game, go on PlayStation and I'll do some art and be on my laptop." Liv trying to add some softness.

I think Roe scared himself. How bad he could feel. He was always that guy who believed he'd never struggle with his mind. He was always incredibly sympathetic to Liv and her struggles, but he lured himself into a false sense of security of it was never going to be him. She just wanted him back. It had been so long since she had seen him before the depression. Anyone who has had a partner who had fallen into a dark place will know what it feels like to lose them, while they lose themselves. Liv worried at the fact that no one knew how bad his mental health had got apart from her, she knew their relationship could very obviously end at any moment and she needed to know he would be safe if that happened. With her or without her, she needed him to be okay. As for the fact that he didn't want his family to know she did the next thing that was the safest. She texted his best friend. She got his number out of Roe's phone when he was in the kitchen.

> Liv: Hi George, it's Liv, Roe's girlfriend. I just wanted to message you. To be honest Roe's been struggling with his mental health since a little before Xmas and it's only been recently that he's starting it accept it. I don't want to betray his trust and explain everything he has told me but he's definitely going through a bad time. He's slowing becoming more open but obviously as this is happening it's bringing how bad he actually feels to the surface where he'd normally distract himself from. I've struggled in the past so if I believed, in anyway, that he'd be better without me, I'd leave. I love him too much to not take care of him, even if it meant that outcome. But I honestly believe I make him happy and maybe even help a little on the bad days. I think I kind of wanted to say he needs help from the people that love him, but he wouldn't ever ask for

LOVEY

> it. I'm sorry as this is all a lot! Hope you guys are well! And sorry for such a long message

George was a good friend. Liv always adored him. Him and his fiancé. She was always glad Roe had him close. He was kind, you could tell, respectful too, but funny and cool. Tattoos and stylish dress sense. She knew Roe thought so much of him but it's terrifying what even the *'best of friends'* don't talk about. They exchanged a few messages to which George revealed his own struggle and had actually been on anti-depressants himself. Roe never knew this. It's so incredibly sad how alone men are. Even from their closest friends. From their conversation and months of losing Roe slowly, there was one thing she didn't realise she needed to hear…

> George: He definitely loves you Liv, I've never seen him like this with anyone else

That's why, she thought. She was special, so was he, and so were they. She carried on her fight for him.

It was a relief to Liv that George knew and felt he was now safe, no matter what happened, if they broke up, someone was there, who knew and would look after him when she couldn't. Beyond telling George, Roe and Liv had in the past spoken briefly about him speaking to someone who could potentially help, someone not in his life, a safe place, where he could say exactly what he thought, without hurting anyone. She searched through a therapist directory she had been on for herself and found a few to contact. Reaching out with a desperate message of knowing he needed help and felt unable of asking for it himself, she'd try anything to get him back to being him.

LOVEY

Hi Liv,

Many thanks for getting in touch

It is very difficult to comment as I am sure you can imagine without having met your boyfriend. It seems to me that there are several avenues to think about. One is that he seeks out therapy for himself so that he can explore his feelings in a safe space, and the second is that you do the same, because it sounds as though you are in need of some support in managing what his low moods mean for you, which will have some sort of resonance with your past experiences. The third option is that you decide together to undertake some form of couples therapy – there are many options available – so that you can explore together the issues which you face in your relationship.

Best wishes,

Katharine

*

Last words

"Can I have the email of that therapist?" one of his final comments as the pair split.

He never did pursue therapy.

⟨ Notes

It's almost like I lived to make him better. I thought if I could stick by his side because as much as you think depression won't end, it does. And we can go back to being us, in a new, better, stronger way knowing we can get through the worst of times

LOVEY

*

The ways we fought for it to be us…in the end

"I have no idea how to do this, but it needs to be us, you, when I'm out of this."

He came back.
Again.

"I know I can't be a full partner, but if there's a way it's us at the end then I'll do it."

He had ended it on one of the occasions she was staying at his in the summer. A week later he asked to speak. They were back.

"I'll do whatever we need to do, for it to us when this is over."

This period of time was confusing. In some ways they were the best they had been in a while.

>Roe: Hang tight I'll be back as soon as I can

It was this promise that was why Liv did what she did. She wanted to hang tight for him. In her heart, if she could, just hang in there like he wanted them too, in return, she'd spend the rest of her whole life with *her person.* Now, that was the easiest decision she ever made.

>Roe: I want this forever

Roe replying to a cute silly selfie the pair took.

LOVEY

*

They saved each other

Roe: You know what's mental... I was in love with you before, and it's like I'm falling into a deeper whirlpool of love and I'm on fucking cloud 9 because of it... like for real you are fucking amazing

Roe: I want to be stranded on a desert island with you

Roe: Don't ever leave me

Roe: I'm gonna become such a better person after all this bub

Roe: My fucking star

I'd love to say we almost made it, didn't we Roe? But we didn't. I thought when he came back, we'd weather the storm together, get through lockdown and his depression, all to not let any of that steal the future we were so excited to have. In the moments that he or I would wobble, we'd often say, 'Same page' and the other would say 'Same page'. It became the way of saying in the difficult times that I love you and let's continue to fight this together.

Roe: Same page 🩶

Liv: Same page 🩶

They were really happy again for a while, but his depression outran his love and eventually, *she fully lost the person she fought so hard for.*

LOVEY

*

She needs saving

During a manic moment, Liv ripped apart her room. She grabbed her suitcase from the top of her built in wardrobe looking for the collection of sleeping tablets she had always kept in case of emergency in her mind. No longer could she cope with how the sexual assault and violence had left her. She pulled a sheet of paper out to remove more of the contents, trying to get to the packets of pills. Stopping her in her tracks, she realised the paper she was holding and about to discard on the floor was an old suicide note she had written years previous. A surge of heartbreak and weakness waved over her body as she fell down off the chair she was using to prop herself up and dropped to the floor. Then, curled up on the floor, she sobbed. She sobbed uncontrollably. She rang Roe. She rang and hung-up believing all she was, was a burden.
"I can't do this," she pleaded, sobbing on her hallway floor, after he called her back immediately.
"Not this time."
"You can." Roe always had undeniable faith in her.
"Everyone thinks I can just get through anything, and I can't."
He viewed her nothing shy of a superhero.
"You can," Roe lovingly battled,
"You're the strongest person I know."
"I don't want to be strong… I want to be happy." she quietly cried.
"I know." Roe with the heaviest heart.
She sobbed on the floor just focusing on the only voice that could part the tsunami waves she was drowning in, of her own mind. His voice always managed to part the seas.

It reminded her of a conversation they had once had.

> Liv: You save me sometimes bub

LOVEY

Liv text Roe after a bad panic attack which he always seemed to rescue her from.

> Roe: You save me too

Roe referring to his depression and how Liv had done everything in her human power to try and save him from.

We know now, it was never enough, it was never going to be enough. But she tried and so did he.

> Roe: We are a team

This text would haunt Liv over and over as the months would go on… in all the moments she needed *her team.*

You see, it's all these times…these moments that built this foundation of rescuing each other.

Maybe that's why it took Liv so long to *let go.*

What would happen in these moments, if she no longer had him?

LOVEY

Chapter Three

Waking up in Camden Town felt like a new chapter

A new but important player, *Elijah*. Elijah is a complicated soul which arrived in Liv's world like he could hear her. He could hear her thoughts, her pain. He was *truly special and one of the most important loves of her life*. His unwavering persistence held a place in her life quickly, so with this in mind, *lets meet Elijah.*

The pair had matched on a dating app. Liv had an undoubtably annoying habit of replying, partaking in a conversation to then go cold and *'ghosting'*. Nevertheless, his reoccurring persistence would later result in making the date happen. In his last-ditch attempts to grab her attention, one evening he sent her a voice note. *His voice. His voice melted Liv to her knees.* It was deep and strong which a touch of cheekiness. He expressed he'd love to meet and take her out but to let him know if she wasn't feeling it. It was instant. The moment she heard his voice, all her attention turned to him. She responded with that she'd love to and she met him a couple of days later, that Friday.

The certainty he possessed for her after just one date was a strange sensation but we're getting a little ahead.

LOVEY

Liv had matched Elijah before the assault and their conversation had sat in her dating app. She had been hot and cold with the apps in general. The weeks that led after the rape, Liv had waves of being sick of lying in bed and feeling suicidal. She wanted to go back to normal. In these desperate moments for her old life, she'd open up her dating apps to see what messages she had been left in her absence. She often took one look and immediately closed her phone down, knowing she was nowhere near ready and to not to reopen for a while. After Liv and Roe saw each other and agreed reluctantly to move on with their lives, she took this as her que to revisit the apps as she understood it was time to move her heart onwards and far away from Roe.

Elijah. He was keen and a good replier. Liv was still unsure if she could bear a first date, but in the moments she didn't want normal life to continue on without her, she entertained the idea. She liked the idea of it, believing there's nothing more fun than a good first date. *The first spark.* That giddy happy feeling that is fuelled by someone new. These moments are pockets of happiness.

> Now spoiler alert, Elijah's presence in Liv's life was full of complications but there was a tremendous amount of love shared.

So, rewinding to the first date. Stood outside of Kentish Town tube station, in true Liv style, making all the clothes she wore, in a top she had manufactured out of a brown and gold monogram silk scarf from ASOS and cream Zara mom jeans which she tailored to fit her short legs. He strutted up a few minutes late which Liv met with a banterous telling off. He instantly found her endearing and more charismatic than what met his eye. They began to walk side by side, him in wide leg Dickies trousers and a tan Carhart jacket that she always wanted Roe to have. He stood over her with his six-foot-two frame, beautiful wavy almost black hair he had slicked back and a confident smile that made him glow whilst also seeming a touch

LOVEY

cheeky. He had surpassed her idea she had of him in her head. He was the classic example of *'trust me, he's better in person'*. Liv would learn he was never much of a picture person anyway. This explained his lack of decent photos on the app. Elijah would become the most attractive person Liv would be in a relationship with in most of her friend's eyes. They'd say Roe's goofy, sweet, but Elijah's handsome and stunning. Liv agreed. The couple later often joked over Elijah's ethnicity, for the fact that he looked like he had a strong hint of a Persian or Turkish background due to his strikingly dark features, but regardless, he's a Brighton boy, through and through. She lusted over his near black, softly waved, thick hair he used to gel and style off his face, his strong brunette eyebrows which framed his beautiful brown eyes. All his features added to his prominent beauty. They connected instantly as they shared the best parts of themselves.

> Flum: Hey you ok
>
> Liv: Yeah I'm in love with him
>
> Flum: I bloody knew you would be!! Haha

Liv texted Flum in the toilet as they were about to depart from the second pub. One thing to know about Liv is, if she isn't texting Flum or her girl group chat saying she's in love with you, after only an hour, she's not feeling it.

Throughout their Camden pub crawl that he had caringly spent some of the afternoon planning, she truly believed there was a possibility his caring personality, which continuously revealed itself, would translate to her life and he would maybe shield her just like he did his sisters. Three younger sisters he looked over. He gushed proudly over how he never let them go without. She could feel how rewarded he felt that he had stepped up in the ways his parents were absent. Paying for his youngest sister's phone contract, ensuring they always had everything they needed for school and so much more. He

LOVEY

was mature and alluded to the experience of real pain in his past. Something Liv could really connect too. This was the greenest flag she could have heard on a first date. His charity work and mentoring for a men's mental health charity inspired her, starting from needing their help to years later giving it back. The more they spoke, from pub to pub, he lit up around her presence making Liv truly believe this could be something good. Finally, *something good.* Elijah's complicated as I have said but Liv wholeheartedly believed every single intention he had was good, but unfortunately, eventually, it sometimes did not get translated that way. He was insistent and often put his worth on not letting her or anyone, down. This was his thing.

They sat cosily a wooden bench in the beer garden of the last pub of the night, The Abbey Tavern. His arm stretched around her, as he said, "I have to kiss you." Then he took her chin and brought it to his lips. *It was a great moment.*

Stood outside the pub as Elijah had a cigarette which they shared, "you're more than welcome to stay at mine." she looked up at him, both locking a gaze with their chocolate brown eyes, Liv's just a touch darker, "…I'm not trying to get you to mine." they giggled a little. "…just know you can if you don't want get the train back to Brighton."
The night was getting late and the idea of spending two hours getting home felt tiresome. She decided she had spent the whole night feeling so incredibly safe and happy that she decided to take him up on his offer. She had four people, including Flum and other Liv on find friends and told them all her plan so people knew where she was.
"We'll get snacks and watch a movie," Elijah said with genuine excitement running through his voice.
"What do you need?"
"…a toothbrush?" he asked.

LOVEY

"We'll also get you some makeup remover." Liv laughed to herself at how sweet and strangely amazing the date had gone.
The newly inseparable pair bounced into a convenience shop round the corner from Elijah's flat. He walked through the aisle of toiletries, picking up a bamboo toothbrush and put it in the basket.
"What snacks do you fancy?"
He took the basket to the till of one of those late-night corner shops that sell the most random items along with weirdly exotic fruit and they departed. She felt excited. Totally content. Safe.
After a short walk she climbed up his stairs and into his flat he rented alone. It was quite big… and nice, she noted. She took her new toothbrush and the t-shirt he gave her to sleep in, into the bathroom and changed and brushed her teeth. Re-emerging, she climbed into bed, whilst he arranged his laptop at the end so they could watch the movie. After some heavy kissing they cuddled and went to sleep. She loved the fact she never felt any pressure from Elijah to do any more than she initiated.

The next morning, she could feel his disappointment as she got dressed and announced that she had to leave. He would, however, see her a of couple days later.

28th August 2021.

> Elijah: Worried I'll put you off by being too keen but I'm so excited for Tuesday already

This was a WhatsApp message she received, leaving his flat in the early morning, walking to Kentish Town tube station, after seeing him twice. Liv had spent months and months feeling like an option, and even worse, a rejected option that no one, including Roe, wanted or respected. But here was Elijah, ready to give her all his love, loyalty and commitment.

LOVEY

*

Field day

Liv: Oh so the offer still stands ;) x

Elijah: You know that the offer still stands every single night of the week

Somehow got me wrapped around your little finger after one date

She was attending a festival a few days after their first date. He had offered for her to stay and not have to get a late train back to Brighton after attending Field Day.

Elijah: Sneakily hoping you get stranded and need to stay

*

Liv: I didn't say it but thank you so much for letting me stay xx

Elijah: Should be me saying thanks to you xx

Their next date was only the day after she left that morning which only added to the accelerated whirlwind romance.

Elijah: Honestly can't wait to have you back xx

I might already miss you a little bit

Text me when you get in safe xxx

*

Morning after their third date…

Elijah: Managed to miss my tube, mess up my beard line and forget headphones

LOVEY

Strong start to the week

Getting you back tonight though so life is still good x

*

It's the little things

Opening WhatsApp to a picture of Elijah holding a box of Oral-B toothpaste.

Liv: Why are you the best

Elijah: Because I'm seeing someone that makes me want to be x

She was so surprised how a tiny passing comment of how she didn't like his special gum protection toothpaste, had translated into a small yet powerful thoughtfulness. This would be a precursor of him taking the smallest comments and moments, creating a note on his phone which he would later use in surprising her with generosity she had never experienced.

*

Third date

Elijah: Spent my day looking at vegan garlic bread recipes rather than doing a massive proposal at work

#priorities

Decided that you're too good to be eating any old store bought garlic bread

Liv: #garlicbreadpaysbills

I mean any garlic is an elite food

Love the effort so much x

LOVEY

Elijah: So do neuroscientists

This evening Elijah started a trend of cooking the most incredible meals for her, wanting to use his genuine talent to impress. Sat at his dining table with the vegan creamy pasta with garlic bread was the first of many spectacular dinners they'd share.

They hadn't had sex yet. Reasons being the first night Liv felt staying at his and having a heavy kissing session and cuddle was enough and the second time she slept over she was drunk from the festival and he was stone cold sober, and the dynamics felt wrong to both. So, a lot of unspoken pressure had landed on their third date. After the meal and a cosy evening cuddling on his brown sofa, in his spacious lounge, they tucked themselves up in bed and began to kiss. Something they knew they were already good at. After a few heated minutes of subtly teasing and touching each other, Liv reached down to Elijah's hard crotch. As the intimacy escalated Elijah stretched into his bedside draw and pulled out a condom. He positioned himself on his back to roll the protection down his hard self. Once he was ready, condom wrapper thrown on the floor, he realigned his tall frame on top of her. The moment had finally come. As he began to place himself inside the girl he had become quickly obsessed with, the weight of the highly anticipated event had crumbled down on his shoulders as he suddenly became unprepared for the act. Laying back down next to her, "please take it as a compliment, I get nervous with you." he began to stress, turning into face her. Liv could tell he had started to worry and felt a little embarrassed, but she really didn't think too much of it. The male anatomy is strange sometimes and he was 100% in his own head. Liv could tell that with everyone else Elijah was an extremely confident, borderline arrogant guy, but with Liv he seemed to crumble under his infatuation with her, showing his soft, vulnerable side, almost immediately.

LOVEY

Elijah: Wanted to say thanks for making the journey up

Really appreciate it xxx

Liv: Nah thank you for making dinner and a great eve

Dinner was really good!!

Also I wanted to sleep with you all night haha

Elijah: You're welcome

I had a lot of fun too

Why didn't you say fml

I was worried the moment had gone and that you weren't really up for it

Liv: I just thought you didn't want to then haha

Elijah: Noooo

Liv I'm actually obsessed with you

Not sure if you realise

Fancy you an embarrassing amount

Oh well no point bugging

Saturday will be good

I promise

Just got a bit nervous as was first time n I do properly like you

The nerves are out my system now though x

Liv: Not embarrassing

LOVEY

> We'll 100% make up for it
>
> Elijah: We are going to be together for a good while anyway so it will all be irrelevant x
>
> Manifesting ^
>
> Liv: V excited for Saturday now
>
> Elijah: Honestly can't wait you genuinely get better every time I see you

*

Fourth date

> Elijah: Everything is just better when you're around
>
> Cringe but my whole week is genuinely made by the fact I have you on Friday

Their next date plan had been for Elijah to journey down to Brighton on the Saturday after her shift at work. After Elijah had sent a voice note explaining he was going to come down on the Friday to make the most of the trip, Liv made sure he knew he was more than welcome at hers.

> Liv: If you are free and in btown I think I'm free, always welcome at mine
>
> Elijah: Wait whatttt
>
> I didn't know a double sleepover was an option
>
> Obvs I'd come over on Friday if allowed
>
> Assumed you were busy

LOVEY

*

Elijah: Can't wait to get my hands on you Friday

Liv: Sameee

*

Elijah: Excited to see your flat

Liv: Me too not as big as yours lol

*

How it started

A screenshot from their initial dating app conversation. Elijah had sent her a message trying to grab her attention again after she had ignored his messages once again, *"How you gonna break my heart like this liv x."*

Elijah: How it all started

Liv: Haha awww

So you have the app back ;)

Elijah: Noooo

I promise

Look at the top

17th August

Liv: That's cute

Liv realised he screenshotted that two days before she saw Roe for the last time. *Weird to think,* she contemplated.

Elijah: Can't remember what the context was

LOVEY

Probs sending to a mate

Liv: You knew from day one

Elijah: Ngl

I was bought in immediately

I remember ranting about it to my friend

Like

Why has she messaged me n is not replying

Kept going on about it

Got a bee in my bonnet

Liv: Haha see!! Annoying you since the beginning

Elijah: You couldn't annoy me if you tried

I'm someone who gets annoyed easily but my threshold seems to be 1000 times higher with you for some reason

Liv: I think this means something really good about us

Elijah: I'm sure it does

*

Friday had arrived

Liv: Morning handsome xxx

Hope you slept well

So excited I get to see you today

Elijah: This made me smile xxx

LOVEY

> Honestly same
>
> We are going to have a lot of fun
>
> What time you going to see Dottie x

Dottie is the daughter of one her best friends, *Lucie*. Liv and Luc have been best friends since they were eleven. She's always been so incredibly grateful for their friendship. They could truly share anything and everything. To combat their distance and busy lives, Liv always tried her best to see her as much as she could.

On the train down to see baby Dottie and her best friend, she got a phone call. The music streaming through her in-ear headphones was interrupted by her phone buzzing with an unknown number. The results from the sexual health screening from the assault had come back. Answering the call, the concerned voice told her everything. The nurse informed her she was positive for chlamydia. *Fuck*. She was sad, then annoyed, then worried. She felt even more violated from that man, that violent unprotected man. She began to contemplate what the positive result now meant. Firstly, she realised she had slept with Roe multiple times since the assault, so she put together a message informing him. It directly followed his previous message of telling her he had chlamydia as all the correspondence after the assault had moved to iMessage after she blocked his WhatsApp. In a strange way it felt like karma for him. Then she realised *Elijah*. They were meant to, for the first time, sleep together that night. And how, not only was she going to have to tell him she had an STI, but also tell him *why*.

> Liv: I feel rubbish
>
> I have something to talk to you about
>
> You'll 100% call this a day

LOVEY

And I just feel shit

Elijah: What's that

Not sure about that

Liv: More in person thing

Elijah: Sure

Don't worry

Liv: I'm just worried

Tbh it'll be up to you but I hope it will be okay

Elijah: I really don't think there is anything that would put me off you tbh

Honestly wouldn't stress

Any way of giving me a rough idea of what it might be about or prefer to just talk in person

Obvs fine either way

Please don't worry Liv x

Liv: I could literally cry lol

Elijah: What's up

Can't tell you what to do but I find that getting these things out of the way makes it easier or you'll be stressing all day

Happy to do in person though

Whatever makes you comfortable

Liv: Basically something happened to me and something has come out of it

LOVEY

> Elijah: Right
>
> I'm not entirely sure what to respond to that
>
> But whatever it is clearly isn't you're fault
>
> It's hard as I don't really know what it is but I promise that I'm not going to judge you or make you feel uncomfortable
>
> Liv: I totally understand if you don't want to see each other anymore
>
> Elijah: It would really help if you said what it is
>
> I get it's difficult
>
> I can't really think of anything that would make this happen

Liv's heart was pounding. She eventually concluded he'd know eventually, better he leave now than later anyway.

> Liv: Just over a month ago I was raped and I did tests a while ago and I got told today I have chlamydia
>
> Elijah: Ahh I'm so sorry Liv
>
> That's awful
>
> If you think I'd stop seeing you over that you're crazy
>
> I'm here for you
>
> I'm just absolutely gutted that has happened
>
> I'm not going anywhere though
>
> You're perfect
>
> It's not your fault
>
> Don't be worried

LOVEY

Doesn't bother me in the slightest

I just hope you're okay

I'm so sorry that you've had to go through this

Liv: You're too amazing

Literally

Elijah: No I'm not

In what world would I stop seeing you

Liv: But I understand if you did

Elijah: I'm just upset you had to go through that

Liv: Cause it's horrible on so many levels

Elijah: Don't think like that

It shouldn't bother anyone that isn't disgusting tbh

I'm here for you

Liv: 🤍🤍🤍

Elijah: I know I've only known you a week but I do genuinely really care about you

Think you're great

Don't panic about stuff like that

Liv: I know and I already don't want to lose you

Elijah: Can't wait to speak this weekend with you n lots more weekends x

Liv: Me too xxx

LOVEY

> Elijah: It's actually so sad that you feel like this would impact how I think of you in anyway

She truly did. Still does. Think it would change the way someone views her. When it does come up naturally, what she's been through, she always hopes for the perfect response. It actually became a little test in her mind, unintentionally. She felt you could tell a lot about a person by the way they responded to the assault. She always wanted to be treated the same. *Not fragile.* But also wanted someone to take it seriously and not like it was nothing. *A fine balance.*

> Elijah: If anything it's amazing that you're still the person you are
>
> Shows how strong you are to carry on with life as normal
>
> I think you're great for having to deal with that
>
> Not going to let you down I promise
>
> You can trust my word I assure you
>
> Thanks for sharing with me
>
> Really appreciate it x
>
> Let me know if there is anything I can do to help or support you
>
> My job is to be here for you
>
> 🤍
>
> You deserve everything xxx
>
> Also look what just arrived

LOVEY

Elijah had made another note of a game Liv had casually mentioned she wanted to get. It was an unsolved case file game where you are given documents, having to figure out who the murderer was of the closed case.

> Nothing too special but should give us something fun to do this evening 🤍
>
> Liv: Omggggg how are you like this?? You make me so happy 🤍🤍
>
> Can't believe you got it
>
> Elijah: I knew you'd like it
>
> Would've kept it a surprise but thought it might be nice for you to know now as you were having a rubbish day
>
> Liv: Yeah it's perfect can't wait to see you xxx
>
> Elijah: You're perfect xxx
>
> Also just looked at flights to Edinburgh in December
>
> It's ridiculously cheap
>
> Liv: Omggg that's so good!
>
> Elijah: First trip away of many
>
> Unless we squeeze in another one before
>
> Liv: 🤍 so much to come
>
> Elijah: Matching jacket pic pending
>
> Liv: This needs to happen
>
> Elijah: Me n you are going to have so much together

LOVEY

Hope you realise xxxx

Liv: Nothing makes me happier this xxx

*

I love you Liv

He fell in love with her, and she fell in love with him.

"I love you Liv." Elijah whispered down into her ear, stood at London Bridge station, embracing quickly but tightly, rushing to catch Liv's train back down to Brighton
"I love you Elijah." the words fell out her mouth with a smile, hating the fact she only got to quickly look into his eyes, before having to run off.
They both knew all along they'd fall for each other quickly. It felt as though their relationship was in 2x speed. They became boyfriend and girlfriend extremely quick. Elijah deleted the dating apps after their first date. Their eyes, from the moment they met, only saw the other.
"There's no pressure but I just know if I was to go out, I know I'd rather be there with you." he added as justification for his speedy commitment.
"Honestly want to be with you all the time."

*

Elijah: Might be in love with this girl.

Replying to a mirror selfie Liv sent showing her outfit.

Liv: She might be in love with you too

LOVEY

*

A near miss

Liv: Can I just say... after what happened I needed an actual reason to live. I didn't know to be here anymore and felt like I had lost everything I had spent 23 years building. Genuinely. I asked the universe for just something good because things were unbearable. Then I met you. Literally. I know how it was difficult, but I started to feel more myself just being next to you. That's because of you and who you are. I know you think you're bad for me, but I could always feel how much you loved me and well that was always enough. You played a huge part in putting me back together and that never wavering support, being by my side is something I've not really had a lot of, that's why I'll always be thankful for you and sad we didn't get more weird and wonderful memories together x

Elijah: Liv I actually can't

That's properly broken my heart

I don't think I can leave this

It feels wrong

You're my best friend

I love you

Liv: You're my best friend. I love you

The couple had a near miss but nevertheless, found their way back and stayed there for a while.

LOVEY

*

Complicated

What we'll learn about Elijah and his and Liv's relationship is that just as it was filled with love and affection it was also tainted with pain and conflicting hearts. Both him and Liv are complex souls. They tried with all they had, to come together and bring something beautiful from the hurt. They did not succeed. I think their relationship could have really been it. They matched on so many levels and wanted very similar things in life and my goodness, *did he make her laugh.* It's easy to let the pain become louder than the good. Good, sweet, soft moments are subtle and quiet and can sometimes be easily forgotten. Elijah was amazing at making Liv feel special and adored. He made her feel like the most beautiful person in every room.

"No one's bigger than the club," Elijah explaining that in football, no one player is bigger than the club they are paying for.
"You're bigger than the club though."
She glowed in how she felt truly irreplaceable to him.

"You look like a Disney couple." Flum said loving Elijah almost as much as Liv did, maybe more.
Liv could admit they matched each other perfectly. They could have been a powerhouse, maybe if they had met at a different time. But he held her through the tough moments. His support was unwavering, and he never gave up on her, even in moments she wanted to give up on herself.
"Do you think you could maybe but a little autistic?" Liv asked on their third date after more revealing traits started to show. These being what the couple would later light-heartedly refer to as, '*An autism attack.*'
 "You're not the first person to have said this." Elijah laughed, being much less offended than Liv predicted.

LOVEY

She could tell he interrupted the world ever so slightly differently. Sometimes he's become overstimulated causing him to feel overwhelmed. That's what they deemed an *'autism attack'*, when he'd become flooded with external stimulus, effecting the way he could process his thoughts. Imagine when you turn off the music when you're driving to *'see'* better and concentrate, only times that feeling by a thousand. He was also a little blunt and said things we are programmed in society not to say out of politeness or acceptability. It took Liv time to learn his character. He had little quirks that could either make or break his day. It all needs to align in his mind. Or he'd become overwhelmed and often angry or frustrated. The quicker Liv learnt his triggers, the simpler and quieter life could be.
"Are you having fun Eli?" Liv's friend Sophie making conversation, stood outside on the balcony of Liv and Soph's mutual friend, Ned. It was his birthday and Liv had been excited to introduce Elijah to her friendship group.
"No, not really." Elijah halting the conversation.
Liv knew he wouldn't lie if he wasn't having a good time and also hated people shortening his name. Usually, I think, most people would be quite agreeable and maintain a level of social compliance, but not him. But as much as it was rude and harsh sometimes, Liv also adored this side, most of the time. His honesty was almost refreshing. He was brutally truthful but fiercely loyal however, he was rude, sharp and slightly arrogant but on balance, sweet, thoughtful, immensely caring, generous, affectionate and never failed to make her cry with laugher.

Their relationship could not have been more different to hers and Roe's and for a while, she liked that. But as time went on and her feelings grew so dark and volatile, Liv yearned for her socially awkward, silly, goofy, soft Roe in the moments Elijah's harshness was cutting her too deeply.

As time went on, she realised the reality of being with someone so soon after something awful happening. It became **the** most

LOVEY

confusing time for Liv. The assault happened roughly a month before they met, and she was in extreme personal turmoil over what this would now mean for her. How to let others treat her, trying to, in so many ways, create boundaries which protected her. The ones she thought maybe could have saved her, had she of had them a little sooner. Whilst also finding a way of letting someone in. Letting someone love her. Letting herself *need* someone. Being vulnerable. She felt numb sometimes. Barely cried which is very unlike her. She was still in survival mode, whilst desperately trying to build a life with someone she knew she loved so deeply. She really did think, *if I love Elijah this much, during this time where I can't feel that much for anything, then after this I just know he'll be everything I never want to lose. We just have to get there.* Alongside her constant internal battle that had been ignited by the rape, Nannie was dying, quite suddenly. Upon reflection, there were many moments she took out all the pain life was relentlessly inflicting her with, on him. It was such a painful, conflicting time for them both but at the end of each argument, end of each day, they truly were drawn back together by the true love and intentions that were behind it all.

*

I feel like I'm going crazy. I feel like a shell of myself.

*

Beauty

"No one looks like you, you're so unique looking. I could go out and find a copy of all your friends but you're special."
Elijah was fantastic at making her feel incredibly beautiful. I can say this comment, apart from finding slightly offensive to her friends, particularly made Liv feel truly seen. He was right, she was unique

LOVEY

looking, with a mix of Filipino running through her genes. Being the reason all men on Tinder loved to guess what part of Asia she was from. Her mum would call her Pocahontas growing up, always complimenting her appearance to be beautiful and special. But her Asian genes to some were subtle which created the mysterious unique beauty that she possessed. She adored that she had found someone that saw her, truly *saw* her, through the crowd of people.

LOVEY

*

To-do list

Date ideas 🐣 🐓 🖤

- ✅ Hampstead Heath
- ☐ Otherworld
- ☐ Duke of York cinema
- ☐ New unity games night
- ☐ Food for friends (Brighton)
- ☐ The Shisha garden
- ☐ Roof east
- ☐ Namco funscape
- ☐ Boxpark
- ☐ Twisted lemon (Brighton)
- ☐ Chaos karts
- ☐ Circolo Popolare
- ☐ Flight club
- ✅ Four thieves
- ☐ The prince
- ☐ Lost in Brixton
- ☐ Vinegar yard
- ✅ London Bridge rooftop
- ☐ Backyard cinema
- ☐ Getting married 🖤 💍 💒
- ✅ Everyman cinema
- ☐ VE kitchen
- ☐ Skylight

LOVEY

Liv and Elijah, from the moment they met, began creating a shared iPhone note of all their plans and activities to do, making the most of all that London had to offer. Each time they found something fun or saw a nice restaurant, they'd pop it in the note. One day she received a notification that he had made an edit. '*Getting Married*' appeared. She smiled brightly down at her phone.

*

Could really be happy

Sat on the kitchen counter, watching Elijah cooking, his favourite thing to do and as we know, was something he was extremely talented at. He stood smoking a joint out the large window in his flat in Camden, wearing a plain white t-shirt, dark joggers, with his beautiful wavy darkest brown hair that had fallen out of its gel a little, which Liv loved. She sat with her legs crossed on the counter by the microwave, she took in all that this moment was and contemplated a thought… *if life stayed like this, right now, well, I'd be happy, I could really settle into this and be happy.* Of course, we know life didn't stay like this, but she couldn't deny these moments really showed her how much she cared for him.

*

Conflict

"You do this, you invest in people, their problems become yours and you stay when you shouldn't."
Liv pondered what a strange thing to say in an argument. If anything, she thought that it could have been a nice quality but instead he was turning it into a reason to tear her down. Making it a weakness, rather than the strength it is. He always had frustration of how Liv handled difficult situations. They tackled them oppositely which created nothing but friction and arguments. We can see now he just wanted the best for her. Didn't want her in a scarcity mindset which she had been encased in. His intentions were pure and were

LOVEY

because he cared so much but his execution was severe and sometimes controlling and hurtful. She liked her life with him though. She loved so many parts of him which she knew were quite unreplaceable. She loved his sisters, family. She really liked his friends. He was sometimes difficult to love and he made her feel like she was too. Maybe she was, *it's hard to love someone when their healing.* Nevertheless, he had invited her into his world with open arms and a red carpet, in the form of a toothbrush, but he sometimes held her by the throat with it, metaphorically.

*

Thoughtfulness

Elijah rang, "are you at home?"
"Yeah, why?" Liv asked.

Whilst on the phone her buzzer started filling her flat with overly loud ringing. She answered the door. To her surprise and amazement, it was a Deliveroo driver passing a big bouquet of flowers through her front door. She had told him that morning the news that Nannie was more ill than they all first anticipated. It was a sweet moment and Liv had never had gestures like this before. He surprised her at every turn and was quickly becoming the only light in the darkening time, that was laying in front of her.

*

The home in Camden

When Liv met Elijah, she was surprised he was able to have his own one bed flat in central Camden, all by himself. That's what you get when in recruitment, I guess. It was big, kitchen was spacious, with a large window he'd use to smoke his joints out of, that overlooked a garden from above. The lounge was made up of tall ceilings and windows which nearly reached the flat above. Then, turning right entering the front door, you step down couple stairs to the bathroom

LOVEY

and bedroom. He had a bath. Oh my goodness, I think he thought sometimes she was with him just because he had a bath and she could sit in her LUSH bath bombs whilst he relaxed in the lounge. It was a plus, I must say. She would later call this flat *home*. Just as he always encouraged her too. During this time, she still had her flat in Brighton and upon reflection thank goodness, taking into consideration how often she'd pack up her belongings and leave after another argument.

*

Flashback to Halloween 2019

"What shall we go as for Halloween?" Liv excitedly asked Roe. Looking through Pinterest, she stumbled upon a picture of a couple in checked brown shirts with white eye contacts and black distressed clown makeup.

    Liv: This??

Sending Roe the picture.

    Roe: That looks sick!! Yeah!

That evening they walked round the main shopping centre in Brighton finding matching shirts to complete their costumes. Roe picked up some contacts and they made their way home. The shirts were Burberry-like, completing the look with the top button done up Liv drew on an imitation of the Pinterest makeup with black eye shadow, and they were ready for the Halloween club night on Brighton seafront.

LOVEY

*

Halloween 2021, back to the present

Going as a character out of The Purge, Liv painted 'X's' over her eyes and the outline of a skull with white eyeliner, pressing over the top of with neon pink eyeshadow, making it look like a glowing Purge mask. It was a makeup trick she had learnt from Pinterest. She brushed the front section of her hair in two high ponytails on each side with just a small amount of hair pulled out to frame her face. After an extensive pre's session, her and a friend went to a house party. The party was at her friends, boyfriends house with all his flatmates and plus ones. After Liv had successfully become best friends with all the random girls she bumped in to, she found herself in an unknown person's shower, finding the quietest part of the house to call Elijah.
"I want to come homeeeee." she wined down the phone.
"Come home then." he laughed.
"Problem is Slug, I don't think I can see out my eyeballs." Liv confessing the level of drunk had exceeded a new high.
"Oh god, I'll get you an Uber." Elijah finding her intoxication amusing whilst simultaneously wanting her home.
"Okay." Liv with a big grin on her face, instantly agreeing to the plan, beaming with excitement at the thought that soon she'll be cuddled up in the bed they shared.
"I want a McPlantttttttt." she moaned.
"I'll run and get you one." Elijah adding to her new lease of energy.
"Yaaaay, oh my god, will you? Oh wait. What time do they shut?" Liv running from overjoyed to concerned in less than a second, all being fuelled by her drunk chaotic energy.
"I'll order you an Uber now, then run to McDonalds and it'll be here waiting for you."
"I love you." Liv whispered, still stood in the shower. *Now I've just got to find my way to the front door,* she thought as the realisation of her intoxication had become apparent.

LOVEY

"...I think I'm going to be sick."

*

Story Makers

Any partner that Liv had knew what it meant if they woke up in the middle of the night to the theme song of the kid's TV show *'Story Makers'* playing out her phone which she would place by her head, on her pillow. It meant she was sick. Whenever she felt sick, or would be sick, she'd put that show on and it would be the only thing that soothed her enough to sleep.

*

Made it home

Liv had made it into the Uber and back home the pair virtually shared at this point. Elijah had physically run to the nearby McDonalds to get the McPlant as they were about to shut. Incredibly proud of the fact he had been able to fulfil his promise of the vegan fast food, I'm sure you can imagine the frustration he felt when a very drunk Liv took one bite and revealed she felt very unwell. He left the room to get a bucket as he knew his girlfriend was a little too drunk to get one herself. When he got back, her face had practically landed in the meat substitute burger. He stood in the door frame and laughed. Then coming further into the room, he replaced the plate with a large grey mop bucket. He tried to be annoyed but it was difficult as he looked upon his little drunk girlfriend with her little ponytails poking out the bowl.

*

You're a Weasley

Barely being able to catch her breath, Elijah was in the heat of an *'Autism attack'*, but this time was the fun kind. Where his weirdness reaches a new high and social norm barely exists, contributed by a

LOVEY

hefty amount of alcohol on this occasion. Elijah and Liv had started walking to the tube station after a night out in Revolution. Elijah, in his manic state began running up to random people, calling them either a *"Weasley"* or *"Potter Potter Potter"* in a funny voice, mimicking a scene from one of the Harry Potter movies. Liv found it a touch embarrassing, yet absolutely hilarious. She loved moments like this, where he couldn't care any less than what others thought of him. It was authentic and a rare quality.

*

I fell in love with who you are now

After the most agonizing period of time that eventually reached to Nannie's death, Liv struggled incredibly with her university work. Up till she passed she was staying at Nannie's mostly full-time, breaking to go back to Camden with Elijah. She was writing her dissertation on Anti-NMDA Receptor Encephalitis, a topic she chose due to it being the human equivalent of her baby Bud's neurological disease. She was often found at Nannie's bedside, juggling her university work whilst feeding water with a dropper after Nannie became incapable of swallowing. After Nannie had eventually past, her mind had never felt so unknown. It all felt like *too much*, *too quick*. Barely having any time to heal from one thing to the other. She felt she had officially hit her limit.

> Liv: I'm scared about what's next. I think I'm totally fucked.
>
> I can't do this

Liv text Elijah minutes after Nannie floated up into heaven.

> Elijah: You can
>
> I promise
>
> Your man has your back

LOVEY

    Liv: I really I love you… I hope you know that and

    I'm sorry

    You met me at the hardest time I've had

    And not the version of myself I want to stay

    Elijah: Don't apologise

    The version I fell in love with…

    I'm not in love with who you want to be

    I'm in love with who you are now

    Liv: I genuinely don't know how to process all of this year

    Sluggy

    I love you

There is something about having someone say,
you are enough.
Who you are,
right now,
even at your worst state,
is *enough.*

Not only enough,
But that they love,
Fiercely

                                        That's how he made her feel.

LOVEY

*

Can I just paint?

Liv's happy place is painting. And if it isn't painting her large canvas' with cream and off-black acrylic, then it's making clothes on her sewing machine or drawing linework illustrations of women on her iPad. She had always been creative and had continuously received compliments for being very academic and imaginative. It was a gift and a curse. She needed both to feel fulfilled. They balanced each other like yin and yang. The days and weeks following Nannie leaving this world, she couldn't bring herself to finish her degree. She'd try, try with all she had but it was as though her brain had just died. She felt exhausted constantly, numb, confused, panicked, heartbroken, all. the. time. She had confessed her difficulties to Elijah one evening. He was always great at sending long voice notes, making the world seem a little more doable.
"Liv, your only job for the end of the year is to paint and try and have a nice Christmas with mum. Uni work will get sorted, I promise, I know it stresses you, but it will be okay, you're so close to being completely done." Elijah trying his absolute best to make the road that laid ahead, as bearable as possible.
"All I want to do is just not think and paint." her empty exhausted voice confessed.
"Then that's what you'll do lil sluggy." Elijah concluded.
So, under Elijah's encouragement, she sat on her floor below her high ceilings, in her beautiful flat on the seafront in Brighton and painted. Painted large bold strokes of black and cream, making abstract art of different compositions of blobs.

Elijah would be right, university did get sorted and Liv did get better, *just like he promised.*

LOVEY

*

Scarcity

Frustration grew with Elijah over her revealing *'scarcity'* mindset. Liv had always operated on opportunities never coming back around. Not just opportunities but, everything. When one good thing came around, she believed nothing else would ever again. That led her to function in way where, in situations she could do 'better', she'd take what was given to her. Elijah was incredibly passionate about her worth. How she should be treated and what she deserved, *ironically.* "If we don't end up together, please know you can do so much better than Roe." talking of her scarcity mindset with men. "You're too special to end up with an accountant from Surrey." he teased but truly believed. You may think that is an odd thing to say to your girlfriend, but it was a very *Elijah* thing to say. He saw the ways her brain had not caught up with who she was now. Whether that be a more attractive man after *'levelling up'* a few leagues after losing so much weight and transforming herself or it be, she had been so incredibly used to having very little control over striving for better than what she was given. Another, better opportunity didn't ever seem to be a real option. He knew they were out there, ready for her to take and live an incredible life doing whatever she desired. Liv took much convincing to be shown this. He was a symbol of better in a lot of ways. Showing her, telling her, *be picky, don't settle, go after the very best of what you want.* Even through Elijah had his flaws, he fiercely loved Liv, would have forever been loyal and strong and have her back, she knew he would.

She'd later conquer this mindset, fear. Once you start to believe there is an abundance of magnificence out there in the world, for you to take and have, it all gets that little bit easier. You hold on to things a little less desperately which allows a whole different side to you to exist.

Met a beautiful, sweet, kind guy or girl but it doesn't work out? No worries, there are thousands more! They simply weren't your person, and maybe, the world might have actually dodged a bullet for you.

LOVEY

Didn't get the job you desperately wanted? Something genuinely so much better is on its way.

If you start believing the world is actually on **your** side, instead of against you, suddenly you can see how it's all working it out for you, the way it needs to. Liv later realised how when everything felt it wasn't aligning, wasn't going the way she so greatly desired, it actually was, truly working it's self out in the background. This new belief took time, a lot and doubt still rises but it creates a sense of calm which she had always wanted.

Nothing that is truly yours will pass you by.

> She'd eventually find a little more peace.

*

Voice notes

"How could anyone not love Liv?" Elijah gushed in his voice note thanking her for meeting his family on Christmas Eve. Liv had left Flum at home while she went to squeeze in a meeting with Elijah's whole family for the first time. As they were all from Brighton and Liv still lived there, it worked out well. They met at a pub. Liv was nervous to meet them all but was excited to see his mum for the first time. After they all collected a drink from the bar, they sat themselves down at a large round table. She found it easy to be bubbly and talkative. After a few hours of more drinks, bonding with his family, and hearing stories of Elijah which were funny and exposing, she left. She adored her time but had to get back to Flum to finish up their Christmas Eve. Walking back to her flat from the bus stop she opened up her voice note from her favourite person, "Thank you so much for making the time and coming Sluggy. You smashed it. Mum loved you but of course she did, how can anyone not love Liv?"

LOVEY

With a massive cheesy grin, she walked back into her flat thinking how it had become the best Christmas eve she'd had in a really long time. Re-emerging to Flum lounging on her sofa, they opened some wine and made some late-night Christmas snacks.

She often thought of this, this voice note. She'd play it every time she needed to feel like there really was someone who truly saw her and loved her, even the worst sides. I'd like to emphasise the voice notes Elijah would fill Liv's phone with. They were most days random declarations of love or random thoughts, but she loved them. They'd later be all she had left of him. One night in particular, he had sent an extra-long one. As it was late at night, she propped it on her pillow by her head... *"Hey gorgeous girl,"* he greeted in his deep voice everyone adored, "I was just laying here in bed thinking and I just can't get over your journey, your childhood, school, college, and now you're in your last year of university doing neuroscience. I guess I'm saying I want to be more like you. I've probably taken the easy route a few times when I shouldn't have and yeah... you're amazing, I love you."
Liv laid there with tears in her eyes. *Someone noticed.* She meant so much to someone, they had laid there in their own bed, thinking in deeply of how much it took of Liv to accomplish what she had. It meant *the* absolute most to her.

Can you see how she fell for him?... she had never met anyone like him. Liv would always think Elijah was special.

> Liv: You're such a blessing
>
> Elijah: My chink
>
> You the blessing
>
> Know your value

All he wanted was for her to know how much she was worth.

LOVEY

*

Come home

"I'm sorry, my stress boiled over." Elijah sent as Liv had taken her belongings and left the flat after a disagreement.

> Liv: I'm sorry too
>
> Elijah: I don't want you to leave
>
> Liv: I think it's best
>
> Elijah: I disagree
>
> Liv: Like you said, this isn't why you moved to London. I'm not going to ruin your time here. I love you too much to do that

Elijah had moved to London only a couple weeks before he met Liv. He had moved up from Brighton and had intentions of staying single and engage in more causal encounters, then he met Liv. He sometimes held it against her. *"I wish that was an option when we met."* he said once after Liv divulged, she had only been in casual situations after Roe. Bear in mind, this comment was months into their relationship. "Are you joking? you do realise you just said that too your girlfriend?" He didn't mean it of course, he was obsessed with Liv from the second they met but it's the fact he could say that, knowing how much it would hurt her… implying he would have wanted to exchange their meaningful relationship for only wanting one thing from her, especially after the rape.

> Elijah: Liv stop it
>
> You're mine
>
> We going to be good

LOVEY

> It's a stressful time
>
> Come home
>
> Go get yourself a matcha and take some alone time

Elijah sent a picture he took of her from Halloween. Of her on the sofa, pink purge makeup on her face, McDonald's on a plate her ponytail poking out as her head hung out of the big grey bowl.

> Liv: Worst person
>
> Elijah: She cute as hell
>
> Liv: I might come home
>
> Elijah: Come back
>
> Pls

*

High Cake girl

"Elijah, I don't feel right,"
"I can't feel my arms or legs."

Elijah started to laugh at Liv's bad trip after they had smoked some weed one weekend they were spending at her flat in Brighton. Liv wasn't a stranger to weed, she had never done any other drug before, but weed was always safe in her eyes. Elijah smoked quite a bit, some weeks most nights, then he'd pull back and only smoke on weekends, so through association, she became more exposed to it after getting together.
"Shall we order some dessert from Deliveroo?" Elijah suggesting a cure.
Sat on her bed with cake in one hand and a spoon in the other, all her paralysis had magically disappeared. The pair giggled over that fact

LOVEY

that she was miraculously healed the minute the delivery driver rang the buzzer with their dessert.

The following day, Elijah ending a voice note…
"You're still my fave person, even if you do eat too much cake and fall asleep without any cuddles."

*

5th December 2021

> Liv: I'm sorry I'm rubbish but I love you so much, more than I've loved anyone. I think we're good for each other
> xxxxxxxxx
>
> Elijah: Oi!
>
> You're not rubbish
>
> Silly lil slug
>
> You're amazing
>
> I love you so much
>
> More than I've love anyone
>
> We are perfect for each other
>
> Have a good night xxxxxx

*

Christmas was always her favourite time of year

Even though there was the absence of a strong family dynamic, you know, the typical 'going home for Christmas', where you're greeted in your family home, by your parents and extended relatives. Her last few Christmases were spent in her own flat with Flum. But to her, this was fine, it was enough. She enjoyed decorating her cosy home

LOVEY

and putting up her own tree. She had always wanted to go to the Edinburgh Christmas markets, adding pictures of the festival to her Christmas Pinterest board. It was something her and Elijah discussed early on. He one day amazed her with his thoughtfulness again by booking flights over the festive season, not long into their relationship. The date of the outbound flight would later be the date of Nannie's funeral. Of course, he wasn't to know this, just the worst of luck. There were many small moments which made the couple feel like they were cursed. She moved her flight to a later time and departed alone. The only way to keep the plan that had been the only good thing to happen in months. He was determined for the trip to be amazing, to be everything she imagined and deserved it to be, after having the worst few months of her life.

It was not everything she imagined it to be.

There were lovely moments. *Christmassy magic.* Moments sat in her red bandage Oh Polly mini dress, in an all-vegan Italian which she had found in the months before going. Or when strolling through the beautiful streets lit by thousands of fairy lights, amongst tall ancient architecture the city was composed of. One of the days of their trip, Elijah found a science museum which he knew Liv would love and she did. They spent hours there. One evening was spent in an intimate, authentic tapas restaurant, having a large glass of red wine, sat opposite her best friend, laughing and being stunned by his endless compliments. She thought she had found her moment. But just as there were these flashes which felt like dreamlike, there were just as many which felt like she was screaming, and no one could hear her.

LOVEY

*

Cornwall for Christmas

Christmas 2019.

She sat in the bathtub located upstairs in Roe's beautiful family home. The house was the perfect size between still maintaining its cosiness whilst also being aware that he was very lucky to call it home. Liv had come from a very different life to a fully detached house with a garden in expensive Guildford. A life where you get a Rolex for your 21st birthday. She managed to reach a level where she didn't feel like a total burden and comfortable enough to let herself enjoy one of her simplest yet most fulfilling pleasures, *always being a bath person.* He always tried to reassure her she was welcome his in family home, that she wasn't intruding and to simply not overthink it and just… *have a bath.* Things weren't always that simple in her head, she wished it was though.

"We're so glad you're coming with us for Christmas." Roe's mum Linda said with conviction as they sat opposite one another on the sofa. She felt included. She always loved Roe's parents. They were the perfect example of what she wanted one day and had very little exposure to, a happy marriage. Linda was silly, a little ditzy but incredibly sweet, lovely, and always wanted to put Liv at ease. His dad, Rich, he was everything Liv wanted her dad to be. His sense of humour was witty, the type of humour where he'd wear a brussels sprout patterned suit on Christmas day. You could also tell he was caring and saw moments maybe someone else would miss. Roe and Liv embarked on their road trip down to Cornwall in his dads Defender, transporting most of the family's luggage and presents. It had taken some convincing to get her to agree to come. She was committed to the belief she'd be imposing on their incredibly close family unit whilst also being aware once there she was committed and couldn't leave. *All she ever wanted was to be part of a family.* To

LOVEY

have a dad to look up to and feel protected by, to have a mum who cooked her dinner and made her feel like she didn't have to carry the entire weight of the world on just her shoulders. Initially, she had been so excited that he had such a strong family dynamic, *maybe one day, they'll think of me as family too,* she hoped.

They arrived after a long journey, but Liv and Roe always found a way to make it fun, laughing for a lot of the way. He was always a good driver, but the Defender could be heavy and hard to drive so he did well. Pulling up at the Airbnb Roe's parents had booked for Christmas break, she was conflicted with excitement and panic. But her lifeline was next to her, so she'd be fine, so she thought. The Airbnb was big. A large remote cosy cottage that was idyllic for a Christmas holiday. Evenings were spent drinking red wine that Rich was consistently suppling her with and playing Mastermind with Roe on the floor by the pop-up Christmas tree. She felt content, maybe a little out of place as her imposer syndrome was in full swing, but still happy.

> *You're not a part of them Liv.*
> *You were only invited as they pitied you for not having a family of your own to be with.*
> *You'll never have a family like this.*
> *You will never feel fully included.*
> …These were the voices that plagued her mind and couldn't escape from.

At the under-sized, overcrowded dinner table, situated in the beautiful, stoned floor, open plan kitchen, an argument broke out. Immediately, the shouting triggered a trauma response. Adrenaline started to course as she sat quietly. Rich, sat next to Liv, felt his son's girlfriends' unease. After the argument between Linda and her brother continued to escalate, he lent into Liv. Roe did his classic response to any conflict, this being, head down and pretend nothing is happening. Lexi sat getting increasingly annoyed the more her

LOVEY

uncle continued to shout at her mum. Liv felt like the catalysis. The frustration had built from how people had joined for Christmas and the lack of room the family were now experiencing.

"I can eat in the living room. I really don't mind!" Liv trying to resolve the seating issue as dinner was being plated.

"No, no, you're eating with us." Linda resiliently making sure Liv was just as included. Again, and always, she thought, the outsider, burden. She was disappointed in herself. She knew this would happen, maybe she shouldn't have come but she desperately wanted to be with Roe, on Christmas day. As the argument intensified, Liv started to pray the ground would open up and swallow her whole, Rich felt the moment and judged it perfectly. He lent into Liv and with a humorous whisper and a cheeky smile he said, *"welcome to the family."* she looked up at him and smiled. She felt like she belonged again, wanted, even only for a split second. It was his way of saying, *this isn't your fault and you're a part of this, like we all are.* It was the validation she needed and was searching for within Roe but never received. Rich was always there even in ways Liv could only appreciate till after the breakup, whilst combing through every moment of her and Roe's relationship. He'd always pop his head in Roe's room, "You okay Liv?", "want to come sit out here with us? more than welcome you know?"

She has many regrets in terms of their relationship but one of them being not spending more time with his parents, but two things stopped her.

1. She genuinely enjoyed sitting in Roe's room, on her laptop staring at the back of Roe's curly man bun he tied to move hair out his eyes as he worked.

2. Her confidence was rock bottom. She felt rejected by her own dad, family, why would his family be any different. They were the perfect family after all.

LOVEY

Spoiler, they weren't, but no family are. They were good people though, and she thought so much of them.
The reception from his older sister Lexi however was always a little frosty. Liv desperately found herself wanting her approval just as Roe did. Lexi had an aura around her. She was a powerful presence, opinionated, beautiful with long blonde curls which framed her stunning face. Her and Roe were both blessed with her bodies, both slim curvy with big bums and small waists. They were both tall, long legs which balanced their physique. Roe was always the quieter one out the two, always being comfortable in the background, watching the happening. Baby videos confirmed he had always been like this, and Lexi had always been *'Little miss bossy boots'*. It's funny, this was Liv's nickname when really little, till life battered all her natural confidence out of her. But with Roe, the more comfortable he was, the weirder he got. Liv adored this quality. When Lexi and Liv would converse, she'd often use words like *"My* family", *"My* mum" in moments that didn't seem necessary. Liv believed she purposefully chose to isolate her brothers first girlfriend from ever thinking *"my family"* would become *"our family"*. It felt as though no one was good enough for her Roe. We now know this isn't true but in a weakened Liv, she believed it. Liv often thought how different all those moments would have been if she had just been who she was now with them. Happier, more confident, believing her place and her worth.

> Once you discover your worth,
> you'll find it difficult being around people that are blind to it.

*

Presents

Not wanting the pressure of each exchanging their presents in front of the whole family, they decided to do a more intimate gift giving on Christmas eve, in their room. Liv has always been obsessed with fashion, men and women, so clothing was always a good bet. She'd

LOVEY

find cool one-offs from Depop and send them to Roe. He'd look to her for her opinion often. For Christmas Liv bought Roe a grey oversized Lazy Oaf Sherpa quarter zip, a light brown vintage puma jumper from Depop, a couple of pairs of trousers that happened to fit his long muscularly legs perfectly, along with an expensive eye cream that came with its own little spoon and a personalised pillow, one side had her face printer on it and the other had his, both having their close-up selfies distorted on the round pillow making it a humorous present. The pillow was both of their favourites.
"Omg you got it." she said in disbelief, gently picking up her new vintage black Fendi bag.
"It's one of the ones you liked on Depop, I got black over brown because I thought it would go with more."
"It's perfect." looking up from the bag to his eyes as she beamed.
Liv didn't grow up with much and this was the most amazing present she'd ever received.

*

Winter mornings

When she'd stay in Guildford, the mornings would start early. They'd get into Roe's Audi TTS and adjust to the cold as the engine warmed on the driveway. Driving through the quiet back roads, pink sunrises would engulf the sky as they drove towards Roe's office. Sat in the heated seat, his hand would grip to her thigh, only to be removed when needing to change gear. Liv was put in charge of the music as Roe and Liv had always had their music taste as another trait in common. His work was next to Three Bridges train station, so the routine was to always drop her off there, while trying to squeeze as much time together as possible and using the drive as another opportunity.

These cold peaceful early pink mornings were her favourite.

LOVEY

*
Bubble tea

Liv stood in the middle of Elijah's living room, wrapped in his vintage Tommy Hilfiger light brown puffer jacket that she loved to borrow which practically drowned her, but she enjoyed the oversized fit. Elijah took out his phone and toom a picture of his girlfriend. He gushed over how cute and small she looked in his coat which she had paired with her forest green Adanola joggers and beige Converse. On the weekend's they'd often walk into central London, making the most of a beautiful brisk winter's day, but beforehand, starting the day with a bubble tea from their favourite place in Camden market.

Liv's order: Matcha with oat milk with blueberry bubbles.

Camden is one of those places that are amazing to live in until it's a Saturday. Through the winter months they had developed a little routine commonly starting out with a bubble tea.
 "*Ayyy* my favourite couple," the bubble guy recognising the well suiting duo. He handed Liv a loyalty card and stamped all the circles. "Next time make sure you get something different to matcha." teasing Liv over her unchanging order.
She'd later use her free bubble tea after the pair were no longer sharing their winter walks. She grew to miss Camden, but the bits you don't see. She missed the back streets, the way it felt at night, she missed the lounge in the flat they shared that was wrapped with tall and wide windows that could sometimes feel a little exposing. She yearned for the flat she began to live in. She craved the little life her and Elijah had started to create in the one bed home he afforded, five minutes from the markets. She lovingly reminisced over the memories of climbing up on the kitchen counter, pretending to be helpful while Elijah cooked vegan masterpieces.

LOVEY

*

Caring

Elijah: Put the heating on

Don't be scared to put the heating on

Don't want you to be cold

Elijah had a remote job, so most of the week was spent at his desk in the corner of his large living room. However, on Tuesdays and Thursdays, he could go into the office which he often did. That left Liv in the flat all day. She'd routinely study and make sure the flat was tidy. At this point she was in her final year of university. So, taking breaks from her dissertation, she'd tidy, clean. Clean the kitchen which always managed to turn into a mess so quickly. Often, as the evening approached, cooking dinner so it was ready for when Elijah got home.

I think quite early on into being together, Elijah knew Liv had an eating disorder or had suffered one in the past but still struggled with how to balance a healthy relationship with food. He did his best to navigate it though. Always being food positive and encouraging.

Elijah: Skinny slug

Get my girl some snacks

You've got to eat

Cooking was his love language. He'd cook 100% vegan for her. Meals like, carbonara, mac and cheese, cauliflower wings, full English roast, enchiladas, sausage and garlic mash, making from scratch the Honest Burger bacon ketchup when they'd have burger night, but he'd often ask for her lasagne, truly legendary. Not only

LOVEY

would he spend hours in the kitchen making whatever dinner they decided, he also always insist everything was made from scratch, *only the best for his bun girl.*

*

Rap Game UK

Inspired by their favourite show they'd cuddle up on the sofa and watch, other than Below Deck and Come dine with me, they decided one night to make a diss track on each other.
 "How harsh are we going?" Elijah gauging the right amount of 'diss' to go.
"Oh, I'm going in." Liv giggling to herself.
Once both performances were done, using a beat boxing backing track from YouTube, it was an outstanding win on Liv's side. Both parties were in agreement.

*

Bun girl

Elijah: Can I have bun girl tonight?

Elijah wanting Liv to brush up her long black hair into a bun on the top of her head. He loved how it emphasised her round face he confessed to loving so much.

Elijah: No makeup as well?

Liv loved her long hair softly waved and falling around her face. She had always been a makeup girl as well. Her and Flum would, every weekend, walk around the makeup counters in Tunbridge Wells, buying the latest MAC foundation or eye shadow. Liv was the makeup artist in the group growing up, her friends wanting her to do their hair and makeup for every underage house party. Flum always let Liv express and explore her identify, always being able to wear makeup whenever she wanted, wear what she wanted and not

LOVEY

only that, but she joined in with her too. Liv questioned, does Elijah just truly prefer her without makeup on her round face, with a bun on the top of her head or did he want to strip her? Strip her right back to basics… was it manipulative? To make her feel less like her? or was it harmless? She thought this till one day, he was genuinely annoyed with her for not wanting to put her hair up and sat in his bedroom doing her makeup. Nevertheless, she became bun girl and for a while, she loved being her. As I've said, Elijah was always very talented at making her feel the most beautiful.

*

The Tyson fight

"11th round." Liv said with certainty whilst handing Elijah's phone back to him. She had always enjoyed watching boxing and MMA. She had watched most of the big fights and had always liked Tyson Fury. Elijah gave her his phone to pick her betting. They stayed up late with snacks and made the lounge cosy with blankets and the duvet from the bedroom. She contemplated over his previous fights and the fights of his opponent, Deontay Wilder, and her thought process eventually drew her to knockout in the eleventh round.
"Oh my god." she laughed as the fight ended.
"I can't believe it, you called it!" Elijah in shock at how Liv had beaten his predictions and got it spot on.
"You've won two hundred quid!"
She grinned to herself over what a good moment it was. Sat up late cuddling her best friend, with a bowl of vegan cookie dough the pair had made earlier in the night, and now had won the fight. It was the perfect cosy evening and she felt so thankful she had shared it with her *Slug, Elijah.*

*

Weapons with words…

Some things Elijah said stuck with Liv, till this day.

LOVEY

"You did go on a date with him," referring to the rape.
In the midst of a heated argument which became more usual than she would have liked. Elijah's frustration grew. He always managed to use the most vulnerable insecurity, that being the rape being her fault and weaponised it against her. The moment the words left his mouth her heart sank immediately. *Nooo,* she thought. *Please don't have just said that.* The person that's opinion had become the most powerful was using the worst possible thing against her. The argument had brewed over him becoming frustrated and couldn't understand Liv delaying her plans in hopes a friend would meet her at Brixton tube station, so she didn't have to walk alone to the Duke of Edinburgh pub. She felt it was obvious but proceeded to explain how the assault had made her feel so incredibly vulnerable. That and just being a woman alone at night. *Again, is it not obvious the world we live in?* "But you weren't taken off the street. You **did** go on a date with him." she was heartbroken over his insensitivity.
"You can't do anything by yourself." he continued to add.
She then grew in anger.
She couldn't understand how he could say that.
She had been the most independent person her whole life and now she was having an agonizing, triggering argument, feeling so incredibly hurt, feeling she had to justify why she felt the way she did to the person that was meant to truly be on her team.
She felt like screaming.
Who says something like that…for one?
Two, *how could you be so knowingly hurtful to someone you apparently love more than anything?*
In that moment she felt disappointed that she had let someone who could be so nasty, in so close. There was a small part of her that felt she had let herself down. The most betraying feeling is the one where you tell a person your deepest secret. The most vulnerable part of your heart and mind, they make you believe you are a team, you deal with it together, to then… drop you. Leave you in a ditch at a second's notice and use the most violating knowledge of your past against you. She looked across the bedroom at him in disbelief.

LOVEY

"That was disgusting. I'm not doing this anymore."
She picked up her small black Fendi bag, packed her lipstick and hairbrush and walked out, making her way to Camden Town tube station to join her friends in Brixton.

> Elijah: Liv I can't believe this is happening
>
> I don't know what to do
>
> What happened wasn't your fault in anyway
>
> I was being insensitive and not factoring in how what I said would be received
>
> Surely we can't leave it like this
>
> Can you call me
>
> Liv please
>
> We can talk it through
>
> I didn't mean for what I said to come across like that
>
> Can you block my number please
>
> Otherwise I'm just going to keep contacting you
>
> I understand what you want to break up and respect the decision
>
> But I don't know how to deal with it
>
> Did you get there okay
>
> I'm sorry for being rude
>
> I hope you've got there alright x
>
> My insensitivity wasn't acceptable earlier

LOVEY

> Can you let me know when you're at the pub please x
>
> Liv?

As she stood at the pub with her group of friends, she watched his messages blow up her phone. She wanted to, *so badly*, believe he had just made a mistake with his words, she wanted to forgive him. She went back this time. *She forgave him.*

Unfortunately, his hurtfulness did not stop...

As I'm sure you can imagine, he was talented at apologies. She simply wished he didn't do the things to be sorry for, in the first place. *She forgave him, over and over.*

"Roe doesn't even want you." referring to Roe finding a girlfriend and moving on.

Her heart broke. She forgave him.

> Elijah: Roe can literally cheat on you and be fine
>
> Liv: WHAT THE FUCK.

This one is quite self-explanatory. She met his text with being purely insulted.

She forgave him.

He seemed to find it so easy to deplete of empathy sometimes. One moment he was the most understanding and supportive partner and the next he'd use those exact vulnerabilities against her like a weapon. I have to say there were more, and worse. But now... it is only fair to feature some of the good... Guiding you to relive them is difficult as often they would come in the form of long voice notes of

LOVEY

conveying his love or random thoughts but here's some messages too…

>Elijah: Stay strong Sluggy

>Bud would be looking down proudly at her mum.

Liv reflecting on how it had been three years since Buddha's death.

>Come home. Or get yourself a matcha or something. But confident we will get back together

>I would like to formally apologise for being a cunt

>You're actually the funniest person I know

>You come first in every sense

>Proud of you every minute of everyday

>Why you such a funny lil jerk

>Thanks for being you

>Want you back potter

>Misses peanut head

>You're so strong my gorgeous best friend, literally amazes me, you'll get through this

>You look stunning in your pics

>Morning small Asian lady

>Bun girl looking like she's up to no good

>Gimmie freshly baked Liv

>Hey muggle, lots of Beyoncé, lots of girl chat, my dream

LOVEY

Want your cute round head

Sit on my face you spicy slug

I love you nugget head xxx

You're too important

I love my queen

My slug my wife

Thanks chinky winky dinky

Want my bun girl back forever, life isn't good without her around

Come here muggle

My gf is better than yours, mine is queen

She fun, literally most fun, N sexy, N kind, triple threat", "N has the most incredibly round head, N smells like freshly baked bread, those 2 are my fav components

My G 🩶

Goodnight my misses xxxxx

Gorgeous girl

Actually your biggest fan

You so clever N creative

You are the most beautiful, kind, funny, strong and loving person I have met
I love you pine nut head

You are my best friend

LOVEY

You are my world

You're my Weasley

*

Anger

They argued often towards the end, Elijah and Liv. I think because he couldn't control her, he needed someone that *needed* him and she didn't and not only that, but it was palpable. She could never let herself need him. Not at that time. Maybe he needed someone needing him because it gave him purpose. His parents had been less than responsible sometimes, and he had to grow up at an accelerated rate, to say the least. Once a little older, he took it upon himself to potentially be the stable figure for his sisters, who at that point, depended on him. he was determined to not let them down, which he succeeded. She was determined not to depend upon him though, so she in turn, started to build walls around her. Sourcing weekly therapy from a specialist in sexual assault, she was overcome with anger, all the time. She had never been an angry person. That was her dad, her brother, but not her. She got upset. She'd run away, escape but never angry. Yet suddenly she was overcome by the emotion.

"Why am I so angry all the time?" desperately searching for the answers within Sarah, at her weekly session.

"I know anger scares you Liv, you've only seen how the emotion can be used negatively but remember, you have a lot to feel angry about." She was right. Liv was so focused on not feeling angry, as to her it represented being out of control and pain, but it can be spun. It can be used in a powerful way.

Elijah always seemed familiar with anger and its presence. He seemed to possess a lot of within him. A past riddled with moments fuelled by the powerful emotion.

Maybe he brings it out in me?

LOVEY

Liv was aware Elijah had done a lot of work on himself. He had attended a men's mental health charity that had mentored him through difficult patches of his life, to say the least. She always admired how impassioned he was to want to be better. He also had a huge desire to do charity work. To change jobs and do good in the world. She eventually thought maybe the reason he wanted to do that so badly was because his worth depended on it. Maybe felt he had something to make up for. *He always wanted to feel **needed**.* She could absolutely tell though that he wanted to help her with her new struggles with the emotion. I think he saw how much it scared her. She had no idea how to channel it. Where to put it. I think he could relate. Elijah came up with an 'exercise'. One day after seeing how much Liv was starting to panic in how she would now live with this new, unfamiliar emotion, he thought of a way to channel it. One where he'd sit on the edge of the sofa and she'd have to push him as hard as she could. At first, she found it difficult to let go. Barely budging her six-foot-two boyfriend. To fully release all the emotion and fuel it outward in a controlled way.
"Come on Sluggy!... Harder!" he'd say.
He persisted and so did she. Eventually she grew to trust herself to let go and release. She couldn't believe it, it actually helped. They'd both smile and laugh after. It was so simple, but it helped.
The frequent disagreements escalated as she continued to stand up for her thoughts. There were times she truly believed Elijah never really knew her, *how could he though?* she thought, she wasn't her, whilst with him. Exhausted by the hard-wearing inner battle she faced, almost daily within her healing, by the end, Elijah and Liv had both contributed to the shell she was. *'I know I'm not a bad person'* whispering out loud, looking into her own eyes found within the large gold vintage mirror.
"Am I love bombing you?" he questioned one night in the lounge. Surely, he wasn't, not that Liv really knew what love bombing was, but if he was, he wouldn't be aware and talking about it… *right?*
The word *'Narcissist'* only really came up towards the very end. Liv found herself googling *'traits of a narcissist'* on the train up to

LOVEY

London, which would later be the last journey she'd take to see him. Some, many, matched. They both knew it was already over by this point, but she gave it one last go. Elijah did always love to say she didn't know when to let go. Turns out she would learn this skill quite soon after.

*

Am I with a narcist?

Liv was by no means an expert, quite the opposite, of what made someone a narcist or to have narcissist traits, but she did her best to learn after she could feel herself questioning her own sanity as a result of her volatile relationship. I am in no way saying Elijah was a narcist, but she wanted to understand any traits that where making their way out in the moments they would hurt one another with words.

<u>Definition of Narcissist</u>: "Often require constant admiration, show arrogance, entitlement, envy, exploitativeness, lack empathy, self-importance and more."

Traits of a Narcissist:

- ◊ Lack of empathy
- ◊ Exaggerated need for attention and validation
- ◊ Arrogance
- ◊ Self-importance
- ◊ Sense of entitlement
- ◊ Interpersonally exploitive behaviour

Signs of gaslighting:

- ◊ You no longer feel like the person you were
- ◊ You feel more anxious and less confident

LOVEY

- ◊ You feel like you're being too sensitive
- ◊ Everything you do is wrong
- ◊ Constantly apologizing
- ◊ Making excuses for their behaviour
- ◊ Constantly questioning if your reaction to your partner is reasonable

<u>Definition of Love Bombing</u>: "The action or practice of lavishing someone with attention or affection, especially in order to influence or manipulate them."

*

My head feels like exploding

My point isn't Elijah was wrong, bad and Liv was always right and perfect. Many times, that wasn't the case, but she was *trying*.

> Elijah: I don't want to break up
>
> I love you

> Liv: But that's not normal to have a list of things your partner has done that has upset you and now whenever I do anything I'll just be thinking of the list. That's why I don't see a way forward. I already feel I have so much in my brain my head feels like exploding and I'd hoped you'd be my safe and easy space where things are a little easier and it's okay to make lil mistakes because you were understanding and my slug. I try to always take on board what you say once I figure out what you mean after it coming out harshly and I'm always saying sorry for being shit. One minute I'm amazing and a great kind person in your eyes and the next, before I know I've done 10 things to upset you which genuinely o of them were intended. It's so up and down and I feel like a horrible evil person when I've done something wrong to you. Feeling like I 'get away with so much it's a joke' feels so harsh as I'm trying so so hard everyday, always wanting to make you happy, always trying to think of you even with

LOVEY

every single other thing that is going on in my life. It's not poor me poor liv but things atm are genuinely awful in a lot of ways and my brain feels... exhausted. And I'm just hoping I've got enough to give to uni, to get a good grade and job, and life I want, enough to give to mum and nannie, enough for you and my friends and then enough for me so I still want to be here. I'm trying and I am sorry I let you down so much and do the wrong thing

*

Jumping hugs

Liv: How great is that jumping / humping thing when arguing haha

Elijah: Honestly might have saved our marriage

Many times they argued they could often tell they were more frustrated with the situation rather than each other but you know, when you're already annoyed and you're in too deep, they needed something to break those moments and they'd often both just start laughing and go right back to being friends. It was originally a TikTok Liv had seen where you hug your partner and jump up and down. There's no way you can't not laugh and instantly diffuse the conflict. Of course, there was a time and place where this wouldn't fix the situation but a rule of it was other ***had*** to do it, even if they are really annoyed if the other said so.

She'd do anything to make it work.

LOVEY

*

I want it to be us

> Liv: Sluggy, thank you so much for leaving work and running with my bag so I could get the bus. I've had the best time with you, you always make me feel incredibly loved, happy, and never fail to make me laugh in my little Jimmy Carr hackle (when it's really funny ;)) you're the best friend, partner anyone could have and please I don't take anything you do for granted, even the smallest of things. I guess sometimes by brain feels really busy but they always catch up but I'm so so sorry there are moments I don't do the same for you and I always completely understand where you're coming from and just know I love you so much and look up to you for everything you have achieved, all the stories you tell me of how different your life used to be and how you've changed it and you. My intentions are never because I don't think the most of you, guess I'm just simply always thinking and trying for everything to be right and perfect I never look at it as an attack on something you've said or suggested. I promise (swear on bud) in the best and even in the worst moments I honestly think you're the most handsome, smart, funny, unique, strong, honest, emotionally intelligent, annoying, loving, freak ;) there ever was and I want to do everything I can to keep you for a really long time, there's nothing I wouldn't rather do with you, I wanna look up at you with my lil round head as long as you'll let me, so again, I know you're not asking for one but I'm sorry and I'll never stop trying to be better for you and be what you deserve

He met her heart felt message with a voice note, *of course.* "Olivia, that was one of the loveliest things, in fact probably, ***the*** loveliest thing I've ever read. That was so sweet and so kind, and I really really appreciate it. I love you *so* much and I know you appreciate me, and I know that stuff so don't think you need to send a long ass text for me to know it, but I do love the long ass text. So, thank you *so* much my little Sluggy, so kind of you. I love you. And look, I know we fall out but sometimes it's just me being grumpy,

LOVEY

sometimes it's miscommunication, it's never anything serious, we're not auguring over fundamentals. Anyway, I love you. I love you. I love you. My G."

A few minutes later…

"I feel like that voicemail was really underwhelming compared to how nice your message was and I'm sorry I will reply properly in due course. It made me smile *so* much and I was so happy reading it. I just want to squidge your little round head and your little bun and just squeeze you and just be annoying."

I think she believed in them. No. I **know** she believed in them, in their good moments and how it had been there from the moment they met, all those months ago by Kentish town station. Her thoughts were, *if we can just make it through this part. Through the worst time of my life, and I get to heal and become my soft person I recognise, then we could really build an incredible life together. Where I have my best friend, who I undoubtedly get to laugh with, every day.*

Liv: I promise I'll try to be the person you deserve xxxxxx

*

There is good and bad in everyone and everything

Point is, there is good and bad in everyone. We all have moments we are not proud of. No excuses, but we do. But it's important to show both the good and bad, that way, maybe, you'll understand why Liv stayed and also why she left. The reason for visiting the six-month relationship with Elijah was not to showcase the ways in which he let her down, not just as a basic human and friend, but, in fairness to him, she met him one week after seeing Roe and six weeks after the assault. She needed kindness, softness, patience, and she was met with someone who instead, functioned differently, but regardless, he

LOVEY

loved her intensely and was an important part of her healing and he became her lifeline whilst everything was falling apart.

She needed him to be better sometimes. She needed him to be someone he wasn't. There were moments she needed him to be Roe.

                        She took responsibility for the last part.

*

Goodbye Slug

18th January 2022, sat on the train leaving the flat they grew to share, back down to Brighton for work in the lanes, she said *goodbye*.

> Liv: I know you didn't want me to message but I just needed to say how much I really do love you. Your worst moments will never define your memory, you're too good for that. I truly, with all my heart wanted to work with you and renew what we have neglected and the bond we have because I believed it was more than worth it. I'm sorry last night happened. I'll love and miss you for a very long time.
>
> Elijah: This honestly breaks my heart
>
> There is nothing for you to be sorry for
>
> Everything that happened last night was down to me
>
> I'm insufferable when I don't get my own way and cannot control my emotions
>
> It's selfish for me to be with someone when I have so much work to do on myself
>
> Genuinely devastated by what I said to you last night
>
> Worst part is that I know how awful it is but still can't seem to control myself in the moment

LOVEY

> You deserve better
>
> Elijah: I completely get why you've left me
>
> It makes sense and I actually agree with you
>
> I do genuinely love you so much
>
> You are my best friend
>
> Just don't have the ability to control my emotions
>
> Liv: I don't want to lose you
>
> Elijah: Feel like I've already lost you
>
> I just can't keep letting you down
>
> You've had so much shit in your life and I'm just the next chapter

Elijah sent a picture of the pale pink and baby blue stuffed teddy that can be turned inside out depending on whether he is happy or sad. He had gotten him for Liv early on in their relationship, and she always kept on her bedside table. He sent the photo of the sad octopus…

> Liv: He's heartbroken
>
> Elijah: Like his mum n dad

They stayed engaged in conversation, straying from their relationship issues but it kept the communication alive.

> Liv: Look I love you
>
> I want to make sure we're both trying our best and acknowledging our mistakes / things to change for the better and are committed to that because you're my best

LOVEY

> friend and at the end of the day I don't wanna be without you, you're too special
>
> Elijah: Look I love you more
>
> I do want to be better
>
> I just keep losing my shit
>
> Don't know what to do
>
> Not sure where to start but want to do it
>
> Liv: I love you
>
> Elijah: I love you

The next few days carried on as normal. The duo slipped back into being best friends, which always was the best way of describing them. When they weren't arguing, they were undeniably perfect.

> Elijah: You are honestly so special
>
> We need to know when to walk away
>
> Breaks my heart that you think I was abusing you
>
> Liv: I'll miss you
>
> Are you sure about this?
>
> Elijah: I don't know Liv
>
> I love you
>
> You're amazing
>
> Literally my fav person
>
> But we bring out the worst in each other

LOVEY

> Liv: You're my fave and I love you. It's not like I don't wanna lose you because I don't want to be alone, it's I actively want you and love you and the person you are. I wanted to create a healthy loving place for us because I believed we deserved that. I wanted to be with the man I know you are, and you may not believe it but I did want to make you feel loved and appreciated
>
> I'm just sorry

The plan was for Liv to always stay the weekend of her 24th birthday. She had planned a dinner at a vegan restaurant by Liverpool street and night out with all her friends. The couple had split for good after an explosive argument and she escaped to her closest friends, making sure her entire birthday weekend wasn't ruined. Elijah did offer to give her the flat for the weekend and he go elsewhere but she didn't want to be there, without him, so she took her suitcase and ordered an Uber to her best friends. Her birthday evening arrived, and she had put on her makeup and outfit she had planned weeks prior, this being a cream corset from House of CB and a black satin mini skirt and heels.

Upon arrival Liv informed the group why her partner was not present at her celebration. No one seemed to be surprised and was mostly met with their lack of enthusiasm for him or their relationship. After a few too many drinks, stood in the queue for a club she rang her *Prince, Slug*. He answered and they exchanged a small conversation and he wished her a good night. As the night draw to an end, she made her way back with another close friend to the hotel she had booked in preparation for Liv's birthday. Her other friend who she had escaped to after the break-up had gone home earlier in the evening, so she decided to end the night with Sophie, in her hotel. After a long-winded journey, stood in the reception at 3am the staff informed the girls it was a single room and Liv could not stay. "So, you're kicking a young girl out on the street at 3am!"

LOVEY

Sophie argued. She took her phone out knowing there was one place she could go, *home*. She rang Elijah and he told her to come home and before she knew she was in an Uber back to Camden. There was a small part of her that was relieved in a way. She got to end the night in her own bed, or that's how their shared bed felt. After waking up on the Sunday, this being her actual birthday, the vibe in the air was strange. They hadn't slept together. He had let her in late as she had left her set of keys with him the day before. He put the pair straight to sleep. In the morning he brought in the birthday presents he believed he'd never give her after she left. It was perfume, one she had mentioned and totally forgot she wanted, a matcha tea set, a Dunder Mifflin mug for her love for 'The Office' and always preferring to drink anything out of a mug. She was glowing in his thoughtfulness and attention to detail. As the day went on it was almost a though the breakup didn't happen. They fell right back into being *them*. In comfy clothes, they went out and collected oven pizzas and snacks from M&S and sat cuddled up on the sofa watching the 'Rap Game UK' with their oven meals, upon Liv's birthday request.

They had a lovely evening.

The following day, 24th January 2022.

Elijah went off to work on the Monday morning after making sure the towel was on the radiator for her. He came back from the bathroom into the bedroom and pulled up duvet, tucking it up under her chin as he gave her a flurry of kisses all over her face as he said goodbye.

> Liv: It's a no makeup day haha

Knowing these days were his favourite.

> Elijah: Niceeee, Bun girl day?

LOVEY

Liv: I'll do a bun haha

She got up shortly after he left and carried out her normal routine. She had a shower with all her LUSH products she had been given by a friend that worked in the Oxford Street store, always starting the morning smelling of 'Snow Fairy'. But as she continued, sitting at his desk, setting up for laptop and revising for her impending exams, she became distracted by a fact she could no longer ignore. He got home and she knew, knew they could no longer do this anymore. They couldn't continue to have explosive arguments, break up, then come back together as if nothing had happened. *It was too much.* Liv wanted a calm, soft, silly love and yes, sometimes that was Elijah, but she had to believe she could find these things, the intense love, without the explosions. *It has to be out there,* she so desperately believed.
They had to finally end it.
She recognised she'd never heal while she was with him. With everything she was, every fibre of her being, all she wanted to do was stay with her best friend, someone who was loving and safe and familiar, but the truth was no longer escapable.

It's as if the entire universe said…

> Dear Liv,
>
> I guided Elijah to you when you needed him. I made sure his persistence was unwavering when the last thing on your mind was to date or find yourself in a relationship. But he proved to you he was different to the others. *He never left.* He had your back. He obsessed over you. Gushed over your struggles and how you had defeated them. He was everything Roe was not. And sometimes I know you didn't like that, but do you see now that was so important? Good in the ways they were nearly polar opposites of each other? Elijah was special. He was funny, handsome, loving,

LOVEY

generous, affectionate, emotionally intelligent and self-aware. He was stunning and infatuated over you like you've never had. He was there to teach you about parts of yourself you didn't know you had, whilst also giving you an anchor when life was falling apart.
I, as the universe, knew you needed him while you cared for Nannie, watched her die, sat holding her soft hand as she took her last breath, and battle your last year of university and all that it meant after someone took a part of your body.

I had to give you moments where you'd go weak with laughter, cuddled up on the sofa or have someone grab your face and kiss you so passionately so all you could feel was his love. Because without these moments, *well,* I would worry about you... where you'd be...

But... you've got this from now. There are things you need to feel, heal, and that cannot happen while with him, so you now must let him go...

I know you loved him, you tried your best, but sometimes angels are not here to stay, they are here to help you through a time that is nearly *unbearable.*

I brought him to you for a reason... and now he must leave for one too.

Let him go

She left Camden to never step foot in the flat she called home, again.

LOVEY

*

Valentine's 2022

Her recent break up meant she spent Valentine's day with her Liv². They got dressed up and went to a vegan pizza restaurant and cheered over a glass of wine. She felt strangely free after the separation from her Slug. She knew what heart break felt like and prepared herself for that feeling to come in like a crashing wave, but it never did. All her friends found it strange how she seemingly went right back to normal, like she was better than when she was with Elijah. She had a day or two that felt like that classic break up feeling, but it felt like she was the best she had been in a while. It was the biggest sign of how much their relationship had been weighing on her. From across the table in the cosy, filament light bulb lit restaurant, her beautiful best friend reached into her bag and pulled out a pink envelope. Liv stretched her arm out to our Liv, handing her a card. Liv opened it up and slid out a Valentine's card that said, *'I love you more than vegan sausages rolls'* with an illustration of the Greggs vegan sausage roll holding a pink banner. They both laughed. She looked up at Liv, someone who had remained constant in her life after she had entered and felt she completely overwhelmed with love. She opened the card and her heart burst with the message. She thought how different it was this time. Break ups are **hard.** No matter what. And Liv really did expect to feel immense loss, but this time she was **surrounded** by people who loved her, people who would never let her feel alone. She thought of how after Liv told Liv² about the assault, her first instinct was to get the train down to Brighton. She did. Roughly a week after she came down and all they did was sit on the sofa and eat food. It was exactly what she needed. It had been less than a year since they began being in each other's lives and already Liv had shown our Liv she'd always be there, be present for the important moments, the moments you need someone there.

LOVEY

Coming back into the room after the mind wondered into all the reasons she was thankful for Liv, she opened the card and her heart burst.

LIV ♡

HAPPY VALENTINES DAY!

I CANNOT IMAGINE MY LIFE WITHOUT YOU. THANK YOU FOR ALL THE LOVE SUPPORT AND ENERGY YOU BRING. THE BEST TIMES ARE STILL TO COME AND I CANT WAIT TO DO LIFE BY YOUR SIDE.

ALL THE LOVE
LIV ♡
xx

Looking up from the card, Liv's eyes filled with love as she looked at her best friend.

LOVEY

*

Reflection

After Liv had a little time to reflect on her relationship with Elijah, it was only then that she could acknowledge there were touches of narcissism which caused a particular type of pain in her healing heart. Not all the time, it didn't consume them, but it was there, nonetheless. She often found herself searching in their memories for the line between the real love and connection she felt and his traits that their relationship couldn't escape from.

Regardless of the moments she hated, she would continue to have waves of missing those voice notes which made her feel seen and like someone was for once, truly on her team.

She had to be alone to build back the person that was taken.

In all honesty, she'd always have love for him.
She'd be lying if she said otherwise.

She desperately knew he was good at heart. Life isn't black or white but for Liv and him, they couldn't find a healthy way of sharing each other's worlds at that time and that's what hurt Liv, because, at the end of the day, he made her laugh to most in the world. And he truly was, her best friend.

LOVEY

Chapter Four

I'm not sure how to start this part but I have to begin somewhere. Before we go any further, we must hold ourselves in the aftermath of losing *Flannie Puff*. It feels I don't have time to describe to you what Nannie meant to Liv, so the easiest way to show you is to leave the speech she wrote and read at the funeral, stood at the altar, in the large cold quiet church, here for you to read.

The day had arrived. Two weeks roughly since Nannie was still on the Earth, today was her funeral.

*

I'll do a speech

She had rehearsed it to the point she knew every word by heart. Flum and Ian, Liv's uncle, were faced with the inability to honour their mum in words. To Liv, it felt so wrong at the absence of anyone honouring the most special human she was. Internally she faced that the reasons for **not** standing up, at that large dark wooden alter, in the painfully quiet church, was simply not enough to not do it. She knew she'd regret not putting into words the declaration Flannie deserved.

LOVEY

"I'll do the speech." she said confidently to Flum with the tiniest touch of hesitation in her voice.

"That would be so lovely Liv." Flum gushed in relief that someone had to strength to honour her favourite person.

Liv smiled and felt a sense of *'I can do this.'*

Sat at her desk, with her legs crossed, tucked up on her black velvet chair standing on gold legs, she raised her head from her notebook. "How personal shall I go?" asking Flum who was across the room, sat on Liv's cream sofa. Flum had almost immediately moved out of Nannie's after she passed and went back with Liv to stay in her flat. It worked well for the immediate fall out. Liv would spend a lot of time at Elijah's which gave Flum space and also Liv would get to be with her mum when she came back. Only problem was, she was never alone. Something Liv learned very early on about herself was that time alone, for herself, was a necessity. Vital for her to feel like *her.*

"Go as personal as you want." Flum encouraged.

"Whatever you want to say to her, say it."

She lowered her head back down and wrote out a letter from her heart. Tears fell from her eyes and on to the cream paper. She wiped them away as the words filled to the page.

*

The funeral

That morning in a black high-neck tight long sleeve bodysuit and cream jeans. Stepping foot slowly in the large, magnificent church, making each step purposeful. She was paralysed by her nerves. Public speaking wasn't a comfortable place for her, but a strange type of numbness allowed her just off the edge of falling apart. After the large number of *Cherry Perry's* loved ones took their seats in the stalls and the priest had led Nannie's chosen hymns, he announced *"Now we will hear a tribute from Ann's granddaughter, Olivia."* She looked down into her lap, collected her notebook she had anxiously been gripping to for the duration, and rose out of her

LOVEY

seat. As she stood from the hard cold wooden stalls, in the busy church that was so silent you could hear a pin drop, she had one thought... *I can't do this.* She walked across the front of the church, looking at her coffin and positioned herself on the alter with the microphone close enough to catch her words. She took a deep breath, looked at Flum past the alle and began.

Flannie puff,

To me, she was a Nannie, but also a best friend, a second mum and whatever I needed her to be, she was. She was my best friend walking down the old town linking arms, she was a mother when I'd be crying on her sofa. She made wherever she was a home. A home where your walls could fall down, and you were safe. A home where I got to laugh till I cried and cried till I laughed.

You made my world a better place.

We'd always leave little notes for each other. That was our thing. Around my 21st birthday I was very low. Nannie asked me what I would like and all I wanted was for some Nannie wisdom. She had the ability to make the world a little lighter. She wrote me a card of four promises, these were about my life and to this day it is my most prized possession.

In all honesty, I wasn't done needing her, I wasn't done laughing with her, or learning more about her life, stories I didn't know yet or advice I was yet to ask for but... what she has done is imparted so much of herself in the people I'm so lucky to have around me.

I know she'd be so proud of me for doing this today and I guess that's where I'll get the strength to do anything I

LOVEY

want to do in life. She gave us all so much courage and happiness when we needed it, let alone just some great laughs. I will always be entirely grateful to have had her in my life and for the bond I got to share.

It was truly an honour to be able to help care for her towards to the end especially, alongside my mum. Nannie looked after us and then it was our turn. During that time, it was astonishing the bravery she showed and the most incredible strength. I'll forever cherish my last Nannie moments I got to have.

I think the bond you share with someone so strongly doesn't just disappear just because they have. It lives within us and it's a blessing to carry it, cherish it and live it, live it for you both.

She scattered my life with special magical moments like it was glitter. And that was something only she could. She was my angel on earth, I always told her I don't know what I'd do without you and I truly meant it but instead, she's left us all with her strength, bravery and courage and witty sense of humour.

I love you nannie

LOVEY

*

The card of four promises

Dear Liv -

I promise you that you will be happy again x

I promise you that you have a great future in front of you x

I promise you that you will always be loved. x

I promise you that one day you will be a best friend and partner to someone who will be the same to you - xx

LOVEY

Sending lots of love to you
Proud of you, i know
That you'll go far.
xoxo
(Flum)

*

She did it

She did it. She managed to hold her devastation in while letting her love out. After she completed her speech, taking another deep inhale, she unfolded a piece of paper Flum had covered with loving words to say on her behalf.
After the funeral was over and everyone started departing the church, Liv was taken off guard at the volume of proudness and awe she received. Even family she had never met congratulated her on being able to push through the moments it sounded like her voice was beginning to shake and the wave of devastation could take over. She kept it at bay.
"You'll forever be so glad you did it." a distant family member expressed.

LOVEY

"Liv, I've never been so proud of you." Flum said as tears fell from her eyes as they said their goodbyes after Liv's need to rush to Gatwick airport was looming, to meet Elijah in Edinburgh.
"I'm sorry I have to leave Mum, I feel awful."
"Don't worry, go and enjoy it. It will be good for you."

*

All the dominos had fallen

It felt to Liv as though it could not have been worse timing. Discovering her cancer had returned after eight years in remission, it resurfaced with a reckoning force. This all took place a month after she had met Elijah, in the last first term of university, while being tasked with her dissertation two months after the assault. It wasn't long, it was quick. Barely anytime for everyone's minds to catch up with what was actually happening. How could she heal from anyone of it?

*

She barely cried.

LOVEY

*

> I'll never forget the small coming from the bed sores Nannie had. She was in so much it was palpable. We all tried so hard but not harder than her.
>
> "Dying wasn't meant to be painful"

These words would haunt Liv.

*

She was everything

She held her soft hands as the tears softly fell down her cheeks. The time between Nannie becoming ill and dying was rapid, a matter of weeks. Flum had moved in to help and be her sole carer. There was no way *cherry perry* was dying in a care home. She would be home, surrounded by her family who brought her more joy than singing with her little ukulele or strolling down the old town after her weekly hair appointments, or finding a new hat to pair with a great pair of glasses. She was the soul of everything. She was the reason everything was okay.

> Anything but her!!!!! Why her. I needed her. I wasn't done needing her.

LOVEY

*

Lost souls

Liv and Flum relied on her like a couple of lost teenage souls trying to find their way in life and she always managed to bring the light. She really was exactly what you needed her to be, just when you needed her to be it. She gave Flum the strength to be a mum herself. It terrified Liv as to what would happen to Flum after Flannie had disappeared from this world.

*

Music

The soundtrack was Frank Sinatra. And when it was not Frank, it was Hauser. That's what played the days, weeks, leading up to her death. She'd be surround by music. It was her love. She learnt how to play the ukulele at eighty after her first cancer diagnosis back in 2014. She'd learn songs like 'You are my sunshine'. Then she'd perform them. She was a special kind of person. She did not have a bad bone in her body. I know people say it, but I promise, *Flannie was truly special.*

*

Last Nannie moments

"I'm so proud of you."

At this point, it was the last time Nannie looked like how she'd always remember. Liv had to leave for a few days, and it was a very real possibility she'd float away in that time. *She had to say goodbye, just in case.* She was always conscious to not cry too much in front of her but this case she could not contain her tears.

LOVEY

Sitting on the dining chair, which was now positioned next to Nannie's bed that had been replaced with a hospital bed that lifted and lowered, she told her she had to leave.
"I have to go for a couple of days, but I'll be back. I promise."
"Okay Lovey." she said in her sweet soft voice.
"I love you Nannie."
"I love you too."
Nannie was quiet for a moment.
"I'm so proud of you." looking deep into Liv's eyes as they held hands. It came out of nowhere and Liv started to cry.
"I couldn't have done it without you." Liv knowing Flannie Puff was referring to Liv's hard and treacherous journey.
"I'm so glad I could be that for you." her soft smile sweetly beaming at Liv.
"Be happy Lovey,"
"Be cherished."
Liv broke down whilst trying her best to smile through the tears to show her adoring Flannie puff that she was okay.
"What a little trio we are," Nannie looked out lost in thought.
"…we were show-offs down the Old Town, linking arms." she continued as she relived her memories.
"We really were." Liv giggled through her stream of tears that reached her lips as she spoke.
It was always a blessing that her, Flum and Liv had been such best friends, their whole lives.

*

You need to come down Liv

Flum had moved into Nannie's to look after her as the family discovered how unwell she'd become. Liv helped as much as she could, dividing time between Brighton to work, Elijah's in London, and Nannie's in Hastings, and in the times she shouldn't be there she'd be on FaceTime with Flum and Flannie, Flum propping up the phone in the lounge while Liv was doing university work from

LOVEY

Elijah's. Towards the end Flum really needed help so Liv started staying at Nannie's more and more.

"Liv, get up, Nannie needs the toilet." Flum gently waking Liv at 12am, 3am, 6am.

It was exhausting, but Nannie had it worse. Her cancer put her in an incomprehensible amount of pain. Flannie wasn't one of those elderly people who seem their age, she was different. Extremely able bodied. Lively, warm. Liv always spoke to her about the latest boy. "Ooooo Liv, he has a lovely smile." Nannie beamed as Liv showed her a picture of Roe for the first time.

"Oh, Liv he's so handsome. He looks like a Prince." she gushed over Elijah. Hence, he became *Prince* to Liv, Flum and Flannie.

Liv always spoke to her about the latest boy. She loved to gossip and tell her all about her dates. She knew how much Liv loved Love.

She was slowly slipping away. Have you ever watched someone, you know you need, not just want, but *need*, slip away? There is no pain like it. *What would this mean for mum?* Liv thought. Mum was a kid who relied on Nannie like she was still sixteen. *Mum will lose it,* Liv terrified of what was about to happen.

I'm not just losing Flannie, I'm losing my Flum.

After a couple of months that Flum was caring for Nannie, flicking back and forth between her home up the road and her mums, she eventually found less nights to leave. The worse she got the more Flum could not care solely anymore.

Walking into the back door of Nannie's flat which arrived you into the blue kitchen, where she'd usually be greeted with nothing shy than sunshine. She immediately made her way through into the large bedroom which was situated across the hallway of the one floor, large, high ceilinged flat. There she lay. A contradiction to how she'd usually find her Flannie puff. She had grown into immense pain, contributed by deep bed sores on the back of her

LOVEY

weakening body. These made any moments which would have already been awful, into absolute agony. Satin sheets and strength were what enabled Fliv and Flum to allow Nannie to use the bathroom. The satin sheets were folded upon themselves, making it slippery and allowing the pair to move their most prized possession with as little pain as possible. It grew to be a comfort to Nannie once Liv stayed more. Her daughter was growing tired, and Liv could offer fresh patience which always came in handy in the night. Movements took her ten times longer. She had to take long recovering breaks in-between each centimetre of movement just to bare the agonising pain. This at 12am, 2am, 4am and again, introduces you the patience you never knew you had.

It seemed to comfort Nannie when Liv would return. Flum didn't understand a lot of what the in-house doctors that would attend, were trying to explain. Flum would often say, "Did you get that Liv? I'll forget." when doctors were prescribing multiple different forms of medication at different doses to accomplish different results. "Yeah, I've got it mum." Liv could understand for the most part and that acted as a relief to both Flannie and Flum. "You understand all this stuff." Nannie would say. "I've got you Flannie, don't worry." Liv would often describe what the different medicines did to her, in way she could understand. She'd google anything she didn't know and translate it to her and Flum. Looking back, this was a way of coping. Liv could be useful and comforting. The only things she strived to be. Eventually, she told university she'd need a few extensions on assignments and her dissertation. These were willingly given as her advisor saw the gravity of her involvement in the care of her grandmother. Soon her only job was to look after Flannie Puff and Flum. Days became managing her pain, talking and helping district nurses, watching Nannie get a catheter put in, feeding her in small spoonful's to then not being able to eat at all and then tasked with hydration which was achieved by dripping a toothbrush-like instrument and dropped water into her mouth after she could no longer swallow. The work is hard. It is constant and relentless. Brutal

LOVEY

and tiring. But adding that she was everything to Liv. Watching your only light in your life, fading daily before your eyes. It was a unique pain Liv had never had.

It always consoled Liv that she spent every moment she could with her. The relief Liv could physically see in Flannie's face when she'd returned was something that Liv would carry with her always and cherish. She got to comfort her just like she had for Liv, so many times.

*

George is back with Cherry Perry

Nearly a year later, Nannie's older brother, George, had passed away. George Perry, he was a kind man. Nannie's side of the family were all so familiar in the way they all possessed that kind soul that reminded Liv of sunshine that lived within Nannie.
After George's funeral was over, the family stood outside waiting to progress onto the wake. Jerry was one of Nannie's closest friends. They had known each other since they were Liv's age and had their kind nature in common. Liv stood talking to Jerry in her stylish houndstooth knitted cardigan and cane. She stayed as long as she could, absorbing her energy as nothing had felt as close to Nannie since her parting.
"You're dreadfully good looking."
Liv chuckled.
"Thank you." she smiled, rubbing the top of Jerry's arm.
"I miss Ann terribly." Jerry gushed over her departed best friend.
"I miss her so much too."

Nannie's funeral felt incredibly numb to Liv. She had spent that day preparing herself for the speech. But this day, she was able to just sit back and feel. It hit her like a wave heartbreak.

LOVEY

"You know, I'm mostly blind and struggle to get around. I don't get out much, but I think to myself, I've been there, done that, I'm happy." she joyfully chippered with a sense of contentment that Liv prayed she'd possess at her age.
Tears fell from Liv's eyes as she smiled so brightly at Jerry. She was so incredibly moved by how overwhelmed she had become from Jerry's positivity.

The same ray of sunshine reminded her of one person.

LOVEY

Chapter Five

I'm back, but too you, the reader, I would never of left. I'm not totally sure where to start so I'll begin with the present moment. Before we do, you need to think of me as a voice coming from Liv's shoulder, to tell her story. As you may have guessed, her story, like many, is painful and complicated but she is also filled with a lot of love.

*

Where are we now?

So, let's recap. Now it was 1st of March 2022 and she had gotten herself to London. Liv lays in her bed, now located in Elephant and Castle. She thought the incredible bond she had formed to her home she had built in Brighton would have been harder to lose and intense to miss but since she left, she never looked back.

Nannie died on the 17th of November 2021.

Liv and Elijah ended their relationship on the 24th of January 2022.

LOVEY

Fliv Puff ♡

The last day of Flum and Fliv clearing out the home she had built in Brighton, Flum handed her an envelope addressed to '*Fliv Puff*'.

> FLIV PuFF! ♡♡
> You have Come So far; breaking through boundaries & Barricades! which will always Serve as a reminder to you never to limit yourself or fear Change.
> Congrats on your new home, new Location & new Job!! WOWW. So Very proud of you always.
> Love you
> FLUMMY xxx

> FLUMMY would Be So Proud, I'm Sure She is with us and always will be, beaming her Magic on us & Guiding us & giving us strength. ♡♡

LOVEY

*

I miss you

26th January, 21:32

Liv: I miss you so much Flannie, wish you were here, I need you

27th January, 22:31

Liv: I wish you were here to tell me it will all be okay

7th February, 16:05

Liv: Missing you so much Flannie Puff, wish you were here, you always made me feel like life was so much bigger than it feels sometimes

*

Nannie Voicemails

"You should really change your sim only plan, there is no point paying for your contract, you've had your phone ages." After Elijah and Liv broke up, she'd act upon his advice.

Now something to know, Nannie always left voicemails.

"Oh, hiya Lovey." she'd say in her ray of sunshine voice.

It was the most comforting sentence that existed for Liv.

After switching over the O2 sim to the Giff Gaff, suddenly her voicemail tab was empty.

Gone.

LOVEY

All of them.

Gone.

Voicemails spanning back years, 2015, that she had purposefully kept, all deleted. She fell to the ground in her Brighton apartment.

I can say, besides the moment when Nannie past, where Flum and Fliv sat at her bed side, holding her soft hands, waiting for her last breath, this moment would be the next worse.

*
The scenarios she lives in

Liv opened up her black air pod dupes and pushed them into both ears. The music resumed playing instantly out of her 'better' playlist, containing all her soft calming sad songs. It was a comfortable place to be. It was peaceful and an escape. The more unhappy Liv found herself with life, the more often you'd find her laying motionlessly in her bed with her headphones squeezed in, so they didn't fall out, with just the illumination of her neon heart light that lit the room dimly pink. Her mind would wonder and walk into different scenarios she wished to happen or just feel. They'd often contain Roe and a reunion which felt like a coming home. *You know the feeling,* the blissful sensation of walking into your home where your soul can rest and finally just be. The chaos would silence, and the room would be still. She'd skip songs that didn't quite fit the storyline she had created and found herself replaying them in her head, so she got them just right.

LOVEY

*

⟨ Notes

I'm broken. The only time in my entire life I felt whole was with him. The only time I've ever felt truly happy. I can't bare how I feel in my body sometimes. Like it's not mine. Like I'm barely existing. I need to feel I have some sort of control over myself and body.

Heart pounding. I've taken some propranolol.

LOVEY

*

After everything, all the loss, she just wanted Roe.

⟨ Notes

Maybe I should text him. Maybe I should just leave him alone. He's probably happy. Happier than he ever was with me and why should I ruin that or impose on his day. How could he love her? Why wasn't it me

She knew he wouldn't reply. What could he possibly say? We knew he had a new girlfriend from stalking his Instagram, and he was done with hurting her. He didn't want to tell her and rub in the fact he had moved on. He was never like that. Roe had a kind, naïve soul. He made stupid selfish mistakes, *yes*. But wasn't a bad person, he didn't have a bad heart. He was just young and had his own journey to fulfil. She always knew this.

"You'll learn all your lessons with me, then use them with someone else."

Liv's worst fear came true.

LOVEY

Chapter Six

Flum: 21:21 make a wish

Sometimes Liv would look at Roe's WhatsApp just to watch him come online. It was the closest thing she had to feeling like he was there. And sometimes there were days that were so hard, she just needed to feel he was there, even in the tiniest way.

*

I feel nothing

A new type of numbness plagued over her mind as more happened. She struggled to cry, this we know but nevertheless, was a big change. But she also couldn't feel attracted to anyone. The desire for someone, anyone, was totally dissipated. She tried to enjoy sex, just like how you're meant to, and she liked the idea of it but once she was actually there, it felt kind of awful. Now after the assault and more sexual encounters she had, the increasingly numb and out of control she felt. She couldn't bare it. When she thought about having sex with someone or a memory, her skin shivered. Now that isn't always because of the men but more the act. Maybe the reality

LOVEY

of sex had finally hit. It is the most vulnerable act she felt there was. By nature, she never found casual easy which is why Oscar was an important symbol. At that time, Roe had confessed he had betrayed their promise. Liv was devasted. She decided if Roe can do it, so could she. She could share that part of herself easily without the emotional attachment, and she was succeeding, succeeding till the date.

*

Worse than ever

Not far from a year later, and she was done. Worse. The idea of sex or men made her feel ill. She wasn't quite sure why suddenly she struggled so much. Was this something that happens when you're raped? It was almost like she felt people's energy and was rejecting all of it. She was desperate for a soft calming connection. She wanted *home.*

>Go find yourself
>Then come find me

LOVEY

> ‹ Notes
>
> To anyone that has told someone to go find themselves and then come find them... doesn't it hurt to love someone so much and know you'll never stop. That you've given them a part of yourself you cannot get back. I'm not sure I want it back.
>
> You'll lay there at night hoping you cast into their mind like a soft cloud, provoking a warm feeling to which they meet with the urgency of contacting you. Then, as you are laying there still, your phone lights up besides you. The name you've willed to see for so long is finally here. He's home. I'm home.

This never happened. The dark lonely room was never lit up by his name. He would never light up her room again.

*

> ‹ Notes
>
> I'm so lost and I can't get home.

She knew she could of course, function without him, maybe even thrive, but no. That wasn't what every fibre of her being told her was right. Bombarded with opinions of those who love her most, telling her, insisting, he wasn't her person, and her love was lost and for nothing.

        She remained silently certain and that was enough.

LOVEY

Chapter Seven

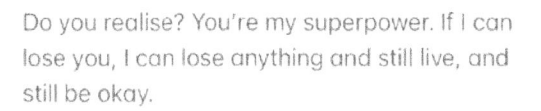

Do you realise? You're my superpower. If I can lose you, I can lose anything and still live, and still be okay.

*

Time heals

Time moved, months past and Roe became a part of Liv's history and that's where he stayed. She finally found peace in his absence. She finally felt like she could hold their relationship without living in it. His smile would always make her smile and his scent would always make her stomach flip like it did in the beginning, but life had moved them both so far from where and who they once were, that she was able to walk past her memories of him and not look back, not look back to see if he would look too.

> It felt like the beginning of something again.
> It hasn't felt like this in so long.

LOVEY

*

> ⟨ Notes　　　　　　　　　　　⬆ ⋯
>
> It hasn't felt like this in so long. I thought this feeling was gone. I thought I was truly broken. I'm not broken… I was just hurt, hurt by people who took too much of me.
>
> But I'm okay now…

*

Maybe I am okay…maybe I'm a little happy

With a sign of relief, it's as if she could breathe again. From all the drowning and suffocating, she was surrounded by air, an abundance of willingness to live, right there ready for her to take. She'd lay in her cosy candle lit room with that vaguely familiar feeling she had felt very few times before, content. Remember the moment she stood outside her flat situated over a run-down coffee shop, glazing up at Roe cooking dinner? She hadn't felt this feeling in so long. She found a present in which didn't make her skin burn with the desperation of needing her future. She felt a warm feeling right now.

> ⟨ Notes　　　　　　　　　　　⬆ ⋯
>
> Right in this moment I'm okay, safe and maybe a little happy.

LOVEY

Chapter Eight

You can't handle the smoke
Oh, hey Russell

Amongst an ordinary day, during an ordinary week, life interrupted normal proceedings with someone quite unexpected. Like a light, Fred walked in the room and from that moment, he lit it up a path which led Liv back somewhere she hadn't been in so long, *herself*.

Let's meet Fred.

It was a Thursday and that meant in terms of living in London, it was the dating Thursday nights which Liv sometimes attended with friends. Thursday is a dating app which as you can imagine, only works on Thursday. The app hires out bars which means only people that are single can attend. It encourages those who don't enjoy small talk to cut out the texting and connect in person. She never attended with an expectation to meet someone, but the girls found it more entertaining than a normal night out sometimes and broke up an otherwise uneventful weeknight. She had previously met a few cute guys at these events which became nothing more than an Instagram follower.

LOVEY

Clapham London Cocktail Club, that's where they met. Walking into the dim room lit up with red neon lights encased in a grand frame, spelling out *'paint me like your French girls'* in French, Liv, Evie and Daisy ordered some drinks, and started to gossip who would be their type as they made their way over to a table in the corner. As Liv sat on the booth side running along the wall she expressed, "they have to be over six foot two," clarifying her none negotiables in a guy. This was no surprise as everyone knew height was a major factor for Liv. "and have dark curly hair, preferably with glasses, someone sporty, gym goers, rugby player vibe." This has always been Liv's type, to which friends would sometimes make fun of, as it couldn't be further from theirs and could never see what Liv saw in the people she crushed on. Roe had dark curly hair. I don't think I've mentioned that yet. Ringlet curls. They were beautiful. She loved playing with them at night, as he fell asleep. He was six-foot-two, with a slim rugby-like build without having to actually play the sport and even wore glasses sometimes.

Back to the event. It's almost as if she manifested him. Everything she had described had just walked in the door and was then sat beside them. First, Eddie. Eddie announced himself in the dark underground bar effortlessly. He entered the room with his six-foot-four stature and handsome face. He led his group of friends across the floor and sat down with a drink in hand on the table besides Liv and the girls. He slid along the bench on the same side as Liv after squeezing himself between the two tables. The rest of his friends collected themselves around the table. Evie, sat opposite Liv, began speaking loud enough for the boys to hear, started commenting on something mildly negative towards the male kind which Eddie took as an *in* to start an interaction. He took on the role of feeling he had to defend the character of all male kind. Eddie was flirty and immediately communicated his confident nature. He was a beautiful boy, light hair, incredible body with tattoos dotted over his physique. Typically, expect for the light hair, he would have been someone Liv gravitated towards. Bonding over their matching line

LOVEY

work rose tattoos, *but it was Fred.* He was the one that Liv clocked the moment they walked into the room. *Him*, she thought. She would continue to only see his face for a while after they met but we're getting ahead. Fred walked ever so slightly after Eddie as they arrived and sat next to him on the booth, further away from Liv and the girls. He let Eddie lead the conversation between the two groups, taking a more *'sit back'* approach. Soon, as the conversations started flowing between more members from the boys table, Evie leant across the table to Liv and whispered, "I like that one." referring to Fred, the one Liv had fallen in *lust-at-first-sight* with.
Fuck, Liv thought.
Fred had moved from his more hidden away position to a more central seat between both tables after a reshuffling following a visit to the bar. Evie and Fred started engaging in a more in-depth conversation. Liv took this as a sign sit back and chat to the others, including Eddie and another friend, Will. Liv believed any interactions with Fred were done. She thought she couldn't peruse him after Evie had expressed she liked him and from Liv's brief interpretation, they seemed to get on. Liv being sat with gorgeous Eddie, she was caught off guard by his unusual accent which she never quite got to the origin of, maybe a mix of Irish and Russian? She could never drop the feeling that naturally pulled her towards to one person, no matter how she tried. She continued to make eye contact with him, not just to grab a moment of his attention, but she thought he was beautiful and felt an undeniable pull towards him. Internally she felt a little sad which she tried her best to disguise whilst speaking with his friends. She was confronted with the fact that she never fancied anyone like this, she struggled before to find anyone attractive but ever since the rape and Roe, she had gone totally numb from men, even the men she had slept with since. Then Fred walked in like a movie, in a moment that hadn't happened for her in so long. He was special in her mind from the get-go. Evie and Daisy got up from the table and went to order some more drinks from the bar, she stayed there to watch their table and belongings. Before she knew it, Fred squeezed himself between the gap in the

LOVEY

tables and relocated himself next to her on the booth and tucked himself in the corner. Their conversation and banterous back-and-forth became even more natural than she could have hoped. She was now not only extremely attracted to him, but they got on, *effortlessly.* As their conversation continued, I actually believe she spent the whole duration as he spoke, purely looking up at him with her chocolate doe eyes. Very unusual for our Liv. She has always been, if it's not a YES, it's an instant no. Things never needed to grow, she knew her own mind, and who she was, from, well, since always, never needed opinions or confirmation from others. She was always confident in the feeling she got, her judgment. It enabled her to call things instantly. So, here she was thinking every single thing he said was just the most interesting thing she'd ever heard. They exchanged their favourite UK rappers and plans for the future. He impressed her with being fluent in French and growing up in the Alps.

"Oh, so you really are blind." removing his glasses off her face and placing them back on his. *My goodness,* she thought. They were the strongest glasses she had tried on, and she wore glasses, had since she was four, only for reading. Her mum did also, and she believed hers were intense, but Fred's were stronger.

She wanted to kiss him.

"I want to kiss you." he said looking intensely into her eyes, still cuddled up in the corner of the booth.
You can read my mind, Liv thought.
"I can't. My friend likes you." Liv stated before she could tell what their strong eye contact was about lead too.
"I'm here with you."
Liv sat in silence for a moment looking down into her lap. She felt conflicted. In that minute she thought how it felt something was truly pulling her towards him. How long she had waited. How the icy numbness had thawed with him. She lifted her head, looked into his eyes and they kissed.

LOVEY

Ahh, that's how it feels, she thought.
It had been so long since she had felt anything but cold.

The girls returned to the table and both groups continued to dance and drink as the night got later. Evie and Daisy proposed they moved to the local busy club which was a few doors down. Liv relayed the plan to Fred and said she was leaving. They exchanged numbers and Instagram's in case Fred didn't manage to persuade his friends to join them at the club. Daisy and Evie made their way up the stairs out of the bar and up the main high street. Liv stood at the bottom of the stairs as she said goodbye to Fred. Every time they pulled away from kissing to speak or attempt to leave, she'd go back for another, always feeling it wasn't enough if she never saw him again.

Reaching the club and onto the dance floor, her phone lit up.

>Fred: Coming to Café sol
>
>Liv: Well I'm happy
>
>Fred: Eddie's getting a burger
>
>Liv: We're inside

Ahh so now they're reunited. She continued their night, this time it was just the girls and Eddie and Fred. The club was its usual busy self.

>Fred: Lost you
>
>Liv: Where r u
>
>Fred: Wanna come back after this drink?
>
>I'm outside
>
>I'll order an Uber

LOVEY

Holding hands crossing the road, they both climbed into the Uber. Smiling across the back seat at him then down at the hands still being held, she recognised something... she was beyond *happy.* She felt simply happy and safe with him.

*

Now, regardless of outcome with the pair, and even though Fred has ever so briefly touched Liv's life at this point, he meant something important without Liv realising.

*

Back to Brixton

Stepping into his bedroom in Brixton after the Thursday night had ended, into a surprisingly beautiful flat, unexpected as the outside looked a little like a prison. They stood in the hallway and continued to kiss, backing into his bedroom. He undid his belt that was built into his cargos and lifted her up. As he did this, they both realise her legs were being restrained by her black satin midi skirt, from locking around his waist. Dropping. her back down, she pulled up her skirt above her thighs and resumed position on his tall strong frame.

Oh my goodness.
The sex.
Out of this world.

LOVEY

*

Next morning

> Liv: I'm alive guys

Liv sent a selfie to the *'Needs therapy'* WhatsApp chat, of her beaming a smile with last night's eye makeup and glitter still on her face. The group chat contained Flum, Harry and her, who had quickly become an unexpected throuple. Mum and Harry had always got on but since Liv moved away, they often met up for coffee dates and became unanticipated friends, it was a strange dynamic from the outside, but it worked. It's a testament to Flum's youthful energy and unintentional sense of humour. The type of comedy that she's unaware she's being which just makes it so beautifully genuine. The name of the group, set by Liv, signifying to the fact that they were all on some level, mental. Making light of their conjoined mental health struggles.

> Liv: I met a boy lol. So funny

Liv quickly followed her picture up by.

> Flum: Obvs.

Flum acknowledging the news knowing Liv was prone to getting into all kinds of situations.

> Liv: Hahaha
>
> Flum: Haha well look at you all cute and alivvve.
>
> Where are you?
>
> Liv: Brixton, not far from home
>
> Flum: Who's the boy?

LOVEY

Liv: Fred

Met him out

Flum: Obvs

The perfect night then

Liv: Loooool

Yeah

Liv always loved how open her friendship was with her mum.

*

Him

Fred was *different*. The sex was *different*. The laughs were *different*. They were *different*. I can't tell you why Fred was unlike any other. Could be his energy, could be a soul thing if you believe in that, but whatever it is, he was, he was unlike all the others. It is still unanswered if he felt the same about her but nevertheless, it felt like she had waited so long to feel like this. She thought she'd never feel like this again.

He held her close all night, every night. After both said "sleep tight", she'd often look over at his glasses which were sat his bed side table and smile to herself, thinking of how there was nowhere else she'd rather be. With a touch of bliss, she'd peacefully drift to sleep.

*

Not broken

He brought her back to her. He lit up a road that had felt cut off, paved over, like it no longer existed. That soft, silly, calm, happy feeling she had faith existed, suddenly had found its way to her. I

LOVEY

think, when you have so much happen, happen to your person, your human body and brain, it is always a fear you'll go cold and be like that forever… she had this thought, so many times. Sounds trivial, I know, but it's true, it's a real fear.

Broken. She concluded she was broken.

> *Maybe I literally can't feel that ever again*
> *Maybe my brain is broken*
> *Never able to feel safe enough to love*

Permanent damage.

…Because that's it, if you haven't guessed. She needed to feel safe to love and that takes a very specific energy for a person to possess, and Roe had it, so did Fred…

But this time she was not cold, not anymore, she was warm. She felt like someone she knew, when with him. She would always be thankful for this. He had an energy which felt safe without sacrificing fun. It was the perfect balance and it had proven to Liv that '*that*' feeling does exist and can without Roe and in spite of the rape.

She could breathe a sigh of relief…

'…*Not broken*', whispering under her breath.

LOVEY

*

Double texts

Liv left that first morning having no expectation or intention of speaking to that man again. They had exchanged Instagram's whilst out and she believed that's all they'd remain.

> Fred: Hickie isn't going

A text from 'Fred' lit up her phone a few hours into the day. He had sent her a picture of his chest, referring to the hickie he was adamant Liv had given him the night before.

> Liv: Oops
>
> I'll put it somewhere else next time
>
> Fred: Somewhere less obvious?
>
> Liv: Defo
>
> Fred: I look forward to it

Now to Liv, that's all she thought it would become. Just some flirty messages to smooth over the one-night stand, then, to her surprise, her phone lit up again…

> Fred: What you up to today?

And that's where it begun, from that day, they didn't go a day without speaking. She was more distant this time. Normally, when she knew she liked someone she'd be less detached, wanting to show her natural, unfiltered feelings towards them. However, this time she was incredibly conscious that it had to be led by him. She was tired of chasing anyone's attention or channelling energy into *does he like me?* This meant she wouldn't fully let herself get that small *giddy*

LOVEY

feeling you get in the moments your phone lights up with a notification of *his* name. It does always find a way in though. You can't help it when you start to like someone. She left many texts being left on read. Just when the conversation had naturally come to end. She didn't want to be the girl keeping a dead conversation going, just to stay in contact. And in her mind, if it fizzled out, it fizzled out. No biggie. But he surprised her. Fred would, every single time, bring it back with some random thought or picture. She would smile down at her phone even brighter in these moments. I think a lot of young women know that feeling of *'I'm good enough to sleep with but not good enough to date'*. It made her truly believe he spoke to her because he simply wanted to.

> That was all she wanted.

*

Barking

A voice note came through. Sat in her bed, late one night as her pink heart neon light and a candle lit her room, she assumed it would be Fred asking her round to his as he had alluded to earlier in the night. The message was Fred, yes, but to her surprise the voice note was not of his growingly familiar voice. She pressed play and barking, like a dog, started coming out her iPhone speaker. She cringed a little and almost got the *'ick'*. I think anyone else would have. She was put off a little in that moment, but he preceded to persuade her in getting her round to his. She deliberated a little in her mind, then found herself in an Uber and on her way to Brixton.

"…Also, what's with the barking?" she jokingly questioned as Fred sat on one of the dining room chairs in the open plan kitchen/lounge. Passing through the hall she was greeted by Eddie who was standing in the open plan kitchen, preparing some food the boys had picked up on the way home. They had secured a feast of pizzas and pot noodles after their heavy night out. Liv, in a brown

LOVEY

crop top and her Adanola black leggings, took off her oversized leather jacket and sat herself onto the squishy sofa. After a bit of small talk between the three, Fred sat directly across from her, eating his pot noodle on one of the dining room chairs. As Eddie began to speak about details of the night they had, Liv noticed how Fred found himself looking at her, ever so intensely. She was aware of the fact this was officially only the second time they'd seen each other, first being the Thursday event, or the next morning, shall I say, but for some reason, the gaze was *palpable*. It was a small moment, but she never forgot it. The way he looked at her. How she felt in his stare as he seemed to tune out anything other than the girl, he had so unexpectantly met. She had felt so often when men would look at her, they'd look through her, look at her body wanting one thing, but with Fred, she always felt intentionally seen. She had gone from it being unbearable to be in the eye line of a man to feeling so quietly electric in his stare. Eventually, he moved over to the sofa to join her as she cuddled her legs into her chest. Eddie was busy deliberating whether to go see a girl from Tinder, not being convinced as she was on other side of London. Both encouraging him to see the girl, Eddie started to spruce himself up in the bathroom. As he left the kitchen/lounge area, Fred escalated their intimacy. Holding Liv as he pulled her hips onto his lap, continuing to kiss. Pressing each other's bodies into one, Fred made sure Liv could feel his hard crouch.

"I can hear you, you know." Eddie's voice emerging from the bathroom. They both let out a small laugh as they held their kiss, giggling into one another's lips as Liv now sat on his lap. They said their goodbyes and Eddie left for his middle of the night Tinder date, followed by Liv and Fred moving into his bedroom. That night she started a tradition she never anticipated would become a reoccurrence. On the nights where he wasn't the big spoon, Liv would tuck herself into his broad back and stroke the back of his head till they both fell asleep.

LOVEY

*

First Fred date

Stood at Liverpool Street tube station in her House of CB burgundy corset and black satin trousers with an oversized black bomber jacket draped over her shoulders, covering her black Fendi bag, Roe had bought her one Christmas, she waited nervously to see his face in the crowd of commuters, climbing the escalator. There was no need to be nervous as they had slept together multiple times and knew they got on like a house on fire, so all the typical 'first date' worries should have been squashed, but she realised quite early on, it was the fact that she actually couldn't wait to see his face in the crowd of people. He became, quite quickly, the only one she saw. In her eyes, everyone else fell to the sides. This fact fuelled the desire to wanting to make their first official date, special. She had planned a whole evening and wanted to surprise him.

> Fred: I'm excited for this, I love a surprise

She had booked the Van Gogh immersive exhibition she had wanted to go to for a while. Stood outside the entrance, keeping it a surprise till they had arrived, they exchanged excitement. He was chuffed.
"I've wanted to go for ages." he said excitedly as they made their entrance. They walked slowly around the rooms of meaning artwork as Liv spouted facts she had googled about the artist throughout the day, soon to have a lot of these facts proven wrong by the plaques placed around the exhibition, to which they both laughed over.
"They have a Harry Potter exhibit too, but that's not till October."
"Just means we'll have to stick around till then, doesn't it?"
You know when someone says exactly the right thing, like the perfect reply, well that was it. She couldn't have thought of anything better than too still be floating around exhibitions with him, months from now. Eventually they reached the immersive room. They sat intimately on one of the bench's that were dotted around the space whilst projected art of Van Gogh ran over the walls. Sunflowers coating

LOVEY

every corner and the entire floor, like they were all of a sudden in a field in Italy or droplets of water and lily pads like they were in a canal in Rome. The room was ever changing but what she felt did not…

That feeling again…Content.

She consciously thought in that exact moment, as she sat cuddled into him with his arm branched across her shoulders and around her…

> *I could stay in this moment for a while,*
>
> *put the world on pause,*
>
> *moments like this don't happen very often.*

The pair left the exhibition in a glowing light of the sun setting over Shoreditch. They made their way over to the next phase of their date. The idea was to go to an arcade pub in Clapham Junction but first, they found themselves stopping for a couple cocktails nearby. Sat close on the bar stools in the Italian eatery, she discovered he had this ability to make her shy. A rare quality these days. All he had to do was look at her with that annoyingly magical glint his eyes possessed that managed to shrine through his glasses, just that one second too long and she'd crack, breaking their eye contact to look down and laugh. Fred leaned into the bar, getting the bartenders attention. "Due aperol spritz per favore." *Did he just order that in French?* She thought, quickly registering it was a foreign language he was speaking. She knew he was fluent in French, but it was unexpected. *There really is a beauty in someone speaking another language.* She had assumed it was French he was speaking, but it wasn't, it was Italian. It was impressive, romantic and a great moment.

LOVEY

After leaving the eatery behind, they cuddled up on the half empty tube to Clapham, moving their date to the arcade pub, nearer home. She noticed their reflection in the tube window. She gazed at herself and him for a moment, being temporarily lost in time at how blissfully happy she was. Moving her look up into his eyes, through his sliver framed glasses, he smiled back down at her, into the eyes that sparkled when looking at him.

They arrived at Clapham Common and started to walk through the park to The Four Thieves. Once completing a very flirty stroll, they arrived. Liv snuck to bathroom to then return to their table which resided besides the bar, where Fred sat with two drinks. They began to play the arcade games, with drinks in hand.

"We should do the photobooth." Fred said enthusiastically.

"Yeah definitely!" Liv in agreement, whilst internally feeling *really fucking good.*

Deciding to destroy each other at the remote-control racing game, they stood in front of the camera, photobombing each other's pictures and out came their 'driving licences'. They positioned themselves on two drivers seats next to each other. They laughed and joked as Liv was winning for a while, as Fred complained his accelerator didn't work and the guy operating the game was helping her win. Eventually, Fred caught up and won the race in the end. Climbing down off the track, they took their drinks and sat at another table with stools so high her legs dangled in mid-air whilst his reached the floor. They continued to flirt and effortless be in one another's company. After back-and-forth flirtatious banter and consumption of more cocktails, Liv slid her hand down over his crotch to feel the result of the ongoing teasing.

"I'm getting you home." he insisted.

He pulled out his phone and ordered an Uber.

LOVEY

*

Driving licence

This driving licence would live in her phone case all while they were dating, then it moved into her memory box, *as that's all he became.*

*

Gummy bear song

"Did you actually just put the gummy bear song on after we've just had sex?" Liv laying naked in bed, looking up at the ceiling, in minor disbelief over what was playing out the Alexa, whilst Fred was smugly proud of his weirdness. Liv knew no one else, none of her friends, would understand this moment and definitely judge him over it, but to her, she actually loved how authentic he was from day dot. His weirdness, ADHD behaviour and pure child-like nature, mixed with his sweet, charming charisma, to which she felt beautiful in. It gave her silly, soft side, a place to escape. These moments only continued to occur every time his name popped up on her phone or his face would light up the room. It left Liv feeling like this would be really nice place to stay…

> …A moment in life
> where she wanted him
> and his weird,
> loveliness,
> to stay for a while.

*

95% Compatibility

Fred had gone round a friend's one evening. He always maintained consistency in his communication, no matter what he was doing. He randomly changed the conversation with texting her asking if she had ever done an astrology test.

LOVEY

Fred: Download it, we can see how we match

Or shall we leave it and assume we're great

She downloaded the app and screenshotted the results after filling in all their details.

Aquarius and Gemini Compatibility
95% Overall

Fred: The sex should be higher

Referring to it being 80%.

Liv: 100%

Fred: At least

*

Is this just sex?

03:03am

Fred: Hi

Hello

Missed me?

Can I call you?

03:05am

Liv: Yeah

Liv had never been a good sleeper, so she just so happened to be awake at the time of his drunken texting. Fred had gone away to Edinburgh with a few friends. Liv half expected not to hear from him whilst he was away, but to her surprise, it had been the exact

LOVEY

opposite. Consistent updates and pictures. *'We're moving here'* was one of the texts that lit up her phone after he had arrived. Liv knew he'd love Edinburgh, purely because it hadn't been long since she was there, and she knew they pretty much liked everything each other did. *It felt as though he missed her.* After their phone call of chatting to a very drunk Fred and his mates, she was left with a thought which she couldn't let go unsaid.

> Liv: Question
>
> Fred: Go for it
>
> Liv: Is this just sex?

Liv prepared herself for the answer as she saw him typing.

> Fred: Genuine answer
>
> I wish it was
>
> But I don't think it is
>
> I wouldn't be asking you out for dinner and stuff if it was
>
> Liv: Okay
>
> Fred: What are your thoughts?
>
> Stop thinking your answer through
>
> Just say it as it is
>
> I see you typing and changing your answer

There were many things that were running through her mind but every time she tried to translate her thoughts into words, it didn't sound right so instead of confessing her growing feelings towards him and how she genuinely felt there was something so genuinely

LOVEY

undeniable between them, she instead went with setting a simple boundary.

> Liv: If it was just sex, I'd have to be out

This was Liv finally being able to set a standard for what she wants and deserves. She was determined to show herself and the universe she had learnt her lesson and that the only way to be happy was to love and look after herself first.

> Liv: What does this mean

Specifically replying to his previous message of '*I wish it was*'.

> Fred: Like I don't want to be going down the exclusive/relationship route as I've just got out of a long term one
>
> But you and I get on so well and I want to see where it goes but with zero pressure

They had only known each other for ten days but it already felt strange to be apart. He was right and Liv thought he had a fair point. Fred had recently come out of a five-year relationship and she could tell he wasn't expecting to meet anyone he clicked with, so soon. Liv felt a little clearer and was glad he knew where she stood. She was also relieved that he was feeling the same pull that was only seeming to grow between them. The pair continued to chat for a little longer till they both decided to put themselves to bed.

> Fred: Sleep tight x

LOVEY

*

You can do better

I know friends always say, *'you can do better'*, their job is to hype you up, make sure you never compromise for a guy but that's all they'd say to Liv. Her friends genuinely didn't understand her attraction when they believed she could *'bag'* someone *'better'*. Liv called it specific taste. Although, there were a few exceptions, many agreed Elijah and Oscar were hands down beautiful men, in anyone's eyes. Sat in a popular pub which was always filled with attractive twenty somethings every weekend, Liv showed Soph a picture of a guy after she had spent a few minutes previous hyping up. Sophie's expression said it all. It was nothing short of *'what are you thinking'* to which they both broke out in laughter over. She tried to explain she had met this guy in person and his sweet and tall presence was what drew Liv into him.

FYI this boy was not Fred.

Sophie was another friend from London, who Liv grew incredibly close too during the time she mostly lived with Elijah. Sat on the floor in Liv's room, Soph took her phone to inspect Liv's dating app as Soph had recently been wifed off by someone she was infatuatedly in love with and wanted to investigate Liv's dating scene.
"You're only replying to the ugly ones," they both giggled.
"You leave all the fit ones on read." Soph's voiced filled with confusion. Liv looked at one of her closest friends and laughed. Sophie never meant any harm. She just wanted to see Liv with someone that deserved her.
"I think I like Fred," Liv confided in an excited yet hesitant tone.
"…but I literally have no idea how he feels." growing a little sadder as she continued to speak.
"Liv you're stunning, like literally beautiful, so fit, and you have the kindest soul, I wouldn't worry about this guy." Sophie was yet another person desperate for Liv to see her worth.

LOVEY

Sophie and Liv are very similar, in the way they are both hopeless romantics, maybe a touch too forgiving and wore their hearts on their sleeve. It was nice for Liv, nice having another soft friend who understood her heart and the way loving so much can lead you down painful paths.

*

Why did he have to say that

Sat on the yellow bench outside a busy bar underneath bright filament hanging bulbs in Clapham, was Fred. Liv emerging from the toilets bumped into Eddie as he stood waiting for his beers. "He's outside." No *'Hi'*, *'Hello'*, Eddie knew there was only one person she wanted to see. She smiled down to herself feeling excited to see him as she strutted out of the bar.
"Here she is." he welcomed her as his face lit up in her presence. She walked towards him in her low black heels and her nude-coloured boned Mistress Rocks corset and black satin mini skirt. She sat down, positioning herself next to him, Sophie sitting opposite. She rested her leg up onto his thick thigh slightly. Eddie arriving a few minutes later, he placed Fred's beer in front of him and sat himself besides Soph.
"Which one is it?" Soph being momentarily confused over which one was *'The Fred'*. Fred quickly picked up on what the confusion was concerning and suddenly seemed ever so slightly disheartened. Maybe he asked himself why Liv hadn't evidently shown Sophie a picture of him. Which she had, Soph had just forgotten, but I guess, he didn't know that.
"This one." Liv laughed, touching the top of Fred's arm.
She had been excited to see him. Soph had come up from Bristol as she had not long moved out of London, back home. As a spontaneous turn of events, she text Liv on the Friday asking what her plans were for the weekend. She responded with being totally free apart from Sunday. Soph made her way up to London for a girly weekend.

LOVEY

"I thought you were my girlfriend." Eddie carrying on the joke that Liv was actually dating him and was cheating on him with his best mate.
"Oh, I am." Liv taking his hand to hold from across the table, knowing it would tease Fred. The night carried on and the group gelled well. Bursting out with laughter at a joke Eddie had made, Liv collected herself slightly for a moment having it caught her off guard. Her reaction took Fred a little back, maybe slightly intimidated that she found his friend so incredibly funny in that moment. Fred, with his hand round her waist, squeezed to nudge her, then looked at her intensely. *'Remember you're mine'* she read from his response as her leg rested up on his.
"I want you at mine tonight." Fred trying to convince Liv to go back with him as the night was drawing closer to its end.
"Soph's staying at mine, I can't,"
"… I'm seeing you tomorrow anyway." she continued.
His next comment I cannot quote word for word, but it was along on the lines of… "if you don't come back, I'll have to have a wank."
Ah, she thought. She was gutted at his slightly misogynistic comment. She thought he was above that, *too sweet*, so she believed.
"I'm not just here for sex." Liv's doe-eyed energy instantly being withdrawn from him. She recalled into herself. It was tense. She sat in silence for a moment going over all the small moments that she had convinced herself were more than just a casual fling and told herself she had been wrong. She wanted more respect.
"Communicate. Communicate." he insisted as he started to panic, realising he might have said something quite offensive.
It was the first time he had felt her doting energy for him, be taken away.
"No, it's fine." she knew she had no technical leg to stand on, as they were only casual, but they *were* dating, that meant something, she believed. But he did surprise her at how immediately he knew the answer was to talk it out and wanted to understand why he had hurt her feelings. A different approach than what she was used to after being with avoidant personalities in the past. The night concluded

LOVEY

and everyone was ordering Uber's. Eddie lives round the corner from Liv, so he went with the girls and Fred went home alone.
Liv watched him as he climbed into his taxi, feeling defeated by how he had changed ever so slightly in her eyes. Walking to their Uber, the three squashed in the back.
"What was that about?" Sophie finally being able to get the full story as to why Fred and Liv had gone from loves young dream to barely speaking.
Soph and Eddie had been talking amongst themselves so only caught the tail end of the disagreement.
"*Ergh* he just said something kinda rubbish, about needing to have a wank if I don't go home with him,"
"…I was like, I'm more than just sex, then he started saying it wasn't like that, blah blah,"
"…what does he actually want?" she continued speaking her mind out loud, talking as if his best friend wasn't there to hear the whole conversation.
"Fred doesn't even know what he wants." Eddie unintentionally answering her question as he looked out the window.
The comment from Eddie stopped her in her tracks. *Of course,* she thought, looking down into her lap. She had forgotten, in how easy it had been effortlessly falling into each other's lives and having nothing but the best times, that he didn't want anything serious, and it probably was just nothing to him, *she was nothing to him.*

> Fred: Just got home
>
> How are you getting on?
>
> I'm still so excited for tomorrow
>
> What time do you want to meet?

She couldn't help but be ever so slightly less excited for it.

She had been looking forward to it for days.

LOVEY

She put her phone down without opening the messages and went to sleep.

*

Portobello Market

Tomorrow had arrived.

> Fred: We're gonna have such a good day
>
> Liv: Excited
>
> Fred: Can we go to a nice café and get a croissant please
>
> Liv: Of course

Fred met her outside her flat. Her main front door being enclosed by a metal gate for added protection on a busy main road in central London but it in fact just made her home look like a prison. He looked nice she thought. She always liked his aesthetic and how he dressed. They made their way down the road to the nearest café and sat and had a coffee and Fred had a pastry. It was a wholesome way to start the day together. Eventually, after finishing breakfast, they made their way to the tube station to get to the portobello markets. The date idea had come from Charlie, Fred's flatmate. Liv had never been so she was greatly excited to share it with Fred, knowing it would make a good experience, even better.

Finally, after a tube ride and overground, they reached their date destination. Soon, on this rainy day, they found themselves wondering through the market stalls full of multi-continental food, clothing, books, and vinyls. Their dates continued to be perfect. They just always felt so incredibly effortless and fun. Liv sat on the barely sheltered benches as rain fell around them, trying their best not to get wet. Fred got up and collected two Aperol spritz and food from one of the many options whilst Liv kept their seats which were

LOVEY

in heavy demand. Sat next to each other, on the same side of the bench, they began speaking about family, which led him into telling funny stories of his nieces and how the youngest one is a *'little beast'* and when Fred would visit her, they'd often greet each other by squaring up to one another from across the room and growl.
They laughed a lot, as usual. They spoke a little about Liv's past, even the assault. They bonded over more commonalities and Fred was on a mission to find the name of the HipHop playlist that had subtly playing all during.

After they were done with the market, they decided to make a stop at a local pub for a drink to then make their way back to his. Fred had promised to cook Liv dinner on this occasion. As the day got later, they made a quick pit stop at Liv's so she could get into comfy clothes for the evening. As usual they took this opportunity to have more effortlessly amazing sex. After, as Liv was rising from the bed, putting on an oversized t-shirt to start sorting herself out before they headed to his, he made a small comment of how the sex was quite different to his ex. One of the first times he had spoken of his past of relationship to Liv. He referred to sex in the past being more *'vanilla'*, him saying it in the kindest way possible.
"I've never been called vanilla in bed." she softly giggled as she lowered herself back onto his lap as he sat off the side of the bed.
"I can tell." he laughed.
Eventually, they made their way back to his flat where he made vegan duck pancakes. Sat at his dining table in his open plan kitchen/lounge, they tucked into the dinner he made. It was the first she had tried his cooking. She always got the impression he was a good cook after the many dinner pictures he'd send her and his past experience helping his brother with his catering company, having a short stint of being a cook. After dinner Liv suggested they watch 'This is the end' in bed. Fred spent the entire time trying not to fall asleep, assuming the movie would be cut short by other activities, but no, Liv was way too into one of her favourite films, reciting all the words throughout. They eventually got to the end of the movie,

LOVEY

Fred just barely keeping his eyes open, finally got what he had waited a good hour and thirty minutes for.
It was always worth the wait.

*

Avocado bagels

That's what some mornings became as the pair grew closer. It's as if he didn't want her to leave the moment they woke. She felt included and for the first time in a while, wanted. You see, when Liv would see Roe once he had moved to Clapham, their mornings went a little differently and could feel that Roe was just waiting for her to depart but she never wanted to and thus created a strong feeling of rejection.
"Don't worry I'm going soon just waiting for it to pass peak time."
"No, it's fine."
She probably built it up in her head, but we know now Roe acted strange the next day as he was betraying her and turns out, it hurt to look at her, lie to her, he would later confess, but regardless, she never felt wanted, not for a long time by him.
"You can work from here." Fred trying to persuade Liv to stay a little longer.
"You can use my laptop to revise." handing over his MacBook to Liv, sat on the bed. She stayed, for a little while. It felt nice. Nice to be desired. Maybe he wanted her to stay as she made outstanding smashed avocado, *always add chilli flakes*. Regardless, he hated it when she left, or at least, that's how it seemed.
He'd occasionally come over to the bed interrupting her work, he would kiss her forehead and lay his head on her arm as she was trying to concentrate. It should be illegal to kiss a girl's forehead if you don't actually want her to fall for you. She'd sometimes reciprocate the affection, standing up and wrapping her arms around him as he worked at his desk. It felt equal, whatever it was they were feeling.

LOVEY

Again, she found herself sat looking at the back of an accountant, finding herself feeling so different to how she felt with Roe. She felt good, really good with him.
Catching him off-guard, she asked, "Do you have people you can really talk to?"
He turned around in his desk chair as she continued to explain…
"they say we're lucky if we have three people in our lives, people we can truly be completely vulnerable with, *ya know,* a proper safe place."
He pondered for a moment.
"I don't think I have any."
He stopped.
"No one I could say *anything* too,"
"…I'm too complicated." he answered.
She looked at him softly, *maybe I could be your safe place,* she thought. She was confronted with again, another man who felt they were so complicated they had signed themselves off as a lost cause.

> Fred: Thank you for such a nice day yesterday and today, I had a really nice time x

*

Sending music is a love language.
I'm convinced of it.

The pair quickly found their love for their shared music taste which rapidly led to filling each other's phones with Spotify links to the latest find.

> Fred: *'Bloody Samaritan' Spotify link*

Liv opened up her Spotify, screenshotting her phone to show him she was mid-way through *that* song and was yet to send. It was the small moments that left a feeling of being so in sync, leading to big moments of feeling connected.

LOVEY

*

Sex with Fred

A few things happened, and few didn't… and I'll explain this because, to anyone who is a survivor of sexual assault, you deserve truth and maybe, *hope*.

1. She didn't dissociate
2. She felt genuinely turned on
3. She didn't feel empty or like something had been taken from her
4. She felt safe
5. She felt happy – it felt like a breakthrough
6. … in fact, it felt *fucking amazing*

It was only later that she found out how common it was for survivors to dissociate during sex. She had experienced this with every guy she'd been with since, including Elijah. Through research she learnt that dissociation in sex is commonly a protective mechanism to protect from trauma. Dissociation in general is the disconnect from, *well,* anything. How you feel, where you are, what you think. Typically for sex it's developed over long-term sexual abuse but of course, it can be trigged by rape. It can feel like you struggle to feel physical sensations, your mind can wonder, it can feel like you're almost outside your body, a little like you're a vessel again but in a different way, and you struggle to connect to what you're physically doing, therefore, cannot enjoy it. It makes sense, your brain doesn't know if this will be another painful, traumatic experience, so it disconnects, shuts down.

Liv's brain knew with him though…

…Being with him, from the moment they met, felt like the easiest thing in the world, and after months of everything feeling so difficult, having him felt like breathing again.

LOVEY

*

<u>Effects of sexual assault / violence</u>

For a while, the effects of what the rape had left behind were difficult to identify, contain, label. All she knew was she was broken and that's all she could describe it as. Sarah and Tara, both sexual survivor therapists, were the key to understanding a lot of what she felt, and how it didn't have to mean her life was over. So, whether you are a survivor and you need to feel like your brain and body is not ruined or that you're not, but you'd like to understand, and I promise that will make you a better friend, better partner, better human, if you recognise some of the ways rape can scar those who live with it.

1. Trauma
2. Guilt
3. Shame
4. Denial
5. Minimising
6. Dissociation (feeling numb, detached, dazed)
7. Depersonalisation
8. PTSD
9. Depression
10. Reliving the assault through flashbacks, nightmares, repeated thoughts
11. Avoidance of the place, things, and others
12. Issues with trust
13. The lack of ever feeling safe

Once she learnt more about what comes after assault, she could recognise that she experienced nearly every single effect. But to her, it all just meant she was *done, damaged, destroyed.*
It started with denial and minimising. Do you remember, pages away, Liv did her absolute best in bargaining with herself that what had taken place was not what she knew, deep down, to be. She did

LOVEY

everything she could to pretend as though it was not rape. She wasn't sure what it was, but it can't be rape, it just can't.

Next came shame, guilt, dissociation, and depersonalisation. Now this is hard. I know no one ever thinks they'll be the one, the one it happens too and if you do think about that imaginary scenario, you have it straight in your head, what you'd do, how you'd reaction but I promise, you can never pre-empt what follows if the worst does happen. Rape culture is spoken about but on the outside, it is so obvious that rape isn't the victim's fault, but my goodness, the shame, guilt, blame... well that crushes you till you're suffocating under the weight of it. Not only do you have that but then you're just floating. The dissociation sets in, detaches you from friends, family, and most importantly, your own body. That's why it's dangerous. That's why Liv was rarely left alone during the fall out. Then longer term, you live with all that comes with PTSD. You live with repeating thoughts. Liv had seen movies, ones where there'd be dramatic flashbacks and believed that they could never be real, that can't be how flashbacks *really* present. She was wrong. Her first was one of the worst moments of her life. Your brain is programmed to *black out* memories which it deems too traumatic to keep stored. It's a protection mechanism we never asked for but is there, nevertheless. However, flashbacks can be the reintroduction of these memories. An error in your protection mechanism. The memories the brain could not bear to keep. They come back with their smell, taste, vividness. Not only do you have the survive the actual event, but you also have to survive every moment it revisits you, like you're back there again. In that hotel. The prison. The windowless prison. With that man. Being violated and beaten. She became selective over who could create physical contact with her being. This is why some people, including Liv, don't want just anyone to feel they can touch her, in her mind, someone still is.

LOVEY

Many will ask,

>*Have you told the police?*
>*Have you reported it?*
>*Did you say no?*
>*Were you drunk?*
>*Why didn't you leave?*
>…and many more.

These are, categorically, the worst things you could ask a rape victim. Any sexual assault survivor. Again, without realising it, you're playing into rape culture instead of treating them as what they are, the survivor, they have nothing to prove to you.

I'd like to say, to those who know how it feels to have a part taken from you, the only part which feels irreplaceable once violated,

You
did
absolutely
nothing
to
deserve
it

This was a huge part of Liv's therapy. She was plagued with anger and guilt and shame. But all she kept saying, looking across to Sarah, in an essential oil scented room, sat in a cosy armchair was, "I was scared… and all I wanted was for it to stop." Liv continued to blame herself for multiple different reasons. She thought, *if I never went on that date, it would never have happened. I should have gone home. I shouldn't have gotten drunk. I should have screamed. I should have fought back with all my strength and ran.* These polluted her mind until it was fact. It was her fault she was so unbelievably damaged. Sarah was a comfort in these times and met her heartbreak with, "Liv, never

LOVEY

feel you could have done something to stop what happened, you did what you needed to survive. Who knows what this violent man would have done if you had responded differently. But also, your brain took over. Your brain did what it believed it needed to do, to survive." Sarah was right, Liv understood that… but it's hard… when you're alone, looking into a mirror at a body you feel is no longer yours. The being you've looked at every single day of your life and now just existing makes your skin feel like it's on fire whilst ants crawl all over you. The vessel you cannot escape, it's the most trapped she'd ever felt. It's easy to blame yourself and delude into thinking, if you had done one thing differently, you would have never had to have this happen, be this person. But it's simply not true.

> Trauma creates change you do not choose.
> Healing is about creating change you do.

Healing is not the journey from something difficult being easy and simply relying on time to move you from it. Quite the opposite. It is the when the journey is agonising, brutal, wanting to give up, feeling you *need* to give up. But beyond every single second of it, you choose you, you choose life, and you not let it be what defines you. What takes you. Because yes, it still terrified Liv, even though she had walked through hell, that did not mean she could again, and she knew that and what life could throw at her still scared her but, she had a 100% track record for getting through all her worst days and as you're reading this, *so do you.*

*

Homeopathy

I have ever so briefly introduced Tara. So, let's meet her. Tara is a holistic therapist who volunteers for the survivor's network in Brighton and also a women refugee. Liv had been referred to different services at the sexual health screening after the assault. The

LOVEY

waiting list for conventual counselling was extremely long, around eighteen months but the wait for homeopathy was slightly less. Liv said yes to most resources offered to her even though none could offer immediate care. After roughly just less than a year, like advertised, they had made their way through the waiting list. That's when she met Tara, *Tara is magic.* Apart from the actual 'homeopathy' part where she'd prescribe different natural remedies depending on what was the main battle in Liv's mind, *she just understood.* Friends try their best. And sometimes the last thing you want to do is talk about the assault but sometimes, she did. She spent so long thinking about it, there was a need for a detailed release of what polluted her mind. She turned it all internal. Didn't want to bother her friends with that she had just had a flashback which put sick in her mouth or that she couldn't walk down a certain road because they'd had been there on the date. This happened once. It was awful. Usually, Liv does her best avoid any place she can associate with the date but on this day, she was aimlessly walking with one of her closest friends down a street in Shoreditch. Losing track of her bearings, she suddenly found herself outside *the hotel.* The first time standing outside since the day she ran from those doors with a body covered in bruises. Immediately feeling panicked and sick, she turned to look away and guided her friend past as quickly as possible. With her sessions with Tara, she made her feel not as broken as she was spending most days feeling. Maybe, some days even normal considering what had happened. She took it so incredibly seriously. She took moments of silence and sincerely apologised that it had happened when Liv revealed more parts of her story. Liv was able to talk freely about how sex had changed for her. How it used to feel good, fun, an act of connection to then, ***nothing.*** Tara taught her about dissociation and how incredibly common is it and now it will **not** always be like this. Liv felt after a few months that the natural remedies helped. She couldn't explain it in words, but they were a comfort to the girl who hated the idea of traditional medication.

LOVEY

Tara uses homeopathy to treat those with mental and physical illness while taking a speciality in sexual abuse. She also offers physical aromatherapy massage and reflexology. *She has a way about her.* She is so incredibly soft and comforting but also safe and certain in her manner. Imagine tingles on the back of your neck and up your to your scalp. There are many things she has imparted on Liv, with her wise and extensive experience but there was one thing that simplified it all.

"Our only job as human beings, is to enjoy the human experience, *to find joy.*"

It was so simple, but it hit Liv like a huge warm wave that washed over her like she was stood at the edge of the ocean, looking for her purpose.

She was determined to find joy and that be it.

*

Pain into power

Liv will forever live with the remains of what that man did that night. There will be moments she never tells a soul. A moment she sees a man on the tube that looks like him and her stomach flips and immediately wants and needs, to run and cry. Times she'll smell his scent again or avoiding a certain part of Shoreditch she can no longer pass. Moments where she'll be with a guy, maybe even a guy she likes but feel overcome with fear, for no obvious reason and she'll be reminded she can no longer operate how she used to. However, these moments don't define her. They are all moments of sheer strength. And eventually, like everything bad, it will become less and less. And yes, it will never be nothing, but she's strong and she knows by now surviving all these moments, now and for the rest of her life, makes her the person she was meant to be. Strong, powerful, brave, loving, a fighter, soft, vulnerable, understanding.

LOVEY

She was still able to own the strength in her softness. Now, that takes a powerful person.

Maybe this gives a better explanation as to why it meant so much when someone, a man, felt safe. Every single one of the life altering effects she had lived with for months, *fell away with him.*

*

Lasagne

After the pair had retrieved all the ingredients for Liv's famous vegan lasagne from the big local Sainsbury's, they got back to Liv's and started making dinner. She stood in her kitchen, over the sink washing up cutlery ready for their awaited meal they had both helped prepare. She had promised him the first night they met that she made the best vegan lasagne. She was chuffed when he'd later say, *"This is banging", "honestly, so good."*

Now this was a good moment… you know, the type you want to last longer than they do…

Catching Liv off-guard as she stood at the sink that overlooked a large window, washing up cutlery for their dinner, Fred softly came up from behind her, wrapping his large strong arms around her waist and lowered his six-foot-three stature down to rest his head on her shoulder. They both stopped, pausing for a moment in their tender embrace.
Liv froze.
"Does this make it hard to wash up?" Fred teased as the washing up halted.
"Kinda," Liv replied sarcastically with a touch of softness.
He lingered for a moment more.
Then let go.

LOVEY

She didn't want him to let go. I'm not sure it came across that way to him, but she didn't. However, she didn't fully give in to these moments either. She didn't allow herself to love these moments. She knew him and they, were not here to stay.

After they finished dinner, they propped her laptop on his lap, and she cuddled into his chest. They continued to laugh, cuddle and kiss till he had to leave as he needed to be at home early the next day.

> Fred: We laughed a lot, sign of a great night

*

Great minds

Fred had gone back to his family home with a few friends for a special anniversary of the tragic death of his close friend. They would every year put on a little festival for him to celebrate his life. Fred always tried to maintain contact whether he was busy or not. He'd include her by sending her random pictures or texts, keeping her up to date. This would sometimes be of his family dog, *Betty,* which was a beautiful yellow golden retriever.

> Liv: I'll leave you to it this weekend, hope you have a really nice time and enjoy Matt fest
>
> Fred: Nice try
>
> Liv: Huh
>
> Fred: Not gonna get rid of me that easily

Again, he said exactly the right thing. She smiled down at her phone feeling that warm glow you get when you really like someone.

One particular night whist he stayed down at his family home, Liv saw she had another picture from him. She opened up her phone to

LOVEY

see a photo of a personalised oval pillow with a close-up selfie of Fred's face printed across it.

> Fred: Do you want to see an ick?
>
> I got it for mum for Mother's Day

Immediately, she closed WhatsApp and started to sift through her camera roll. After scrolling back to Christmas 2019, she swiped up to share a particular photo. She forwarded a picture of the same pillow, just this one had Liv's faced printed across it.

> Liv: Great minds

She was proud they shared the same weirdness, having another one of those moments where they feel so sync. It's difficult to put it into words but they had lots of these little moments which made Liv feel he was the boy version of all the parts she liked about herself. Once she started living a life that intertwined with his, it started to feel every other day was a sign from the universe whispering... *'You're on the right path'*.

> Fred: Wish you were here
>
> Liv: Me too
>
> You miss me?
>
> Fred: I do a bit, ngl

*

> Fred: You can't handle the smoke
>
> Liv: I can handle your smoke

LOVEY

*

A montage of sweet moments

I wish I had time in this book to take you through every moment that made her smile with him. But I don't but here's some soft, sweet moments which filled her heart with the feeling that makes you feel giddy and happy whilst also peaceful and calm with happiness.

> Fred: *Video* All this is happening but all I can think about is you

He had sent a video of the nightclub he was at, music blared from her phone speaker as she pressed play, watching his friends dance around him.

*

> Fred: Gonna feel weird sleeping alone tonight
>
> I actually can't believe we slept properly spooning
>
> I never do that, really rare for me
>
> Liv: Really?
>
> Fred: Yeah, I like it tbf, nice to wake up like that
>
> Liv: Me too

Liv was left smiling at her phone.

*

> Fred: Sleep tight x

*

> Fred: Wish you were here

LOVEY

*

Fred: I told you, I'm addicted to you

*

Fred: I'd feel awful waking you up that early

Fred went to the gym pretty much every day at 5:30am. You could tell from his body. He was tall, six-foot-three and had a broad frame. Thick thighs that a lot of girls, including Liv, liked. So, the gym became a part of his unwavering routine. It wasn't just his body, but he had one of those smiles too, the ones that light up their face. He may not have thought so, but she thought he was incredibly handsome, with or without his glasses. He was never a massive fan of himself without them.

*

Fred: Excited to see you

*

Fred: Might have to stop texting you but I don't know if I can

*

Fred: Good luck with the exam, I won't distract you until you want me to

*

Liv: Never cuddling you again

Fred: I'd like to see you try

*

Liv: Miss me?

Fred: Annoyingly yeah

*

Fred: Have a nap on my chest and then go out

LOVEY

… and these were just some of the texts that lit up her phone under his name.

*

Shall I miss the gym?

Rolling over from his side of the bed, he slid his arm through Liv's and scooped her up tight into his body to face him.
"*Mmm.*" he moaned.
"Shall I miss the gym this morning?" he sighed slipping himself further into one another's bodies. Liv tucked her head down to his chest and nodded, being barely awake. There they laid, entangled into each other's bodies and lives. Probably important to add it only took something *quite important* for him to skip his regimented gym schedule.

*

Fred's birthday

Happy birthday you walking ick

You've not yet achieved your mission but with more barking and gummy bear interludes I'm sure we'll get there

Thank you for being one of the weirdest, funniest, and most authentic people I've met

I hope you have an amazing birthday

Liv x

She got him a card referring to the inside jokes they had built up over him having a million and one '*icks*'. They often teased that he '*gave her the ick*' but he always responded, "you're still here though." and laugh, to this she'd think, *of course, course I'm still here*.

LOVEY

Another thing I've only briefly mentioned about Liv is she creates and designs clothes. Not just clothes but she paints, draws and writes too. She had designed a black oversized ethically made t-shirt with her thin cream line design printed on it, of a woman with graphic eyeliner, holding a dagger. She wrapped this one-of-a-kind sample t-shirt, hoping it would fit, in baby pink tissue paper, packing it and the card into a bag, incredibly excited to give it to him.

*

LAR Studios

LAR stood for Liv's first and middle names and became the name of her creative side hussle. Starting it in the winter of 2019, it ranged from graphic design of linework women to large canvas paintings to also handmade clothing she'd design and create on her sewing machine. Maybe her need for art in some form came from early in her life. It has always been her escape. This is one of the reasons Flum was amazing. She had always given Liv totally creative freedom. Fourteen-year-old one Liv took all her acrylic paints and started to outline a panda in black across her entire bedroom door, on the outward facing side, so anyone passing the upstairs hallway could admire her art. Once the panda was filled in with thick black paint, she began to stroke different shades of green upon the sides, creating its grassy habitat.
"That looks amazing Fliv!" Flum praising her creativity. She had a particular freedom I think a lot of kids probably wished they were given.

*

I just want to make him feel special

The day before Fred's birthday Liv was going to a music festival in the park opposite his house in Brixton with a group of her friends. They had always planned for her to stay so that meant a quick stop off at his to drop her bag before the event, accompanied by his

LOVEY

favourite beer she stopped to collect on the way to his. In the hope to cheer up his day of working.

>Liv: Wine drunk already
>
>Fred: What a legend
>
>*photo* Like the trim?
>
>Liv: I love it
>
>You look fit
>
>Are you giving me side eye
>
>Fred: You can't handle the smoke
>
>Liv: I can handle your smoke
>
>Fred: I want an ice cold beer
>
>Liv: I'll bring you one
>
>Fred: You're the best

Liv smiling at her phone after she sent him a photo of 'sed' beer.

>Fred: I could have a nap
>
>Liv: Don't nap I'll be round soon
>
>Fred: That's good news 😍
>
>Liv: Fucked
>
>Fred: Alcohol abuse isn't something to brag about
>
>Liv: Deep
>
>Fred: *That's what she said **meme***

LOVEY

Liv: You're funny sometimes

Fred: This wasn't one of those times?

Liv: I think it was

I laughed

I'm going to try and act as sober as possible

Fred: You're the most obvious drunk as well

Liv: This is just rude

I'll stop

Fred: I find it hilarious

Liv: I'm not here for your entertainment

Fred: Where's this sass been all my life? 😍

Liv: She's arrived

Sassy as hell

Throughout the festival Liv kept in contact with her consistent drunk texting.

Liv: Can you speak French while we fuck

Fred: I can yes

How drunk are you?

Liv: Yeah I'm fucked

Got someone's sunglasses on

Are you excited for your bday present

LOVEY

> Fred: They nice? I need some new ones
>
> Very excited
>
> I'm intrigued

As soon as it turned midnight, a very drunk Liv jumped excitedly on top of Fred, having recently gotten back from the festival.
"Is it midnight yet?!" leaning over to the bedside table.
"Omg it's your birthday!!" Liv overjoyed.
"Do you want your present now??" Liv flung herself off of his lap to retrieve her black tote bag from the floor. Fred pressed his touch lamp on his bedside table to illuminate his room slightly and slid his glasses back on. He seemed surprised she had gotten him a card, let alone a present.
"Of course I got you a present." she said *softly*.

*

Whiteboard

Bouncing out of his room in the morning, she picked up the black whiteboard pen and scrubbed off the remenance of an old message and wrote *'Bday Boyyy 24!!'* on the whiteboard that hung on the wall facing the kitchen.

*

Sleepless night

He is probably unaware that his birthday night out was the night that she decided to stop seeing him. She knew she had no right to be upset over his following / followers going up as the night progressed and the drunker, he got. No text. He didn't contact her the whole night. The silence was so incredibly loud. She knew he'd never be hers and she didn't want that. After everything that had happened,

LOVEY

she deserved someone to choose her. She was worth so much more than the causal life he wanted to maintain.

*

"You're over thinking."

You have no idea, she thought.

*

Ah, so now it feels like we're falling

She had recently discovered a new power. It was one she never thought she'd possess but a power, nonetheless. She had started to find a strange sense of strength in the ability to **lose** something that she felt she was starting to fall for, rely on, would miss, in the cases where, <u>what she wanted</u> and <u>what was actually being given to her</u>, were **two different things.** It was *freeing.* She thought maybe she didn't have to settle for a casual part of someone's life anymore, just so she didn't lose them because, in a mind-blowing turn of events, *they would lose her too.* And just like that, there was a revelation. She had never thought *'well if they can lose me and be okay then I can do the exact same'.* And with that belief, she was *free.* She was finally finding her worth. Of course, she didn't want this but it's something she couldn't do before. Something maybe if she had been able to, life would look so beyond different. But she found the ability at time, for a reason, and she wasn't going to waste it.

LOVEY

*

> Notes

> 3 things to remember:

> You can push people harder than you think, and stay and it they don't, they were going to leave anyway.

> Like Nannie said, you deserve to be cherished.

> With it without, you'll be okay.

*

The change was starting to show

Now these things sound easy but in reality, they really aren't. Liv never wanted to push people she was terrified to lose but more often than not, this would create a dynamic of being too overly available and people being used to Liv always being there, no matter what. She was often taken for granted and it emptied her soul. Drained all she had. But she was done, and it was almost as if a cloud had lifted and she had new superpowers. This had to be the beginning of something better, of something good.

> Notes

> I'm so close. 3 more exams then I'll have a degree in neuroscience.

Sat on Fred's bed revising for her remaining exams, she couldn't believe how close she was to finally being done. Finally having her golden ticket that everyone promised would make her life whatever

LOVEY

she wanted it to be, and even though Liv knew it wasn't this simple, she did know how much it meant to her to have accomplished and proven to herself she could do it. She could do all that work, survive the worst of times and still stand there with her degree in her hand knowing she was a stronger, happier person than how she started, and she can now go and do whatever she desired. It felt like a new chapter was beginning. It felt university coming to an end was more than that, felt as though it was a metaphor for all that happened during being put in the past and having control over what she allowed in her present and future. She was collecting all she had learnt over the past four years and reflected on what she wanted to take forward and what she wanted to leave behind.

*

Fluffy Suzie

Suzie is Fred's slightly raggedy stuffed hedgehog that lives on his bed. Liv found herself clinging to her the more nights she found herself at his. One morning, before Fred needed to get up and start work, he came in close to Liv, removing Suzie from between them as he'd often find Suzie in Liv's arms. He positioned the childhood toy up and out the way. Immediately Liv, following Suzie's relocation, reached up, above her head to retrieve her from his hands and placed her back into her chest.
"That was adorable." Fred looking down at the pair, gushing over her new attachment to her.

Everything was so safe with him. She wanted to feel that safe for as long as life would give her.

*

Graham

"What do you think is the worst name to say in sex?" he asked as they laid in his bed in the early hours of the morning.

LOVEY

"Graham," she laughed.
"Oh Graham." she fake moaned.
They both laughed as they cuddled, Liv laying in his arm as she tucked herself into his chest.

*

He had no idea what a symbol he played in Liv's life. Time no longer matters or exists when it comes to how someone can make you feel. It's just *there* sometimes.

> ⟨ Notes
>
> I understand roe more now. I understand him and mollie and how it really didn't reflect me. It wasn't he didn't love me, but more the bond they found was what was right at this time and life sometimes just goes that way.

LOVEY

Chapter Nine

Restless
Skin on fire

Imagine walking along a fire pit. Hopping from one painful step to another. It rarely got to this point for Liv anymore but nevertheless, today it had. *Monday.* The first day of the rest of her life. Yes, I do admit it seemed like any other start to the week, however, it was the first day of no work, and no uni. Liv had sat her last exam and the rest was up to fate. No one talks about how lost you feel after university. How anti-climactic it is. How you build up this one moment, so much that, on the other side is just a void of nothingness.

Fred had become distant, and she really cared. She didn't want to. She really didn't, but as we know *'you can't not care about things you actually care about'* as Ricky Gervais said in Afterlife. Now at this point, she would have normally probably gone over every single possibility as to why his feelings may have changed but she didn't. Not this time. Time had taught her that, what's the point when you can't change it, but she could control her, and what she did next. Let's make a plan, a plan for the future. Sat in a random Pret A Manger in central London, she made the decision that Christmas

LOVEY

was the limit, the cut off for still being in the UK. Get a full-time job, save as much as possible and leave. It was simple and in her and Sarah's, her therapists', opinion, felt it needed to happen to prove to Liv she could truly do anything. But before that, it was time to mourn…Mourn university, and everything it had been for her, her lifeline. Mourn Fred and how much he did and could have meant. She opened up her WhatsApp chat with *'Flannie'*, with a sunflower emoji next to her name.

29th May, 21:03

> Liv: Nannie I just want your promises. I just want to be happy and have a best friend and a love all in one. I just feel so lost. I wish you were here. I don't know why I care so much but I do, and I can't stand how I feel and have no idea how to feel better. It's all so hard when it's like this

LOVEY

*

I think life is about to look quite different to how I've imagined so many times. And that's okay, just as long as a few things happen.

I want love. I want a hopeless romantic, happy, soft, silly, weird, love. I want a home and I want to be a home for someone.

I want to see the world. I want to stand on the beaches of Australia I see on Pinterest. I want to swing in Bali and eat açai bowls. I want to swim in the blue lagoon in Iceland and ski in France and whatever else the world has to offer.

I want to find those moments that make it worth it. The moments that feel comfortable, just existing in.

*

It needs to feel just a little easier

She was desperate to feel content. To feel like normal, where everyday life wasn't a constant battle of reminding her, she's underachieving and isn't good enough, smart enough. Her theory was, episodes of panic attacks, crying yourself to sleep till your head is throbbing, can have an effect on your brain. Things like memory and how you take in and retain knowledge. Her memory after a set of panic attacks was always impaired. She felt stupid for not remembering silly things, things she would have definitely not had any trouble recalling, had life been a little softer to her brain.

LOVEY

She had however, grown a perspective, a perspective younger Fliv would have yearned for. It allowed her, in situations that would have temporarily drowned her, to keep her head above the water. *Rejection was redirection. You can't mess up something that is meant for you. You can push people harder than you think and if they leave, they were going to leave anyway.* It's a balance always though and I guess that is why things with Fred hurt more than she would have liked. For the first time since Roe, someone led her back to her hopeless romantic, soft, silly, happy, self. All the parts that were missing with Elijah. She liked who she was around him. She felt funny, she felt content. She was safe. Of course, Liv wanted to stay here, in the arms of someone who made her feel like *her* again. A person she thought, was *gone.* Liv's not afraid of hurt but she wanted to stay in the light a little longer than what was given to her. *It was one of them, that just felt like a shame.* A shame they couldn't have shared something lovely for a little longer. Very well, it may be rare, but it does exist and that's all that mattered to her.

It wouldn't be special if it wasn't rare.

> Mourn it Liv. Then go live life. Feel. Cry. Run. Because there will be so many moments that standing still feels amazing.
>
> It's not a dream, it's the future and the future can look a lot like you want it to.
>
> P.s isn't it amazing you don't want Roe anymore.
>
> Yes. I thought I'd never get there.
>
> Anything is possible.

LOVEY

Chapter Ten

I have no idea what grounds me anymore

For the first time in a while Liv started thinking about hurting herself. I can't really explain why her brain had paved this pathway from an early age, but it had, and it devastated her that she could still slip back even at the age of twenty-four.

*

Everything but linear

I want to take a moment and say, healing is not linear. You can feel like you're on the home stretch, you can see the finish line, running along, giving it the fight of your life, till suddenly, you stumble, you'll fall, and you'll land on the hard ground believing you are at the start again but now you're exhausted and even hurt.

You'll think you need to start from scratch.

LOVEY

But. You. Don't.
You are so much further along than you think. And those knock backs don't set you as far behind as you may think, it may have just been what you needed to realign your journey.

I promise. You're closer than you think.

LOVEY

Chapter Eleven

He makes you happy

She wrote in her phone notes *"he makes you happy"* and that's where she fell. That was the moment where her power had fell through her hands like it had turned from solid to liquid. She had tried so hard to keep her head from tilting up into the sky, gasping for air, while inevitably drowning in the sea of emotions you can't fight. No matter how many times she insisted to friends and Flum that *"no matter what, Fred was a positive thing and it'll be alright."* trying to protect herself. It had gone further than that in her heart. But remember, she's a hopeless romantic and if there's anything she believed in, it was love. Feeling that feeling that only rarely someone can give you. She would miss him more than you would think for knowing someone for two months. But it wasn't really about time in this case. He had *something*, she thought they had *something*. Nights became hard, *restless*. She would later remove him off social media. She didn't want to see him. *What good would it bring her?* And it would just highlight that she no longer had moments with him, the moments she missed deeply. Seeing his following / followers go up

LOVEY

after a Saturday night? No. she wasn't going to do it. It wasn't out of anything negative towards him, but quite the opposite.

It was so important to her to prove to herself and others that she had *one,* learnt her lesson. No longer was she going to settle for less than makes her happy. *Two,* she could walk away sooner rather than later. *Three,* to truly pick her future happiness over temporary people <u>who are completely content with losing her.</u>

You see, in this book you'll watch her grow. You see her fall, fall in love, fall to the ground, fall into sadness but she finds a way up. Even if it means just existing for a moment. Now this isn't advice but if there is a time in your life you need to just exist and it's so painful to do so, can't sleep, can't sit still, it's okay to take a sleeping tablet just to makes sure you aren't up all night in heart palpitating pain, Liv has **always** struggled with sleep, so this acted as a relief. It's okay to spend money you don't *really* have spare, to take yourself to the cinema, so the world is shut out for two hours. *It's okay.* It's okay if these things keep you from floating up into heaven while life remains a little unbearable.

*

The key

…In the ways Roe and Fred were similar, such as their goofiness Liv adored, their softness, humour, and the way Liv felt like their personalities effortlessly fitted into the other, they were alike in the way they both couldn't fully give themselves to Liv the way she wanted… like she deserved. Their emotional unavailability, the walls they had built. Maybe they were so scared Liv may have the key that unlocks it all. And well, this would make them the most vulnerable they could be and losing Liv was worth not feeling that. And that's what makes them wrong. Liv's person will hand her the key like they've been waiting, and she'll do the same.

LOVEY

As much as it was agony, she did what *this* Liv would do, she left when she should. Roe wasn't for nothing, he had taught Liv, her worth, value, the love she had to give, and he did this all by giving her the exact opposite. He showed her how it feels when that amount of love is misplaced.

*

The last date

On the excessively warm tube, un-helped by the humid air clouding over London as on and off thunder and rain struck. She was aware this would be their last date. This put a pit in her stomach. The thought dawned on her how much a relationship right now would have to survive. She wanted to travel, she had no idea where she'd be this time next year and it would have to be pretty perfect for someone to want the same as her. Maybe she was trying to convince herself a little more, just to make it easier. Regardless, it felt like a breakup. Liv hated break ups. *Doesn't everyone?* She had felt this feeling before. She prayed the universe would stop now, she had learnt her lesson and was about to sacrifice any more time with the one person that made her glow, just to prove it.

*

The Roe breakup

You would have thought after everything, it would have ended in a big momentous way, but it didn't. That day, the 18th September 2020, started like any other.

> Roe: Morning bubba!!
>
> How did you sleep??

At 12pm he was asking her what she was having for lunch. By 2pm he reminded her to buy her train ticket for the next day as the plan

LOVEY

was for her to go up to Guildford. Getting to 4pm, the conversation had escalated into a disagreement. By 6pm he texted that it was over. Ended it, it was done.

She begged and begged for him to answer the phone, but he didn't. He stole the entire ground from under her. She texted him saying he owed her a phone call, pleading for the last point of contact to not be a text message. It couldn't end it over text. Not after everything. He finally answered but he was *gone*, checked out, over. He was silent as she spoke for forty minutes about them, their love, journey, future. She spoke of the journey they had been on, how much love and themselves they had put into building their relationship, to not let his depression, his worst time, steal the bond they were so lucky to have found. She painted a picture of what the future could look like, living together in London, and then maybe Australia, traveling the world together, have adventures with their best friend and then settle with a family and the German Shepard pup, they both had always wanted.

"…This is all really nice Liv, but I can't do it anymore."

That was it. She had lost the fight, him. She had fort so hard for him.

*

My promises

Sitting upstairs in a coffee shop in the lanes Brighton, by a large open window, peppermint tea on the table, she opened up a new word document.

> A letter to myself,
>
> So, it's the 22nd of September 2020. This year has been extremely difficult to say the least. Today is 4 days since me

LOVEY

and Roe broke up for good. Scares me to even type that. So, this is my promise letter to myself and him, from a distance. I promise to carry on with whatever it is that's important to me such as university, LAR stuff, work and just trying to stay me. I also promise to let Roe do whatever he needs to do without reaction. I promise myself that no matter what actions follow I will not lose myself. I promise I want Roe to be happy and as that's going to be without me, I'll be ok with that. I promise that time will heal this heartbreak and painful days are ahead and things will happen that make me shake and feel like I'm completely out of control and just the worst pain, but it won't last. I promise it won't last. Just let him get on with it. Whatever 'it' is, it's ok.

Lastly, I promise that I think I'll always love him and wish for a different outcome but It. Will. Be. Ok. One day the pain will be a little less, he'll cross your mind less, till he's just a memory and by this point I promise you'll be ok with that fact.

You are allowed to love him from a distance and hope he gets help and gets better but expect him to forget about you.

※

Buried in Roe's chest. She hated the underground. Always struggled with claustrophobia amongst her anxieties. He squeezed her tightly into his chest, creating a bubble of safety.
"We'll be off soon." he whispered into her ear, Liv tightening her grip as the tube rocked while releasing a slight amount of tension as her nerves eased. Warm stuffy, overcrowded, Roe squashed into the corner where he ducked his head to fit.

※

Sat on the tube, she thought of this moment. One thought being how the tubes didn't bother her at all now. *Feels like second nature and two being.* Another thought walked into her mind like a subtle ghost, *'I wish I could just bury myself in his chest and shut out the world'*. And a third thought arrived straight after like a train arriving right

LOVEY

on time, *'I've lived this far without it, him, that bubble. I can do a bit more'*.

*

Last Fred date

Back to the last date with Fred. They embraced as both stood outside the restaurant, under their umbrellas in the rain. She felt calm and slightly sad. He looked handsome, as usual, Liv thought. They were seated in a booth of the cosy warmly lit vegan restaurant. They shared their meals and bonded ever more over red wine and cocktails.
"I saw something recently and it got me thinking. It was about picking highs over happiness," she continued, "highs are when you choose something to feel good in the moment and picking happiness means sometimes sacrificing the highs to get to true lasting happiness." He looked across the table at her in a glow. Now I can't tell you Fred's thoughts or how he felt about Liv, we'll never know that, but we do know how he looked at her. How he gazed at her with a stare of *'she's quite special'*. I think he liked how she was so confidently different to others and how she would never shy away from the moments which showed the depth of her thoughts or moments which most others would protect their vulnerability. He would only later know that night she'd pick her true future happiness over anymore highs with him.

"Tu es beau." stepping down the stairs of the cosy restaurant, Liv quietly pronounced the small French phase she had learnt a couple of hours before the date.
"Aw you just called me pretty." Fred lit up after realising what translated in her comment.
A few hours before Liv left for their date, she had google translated '*You look handsome*' in French and practised it over and over till she remembered it. She thought it would be a sweet gesture for the man fluent in French.

LOVEY

After a short tube journey, they extended their date back to Brixton. Stumbling into a local venue near his flat, they collected some drinks and sat and watched live music of a band play on stage. After their set was finished the stage was taken over by a young singer which to Fred and Liv, seemed to have a strong *Jorja Smith* vibe. Before entering the pub, they had bumped into Fred's flatmate to which, he and his girlfriend joined the evening. After more drinks and more songs, the audience found themselves standing watching the surprisingly talented artist. Liv stood from her chair with a gin and tonic and thought one thing after catching herself enjoying her last night with him all too much. *'Remember Liv, you're ending it for a reason. Anyway, he's not that affectionate, and you want someone that is.'* And in that exact moment, as if he could hear her, he grabbed her by the waist, pulled her in and swayed them from side to side in unison, to the rhythm of the music, bumping their hips into one another, laughing, while his arm gripped around her. After the moment passed and the song changed, he let go and looked down deep in her eyes and she remembered, he wasn't hers, and he never would be. She forgot for a moment that this was the last time they would feel any resemblance of a couple.

*

I'll miss you

"Fred…" Liv whispered into the nearly pitch-black room as she stared up to the ceiling.
She had promised herself it would be tonight.
She'd end it tonight.
"Yeah." he moaned, half asleep.
She took a tiny moment, preparing herself to ask the very thing she had dreaded.
"Where's your head at…?"
Immediately he knew what she meant.

LOVEY

"Let's talk about this in the morning, probably best when we're both not drunk." he slurred, turning his body over, pulling her into him. "I want to know now." she timidly insisted. She recognised she now wouldn't be able to sleep, and a part of her believed being a little drunk might induce an increased about of vulnerability on his part. "My heads in pretty much the same place as before." he said reluctantly.

There it was. The words she knew she'd hear.

She took a couple of moments to collect what she prepared to say when she knew what his answer would be.

"…well, that means we can't see each other anymore."

Fred propped himself up slightly, suddenly realising what Liv knew all along, that it was ending. Maybe he thought she wouldn't truly call it a day.

She did it. She ended it. She knew he didn't want it to be over. But he didn't want a relationship or was not at the least bit open to not sleeping with other people which seemed strange as he once said she was the first person he had slept with since his ex, and that had been months so why was this such a tremendous ask? *maybe he lied*, she thought. He really didn't seem like the type to lie, but I guess you never really know. Not sleeping with other random people felt like the easiest thing in the world to give up for him. He had always alluded to his lack of wanting commitment being because he came out of a long-time term relationship six months before and Liv understood this, she really did. But on the same hand, she knew that everyone breaks their rules for someone, someone you don't want to lose.

Look at Roe and Mollie.

LOVEY

He held her tightly all night. Tighter this night than any other before. They both knew this would be their last night together, of whatever it was they had shared. Liv truly felt the feelings had been mutual and he was hurt, just as she was. But he just couldn't, couldn't give what Liv deserved. He wiped her tears from her face softly whilst she was nuzzled under his arm and into his chest. Yes, she cried. Because I guess Liv will cry when it really hurts. It surprised her too.
"This is weird, I never cry." laughing a little in amazement, mixed with undeniable sadness.
She wanted the night to last longer than she knew it would, the sort of moment you want to stay in a while, not like the others, not because it's a beautiful moment, but because she knew leaving would be worse.
"Tomorrow is going to suck." she said finally achieving dry eyes.
"It is." Fred seemingly lost in the thought of it.
"You're a fit neuroscientist, you can do better than a visually impaired accountant", Liv laughed at his comment.
In that exact moment one thought walked across her mind with all the sadness it carried, *'I don't want to do better, I like how life feels with you'*.
"I'm sorry." he added.
"I'll miss you." her voice quietly revealing her minds truth.
"You're honestly amazing." he followed up the silence with. He said in such a deliberate manner, it seemed he wanted to make sure she knew it.
She wanted to say, *'I'm pretty you feel the same about me, as I feel about you'*, and *'was it worth throwing away such a natural, genuine bond?'* but she appreciated there was no point in this. If he couldn't see it for himself, she was no longer in the business of reminding those couldn't see how she wasn't replaceable.

I think Fred always knew Liv was unique. She was funny in the way she's sarcastic and will give all your banter back and more, whilst staying gentle and witty. He found himself telling her things I think

LOVEY

he wouldn't expect to leave his complex thoughts. Maybe she could have been a safe place for him. Whilst also being a girl who could recite all the words to his favourite rap songs. For someone out there, she's the perfect balance of fun, weird, but safe and the most loving partner you could have.

*

That's presumptuous

While Liv's famous vegan lasagne was cooking in the oven, the pair began to mess around in Liv's fairy light illuminated room, scented by her vanilla candles. In a matter of a few moments and after a decent amount of heavy kissing, he positioned himself on his knees in front of her, and started to lower his boxers…
"That's presumptuous." Liv said sarcastically in a humorous tone, breaking the intense sexual tension.

They did always have the perfect balance of the exact same humour, tenderness, and intense sexual chemistry.

He fell off his knees and down onto the part of the bed besides her. "Oh wow," catching his breath he had expended on laugher. "That really got me" continuing to gather himself as he giggled.

Their shared sense of humour shone through from the very beginning.

*

It wasn't enough though.

It broke her heart a little. The exchange, break up, whatever you want to call it, it was soft, sweet, just like them. Liv was honest, open and vulnerable and that's how she wanted to be remembered.

LOVEY

*

The final morning

The last avocado on bagel, this time was a Warburton thin, but nevertheless, it was the last one.
"I knew it was coming…you asking…I was just hoping it would take a little longer than this" he revealed as he walked back into his bedroom, standing over his desk, looking down at the driving licence from their first date. Every time she had come round, she found it still living on his desk.
"It got to the point where I needed to know." knowing, any longer and she'd fall.
"I just need to sort myself out. Half of it, I wouldn't know how to put into words." revealing his internal struggles.
This was genuine, she believed. She desperately wanted to be there for him, but she knew it was not her place.

*

To men

To men, I'd like to say, every man Liv has ever met, has struggled. The fear of your own complex thoughts is real. I promise you are not alone, no matter how much your mind convinces you otherwise. You are not too far gone or as *fucked up* as you think. But I also promise, you'll miss out on someone amazing, the longer you don't tackle your demons. I just hope your battle in your mind doesn't rob you of someone truly irreplaceable, because there are people who aren't, *aren't replaceable.*

*

"I should get my bus soon." Liv forcing herself to part from him.
"Whyy?" he said softly whilst slightly extending the word.
"...Don't you want to drag it out?"

LOVEY

Of course, she thought, but she knew how this went, it would never be enough time.
"I have to leave sometime." looking at him with a soft smile.

Collecting her bag and belongings, she took one last look at his room while he went to the kitchen to pop their plates back. Sat on the edge of the comfiest bed she'd ever slept in, she looked down at his vintage-looking union jack truck that acted as a bedside table where his glasses would live while he slept and where her phone would lay after he put it on charge for her. She gazed up at his desk where she got used to watching the back of his head playing with spreadsheets which would quickly be followed by him calling for a break and cuddling up to her on the bed. She looked down at his fluffy shaggy teddy *Suzie* and felt overcome with saddest at the thought of leaving Fred in the past. Finally, after saying her internal goodbyes to his room, she made it to the front door. Neither knew what to do so, stood in the doorway of his apartment building in Brixton, they embraced each other tightly. She let go of the man she wanted to keep for a little longer, looked up at him, and said goodbye.

Thinking back to the first night in Clapham... even though it felt like their worlds collided in just the moment they were meant to... she left.

I think deep down Fred really is a relationship guy. But his brain, his emotions just weren't where they needed to be to follow his heart. She felt it though, through all his actions. That's why she felt how she did. For some reason, unknown to her or him, her heart could feel his, from the moment they met.

And just like that, she had her power back. It was the very definition of bittersweet. Sat on the bus, she smiled to herself while a tear fell down her face which she quickly wiped away wanting to conceal her emotions whilst on public transport. It was bitter in that fact that,

LOVEY

from that day, she knew she'd miss him, *a lot* and she had no more *'Fred dates'* to look forward too. But she was overcome with how much she had grown mentally. Strong enough to truly choose her future happiness over a temporary high. Because that's all he was. That's all he wanted to be. She comforted herself knowing that this was all temporary and life had *so much more* than this small moment, in store for her. And this is exactly what it would become in the wider multiverse of her life, *a small moment.*

> For something so brief, you meant so much...
> more than you'll know.

*

She finally got back to her room and collapsed on her bed. She started to cry. Crying more than she in months. It felt like a release in a sense. She missed him *already*. But she knew she had lost so much more in the past. She could do this. It was just a *shame*. After laying with all the feelings of the immediate loss of him had brought, she pulled herself up off her bed and sat on her wood laminated floor of her room and began cutting up an old t-shirt, repurposing it into a skirt with her sewing machine for the festival she was about to attend the next day.

*

"He's typing, he's typing!"

Liv had made her way down to Sophie's in Bristol for a festival spanning over the following weekend. Laying in Soph's bed the night before day one of the festival, filling her in about what had happened with Fred and how she was already missing him, she threw her phone onto the duvet. Then cautiously picked it back up to see what he had sent her.

LOVEY

> Fred: Hey, no need to respond if you don't want to but I don't want the message above to be our last. So I hope you've got down to Bristol okay, and I really hope you have the best weekend! I've really enjoyed our time together and am sad it had unfortunately come to an end. It's time to work on myself a bit. The friend I was out with tonight has genuinely recommended I speak to someone and I will as soon as I can. But have the best time down there, and if you can be bothered, please send photos/videos of the event x

*

> Fred: You okay?
>
> The signals not great
>
> But I hope you're okay
>
> I hope the festival is a lot of fun x

I will say, Liv had never, in her life, been as drunk as she was at this festival. Her behaviour made friends around her believe she was spiked which was alarming as she had never done a class-A drug in her life. She had gotten blackout to the point she only remembered the beginning and very end where the girls were walking, leaving the festival. She felt sad as there were music acts she had been excited to see, but she knew herself and knew that she wouldn't have gotten that bad unless she was trying to outrun something in her mind.

> Liv: Sorry for calling. Hope you have a good night
>
> Had a really good day
>
> Fred: You okay?
>
> Liv: Yeah don't worry
>
> Thank you for the message. It's a shame we couldn't / didn't have a different outcome but I really hope you feel better and get to a good place within yourself, you deserve it. Good

LOVEY

luck with your exams, you'll smash them. Wish you all the best with everything in the future x

Bye Fred x

Fred: Thank you so much for that

Was really kind of you

Also this isn't legit I hope

Replying to her goodbye.

I hope this just means good night x

LOVEY

Chapter Twelve

Aeroplane air conditioning ran over her skin, giving her goose bumps from the chill. A couple of weeks later she was headed to the sunny destination of Turkey with a friend. Sat in the middle alle as she gazed out the window, she reflected on all that she wanted to leave behind. She was so incredibly ready to escape London and everything it meant. The past few months had been *a lot*. She had met and left Fred. She had finished her four-year degree in Neuroscience. It felt like a period of change, transition and also **loss**. She sat knowing she was soon to be hours away, where everything that had plagued her days, could fall away and be put on pause. It felt like a hopeful time, for the first time in a while and she desperately hoped this would be the break in the tides to which then led to something good.

Out of her beige Burberry carry-on she had gotten from Depop a couple years prior. She pulled out a book she had been meaning to start for a while. It had been lent to her after the assault by a close friend Kate, she worked with in the shop back in Brighton. She was going into it blind, unaware of the plot but knew if it came as a recommendation from her beloved Kate, then she trusted she'd enjoy it. Cozied up on the plane, she sat taking in the beginning

LOVEY

outline of the plot. With each turn of a page, it surprisingly hit closer to home than she expected. The story was based in London, main character being a girl fighting for her failing relationship and the aftermath that fell along with it. It followed her as she fell apart into a person she did not recognise. Liv could relate. Many of the things we've seen Liv do, feeling angry, numb, casual sex, getting black out drunk, would not be what she'd seen herself doing but she found that *hurt* can drive you down different roads. Sometimes roads you're lucky to survive. It was nearing a year since the final ending of Liv and Roe and therefore nearly a year since the assault. She couldn't stop thinking about it. Thinking about it more than usual. Tara said that was 100% normal, this relieved Liv. She thought it was scary really. There's no emergency care for rape victims. And quite simply, if it wasn't for Roe stepping back in, and she later acknowledged Elijah as well, Liv wouldn't be here. She knew this. In the immediate fall out, Roe was her life jacket, one last time.

*

After some back and forth between Liv and Fred as they attempted to untangle their lives, she bluntly asked in amongst meaningless messages if there was any point in speaking if they were no longer seeing one another. He replied with that he was still in the same place as he was when they ended which led Liv to question how much damage it would cause still having his name lighting up her phone and *heart.* She knew to fully heal she'd have to properly say goodbye. They both reached a mutual understanding which ended in a long paragraph, *"you're amazing"* …but it ended like this,

> Fred: …it just didn't work out for us in the end

Liv was so incredibly done with the amount of emotions and energy she had invested. She had lost so much more than a man she knew for two months, who saw no value in her, to stop seeing other girls, along with a few red flags that turned pink the more she liked him.

LOVEY

> ⟨ Notes   ↑   ⋯
>
> Look at what you've lost! Look at every moment with Roe and you've lost that and you're okay!
>
> My superpower always, thank you roe

*

It's interesting the timings of almost everything. That book was lent to Liv almost a year ago to read from a dear friend. It had been sat in her flat in Brighton and then in London. It's interesting because, if she had read it then, it wouldn't have contained the tiny details which felt like they were meant for her to hear, after she had lived her own. The Gemini boy who lived in Brixton, that turned into Fred whilst escaping into its plot, her failing relationship she matched to hers with Roe. Insignificant details which made Liv feel she was where she was meant to be, doing what she was meant to do. Her journey had led her here, reading this book, feeling the words deeper now, than she would have.

*

Let go

Standing in the Turkish sea with nothing but the beaming sun on her usually pale olive under-toned skin which she'd routinely darken with fake tan and the calm blue waves reaching her knees, looking out upon the bushy mountains which spanned the entire landscape, she felt *free*. No matter where you are, you're still ***you*** with all the same problems and believing you can run away is a mistake, but it ***is*** possible to feel relieved by the physical distance between you and home, where life holds you captive with your issues. It allowed her brain to unlock and let go. She had let go of Roe and Fred, both representing different parts of her.

LOVEY

*

23rd June 2022.

> Liv: Hey, so I'm graduating next month and I got my final results while I've been away and I just wanted to thank you, ofc I wouldn't expect a reply and I don't want to disrespect you and your relationship but I couldn't of done my degree without you so I owed you a thank you. I hope things are good for you, always routing for you. I'm so glad you're happy Roe

A few minutes past.

> Roe: Well done, congratulations!

We're done now. We have reached the end. She could leave him in the past now. It can be left on her unwavering gratitude for him. Because yes, he hurt her. Yes, he betrayed her but as you've heard, he's also saved her. Sometimes in small ways and others being saving her life. So, she was grateful, she was allowed to be grateful.

A small part of her wished he had said *'I'm so proud of you'*, *'You could of course, have done it without me'*, but she knew, she knew he thought this, but it probably would have overstepped a line.

Somethings don't need to be said and only known.

On the plane home, she sat by the window of the middle row overlooking nothing but flashing lights in the black night sky. She felt at peace with the life she was about to go back too, the life she was going to make.

LOVEY

The next days were defining

… The new start she had desperately hoped for was about to descend deeper than she could have ever anticipated.

LOVEY

Chapter Thirteen

<u>Scrambling. Scared of herself. Calling for help. In front of a train track. Wandsworth Town station.</u>

I'm not sure if you've ever been so low you become scared of your own thoughts or actions but let me tell you, in those moments, you do what you've got to, to survive. So, if that means calling random people or hopping on the train to somewhere less scary because going home would mean something far more final, just to stop the weight of your mind from actually crushing you, from truly taking your own life away from you, then you do it. She wanted to call one person. No, not Roe. Not Fred, *not really.* I mean, she did call him, but no answer, and only because she thought the one person she wanted, wouldn't pick up. *Immie.* She wanted to go home to Flimmie. Now I know I haven't introduced Flimmie yet. She, in short, was Liv's best friend from her days in Brighton and she saved her sometimes too. They drifted as Liv was yearning to move to London. Life brought the pair to a T junction and off they went in opposite directions.
"What's wrong darling? Where are you?" Immie with an incredibly concerned voice answering the phone, almost immediately.
"I want to come home…" Liv sobbed down the phone.

LOVEY

"I'm so sorry, I don't deserve you being there anymore." Liv referring to the ways she had let Immie down and the total absence of communication, whilst she cried next to the train track.

*

> Liv: Hey lovely, I move to LDN tomorrow wanted to message you. I just wanted to thank you for the endless moments you've been there for me, the fun we've had, and I'll always love you so much. I'm really sorry in it ending with us drifting apart. I want nothing but the absolute best things for you and you'll make it all happen, you're too strong not too. You were such a massive part of what made Brighton a home. Thank you for just being you

This being the last message she sent to which Immie met with nothing but insisting it did not have to be the end, and their friendship could continue. Liv never replied. She felt totally lost by the time she moved and had no idea how to take their distancing friendship with her.

*

"Don't be silly. Come down, get the train to Lancing, I'll pick you up."

*

Bathroom floor

Earlier that day she was expected to be at a popular pub in London for a friend's birthday but instead she was sat naked in the bathroom. She had been struggling every day that went by, but she was still being able to function, *barely*. Stood in the bathroom after a shower, she found herself falling to the floor, being unable to get up and get back to her room. Being in a house share meant she rarely spent any time in the communal areas longer than was necessary. But on this day, she held her legs up to her chest becoming terrified at her inability to move. She desperately didn't want to let her friend

LOVEY

down by not going so after an agonizing amount of minutes and all the energy she had left in the world, she crawled up to her feet and carried herself back to her room. She sat and wiped tears from her eyes as she attempted to do her makeup, trying not to let her cries roll down her face and ruin her foundation. After needing to take many breaks to catch her tears with tissue and take multiple deep breaths, she managed to finish her makeup and dress herself. Upon reflection, she never should have gone. She should have stayed safe in her room. Taken the day to rest. She realised as soon as she left the house, it was all about to be too much for her.

*

Back to Brighton, back home.

And just like that, she was *home.* After crying herself to sleep on the train to thankfully waking up one stop before Lancing, she realised life had brought her back down. Back to Brighton. She got in the car. They looked at each other like no time had gone by, no long months. That's the beauty with Immie, she was family and felt like home. Before heading back they stopped to collect snacks from the nearby ASDA, hummus, paprika Pringles, party rings and vegan chocolate milk, *Liv's favourites.* After a short drive, the reunited pair walked into Immie's new home. In the time of her absence, she had bought a house and was living with her boyfriend. Upon walking through the front door of her new detached home, two small dogs lit up the living room. A puppy and Flimmie's family dog from home. Liv was confronted with how much had changed but with the confusing feeling that even though she'd never been there, she felt safe. That's a testament to Immie and the person she is. She had forgotten what it felt like to be in a place where things stood still. It was bearable.
"Life's so overwhelming there." Liv referring to London, not knowing where to begin.
Sat curled up on the sofa she had been oh so many times, the sofa being one the things that was the same as before, cuddling Moose,

LOVEY

the black spaniel puppy. She tried to explain how she had got to this point. This point being not okay. Trying to examine what had to have happened to get here.

Really, all Liv is doing is trying to find a place where the world felt a little lighter. The more she can't find it and the more that happens, the more she panics and it's too much and now she's drowning.

Can you see how it escalates?

Passing the Pringles to Immie whilst dipping them in the hummus, "it's all too much" as she started to pick a part all the events that had played their part and led her there.
"Tell me, please, am I a bad person? Liv desperately feeling lost in who she was or had maybe become.
"No." Immie answering immediately in absolute certainty.
This brought comfort as she knew Liv, she knew the ways she wasn't the perfect person or friend, but she knew **her** and the person she was.
"I feel like I'm going crazy."
"You need to do day by day, little routines, little plans. You need to just sit there with your baking shows."
With a sign of relief, she felt seen again. Immie had remembered the ways she used for salvation better than Liv had. This was reminiscing over the fact that during their friendship, Liv was either watching The Great British Bake Off over and over or Cupcake Gemma videos on YouTube. Not because Liv baked a lot, she liked it but wasn't something she did often, but they were soft and comforting. She had totally forgotten about them. She wondered what else she had forgotten, forgotten about herself.
After a comforting chat that creeped her back off her ledge and Immie making sure she was tucked up all cosy on the sofa bed, they said good night.

LOVEY

"I'm embarrassed I rang Fred." Liv said the next morning after never receiving a reply or answer.
"That's the least of your worries." Immie said stood in the kitchen, both holding a mug of tea.
She was right. Her life felt as though it was totally unravelling, and Liv was worried how she looked to Fred.
It was time to not care.

She deactivated Instagram, determined to take a step back till she was better.

*

Replaying all the small moments which led to the big ones. Again, how have we got here?

*

With all the energy drained from her body from her panic attacks and prolonged period of feeling miserable which had reached its head, she wondered if she'd ever arrive at the destination. The destination of having a house, partner, dogs. All the things she ever really wanted. Don't get me wrong, she loved London and she wanted fun and adventure, but she needed to believe one day it would her turn. Her turn to be happy.

*

Stepping out of Immie's car at Lancing train station. *Something has to change.*

No social media
No alcohol
Be forgotten, focus and get better then come back.

*It's okay to disappear until you feel like **you** again.*

LOVEY

Chapter Fourteen

⟨ Notes

I'm taking a step back. I've deleted my Instagram. For some reason that makes me feel slightly lighter. Knowing I can't accidentally go on it out of habit or have people see my pictures. I kind of want to hide. I don't want to look at Fred's followers/following or everyone's stories. I don't want to see Roe and Mollie and how they've started their life together after moving in together. It's hurts. Seeing him give the future I wanted and worked so hard for, so effortlessly to someone else in under a year.
I haven't felt like this before. I've felt depressed, anxious, scared, restless, numb but never like this. Can't really put it into words but it scares me and I can't feel like this for long.
Flum and Harry want me to go on antidepressants. I've always hated the idea. I've always found my way out every single time but I don't think I can this time. Roe helped me before, but no one's coming this time. For the first time, I truly have to get myself out of the time.

I'm tired. I'm tired all the time.

LOVEY

The days that followed were dark. Black. Empty. She had officially hit her deepest depression. She now couldn't function. She spent her days laying in her room which she made dim at all points of the day with the blinds down and curtains drawn over them, to keep as much light out as possible. No one tells you how ill anti-depressants make you feel. The thought or sight of food she now couldn't stand. In reflection, it was quite unbelievable and an achievement that she had gone this long having never being medicated. Liv was never against anti-depressants but for her she always wanted to get better because things were truly better, but she knew this time it wouldn't go that way and no one was coming on this occasion, no Roe life jacket.

*

A year since the rape

She became consumed. Obsessed. Suddenly she could not stop looking at the photo evidence of that her body had been left in last year. She rarely looked upon these photos up till this point.
"Is this normal?"
"I can't stop thinking about it."
"I haven't thought this much, in so much detail, since it happened."
She was desperately searching for the answer within Tara.
"Liv, it is very common that around the anniversary of the assault, you begin to revisit it all,"
"The seasons being the same, your body remembers things you don't,"
"It responds to the temperature, day light, all these things being the same for the first time since."
The way Tara described it made sense. She continued to comfort Liv in the way that "It's still fresh," "Just less than a year," "It's a long process." Most importantly, Tara made Liv feel truly normal. She could finish her sentences. Predict how she felt, which only made her feel like nothing of what she was experiencing was any different to other survivors, and that, that she could live with.

LOVEY

the rape will
make your insides rage with fire
till
they turn
to ash
and are
numb
then
you think
feeling is bad
but
you know
numb
is worse

but
it will not
drown you
it will not
be what takes
you

LOVEY

*

Make it stop

In silent screaming pain on the floor of her dark room, she hit her low. Sobbing into her cream rug, she sent four texts, repeating the same two words.

23:46pm

Liv: You awake?

Sent to her twin flame, Liv^2, Harry, Fred, and Elijah.

No one replied.

*

One more day

She needed an escape. But maybe she truly didn't want to be saved in that minute. Maybe that's why she didn't call anyone. Didn't call Harry who she knew would pick up and talk to her till she fell asleep, through exhaustion. He knew how these moments felt all too well. Eventually she took herself to bed, the only reason being was that she knew she didn't have enough pills or means, so she was stuck, for that night she had to somehow settle her agonizing pain. She told herself *one more day* and that was the heart-breaking truth of this night.

"Why didn't you call me?" Harry panicking the next day over the phone as she explained her late-night text message.
"You know ringing will make me up." frustration running through his voice. He never wanted to lose her to one of these moments.
"…I'm not sure I wanted you to pick up." she said quietly, changing the tone of the conversation.
Harry went silent for a minute, knowing entirely how that feeling takes you.

LOVEY

Remaining quiet he said, "we have to do something this time Liv, medication… I know you don't want to, but it helped me when I got to this point, you said the same thing to me that time, I don't want to lose you."

He was right, she had said the same thing once before.

*

The time I nearly lost him

She couldn't explain why it didn't work. But by the grace of the universe, it didn't.
Why didn't he call?
He always called.

Liv had phoned Harry just like any other day. He was at work, sat in his van, on his way to his next job. She asked how his evening had been. He started to reel off the ordinary events of the previous night. Getting in from work. Having a shower. Then… quite underwhelmingly, in a downplaying type of way, he started describing the happenings of the rest of his evening.
"I took my duvet into the living room,"
"I unhooked the gas and channelled it into the front room,"
"Duct taped the doors so it trapped it in the room,"
"… and went to sleep."
Liv was shocked into silence.
"*Wait.*"
"What?"
He remained in silence for a moment.
"Then I just woke up this morning… disappointed."
So many things ran through her mind.
He had actually tried to die.
How did it not work?
"I actually don't know why it didn't work." he added in the quietness.

LOVEY

"…You can't go on like this."
Liv knew he wasn't well. Knew he was struggling but there's a sense of false security that you convince yourself with, that they'll call you, if they feel like that, like they always do. But never underestimate how your mind can steal you from the ones you love.
"So… you've just gone to work the next day?"
He let out a laugh. Not in a funny sense, but in how purely insane it felt to just get up on a morning you 100% believed you wouldn't be here for and put on your uniform and go about your day as normal.
"I know, it's mad."
She knew the ways his mind could fall but this was it.
"I had been thinking about it for a few days" he revealed.
"You need to call someone this time."
They stayed on the phone for a while, hours, as they spoke of options and a plan.

He did. He called and was admitted as an emergency outpatient. He was put on an emergency dose and was monitored twice a day by the outpatient team.

He slowly got a little better after that. But it was hard.
It scared Liv, she was the only one he told about that night.
If he tried again, and was successful, was it then her fault? Should she have done more?

I nearly lost him

*

It's Harry… *again.*

> I didn't tell anybody about my plans because I didn't care. I didn't, couldn't, care about anyone else but me. Not my family, friends, or even Liv. I was done. Just done and my mind went into a place for seventy-four hours where not being here anymore was my only focus.

LOVEY

*

Let me feel something

Being sick, dizzy, tired 100% of the day. She had started sertraline. This, for those who don't know, is an anti-depressant. An SSRI (Selective Serotonin Reuptake Inhibitors). The initial period is tough, and she was told it would soon level out. The beginning is the hardest. A few days into the full dose and she was struggling, knowing that going back wasn't an option and her only way out was forward. She did feel a little better though. She wasn't sure whether it was the medication, not plausible as it was a little too soon to be having an effect or the potential of a job which felt doable, or a combination of life being a little bit more manageable. Regardless, it was enough, enough to keep her safe in her four walls in Elephant and Castle.

She had officially fallen into herself again.

Depression is complicated and for anyone who hasn't been truly, chemically depressed, shouldn't delude themselves into thinking they know the complexity of how it alters your entire world. Words are thrown around and because of that, they lose meaning, *power*. So, I will not try and describe the places Liv's mind went. It was the first time she was depressed to the point she was just barely existing since the rape and her very first experience with the disease at fourteen. This time it meant she couldn't move. Couldn't eat. Couldn't get out of bed. She willed her brain to feel something, *anything*. Anything other than absolute despair and misery. She could physically sense she had no serotonin in her brain, or that's how it felt.

*

and there they were

...there they were. The tears she had waited months for. The loss of Elijah tore through her heart and into its last pieces.

LOVEY

It was a debilitating month, but it felt as though a cloud had lifted in one specific part of her past. She started thinking about Elijah. *A lot.* It was strange in all honesty, but she always felt a little numb when it came to him, wasn't upset or heartbroken after their breakup. She thought she had got away with it. Away from that heartbroken feeling. However, that had all changed now and the decision to delete all their photos and memories had come back to bite her. It was strange really; she was the **most** sentimental person usually but all she wanted to do after the breakup was forget. She truly believed she'd never be able to view them in a positive way and if anyone had told her six months later, she'd be heartbroken over him, she would have never believed you. It was the one thing she was certain about. *I guess you can really never say never.* What she was starting to realise was it wasn't Elijah she wanted to forget. It was everything else. That entire period of time felt she was drowning, suffocating. But it was Elijah in fact, that brought the light during that time. By putting what that happened in those six months in the past, she in turn had to do the same with him. And now all their moments started to climb through the cracks. Each tiny memory started falling in her mind, she felt happy, sad, guilty, lonely, everything under the sun, processing the relationship from a place where she could actually feel how she was meant to. Suddenly she'd replay how he had coped remarkably well. She truly began to acknowledge how difficult it must have been to be with someone while they were in the thick of healing. Especially from rape. That road back to yourself is one full of torture, anger, fear. That soft, loving person she recognised and was so fearful she had been taken forever. I guess that's why there's that saying, *To the boy I met when I was healing, I am sorry.*

You see, Liv finally discovered how emotionally unavailable she really was when Elijah came into her life and suddenly, she could feel *everything*.

She often thought how it could have been different now. How so many of the worst moments wouldn't now happen because she was

LOVEY

so much closer to the girl she had promised him she once was and would be again. No longer did she operate the way she had when together. Less anger, less frustration, more love, more laughs. She found her happy soft soul that had previously raged with fire.

If only we had met when I was truly me...

LOVEY

Chapter Fifteen

The day is finally here…Graduation

Liv had stayed alive purely for a few hand-picked moments in her life. The things that saved her when the sky had turned to black and she couldn't see or feel. Graduation was one of them. It represented more than having a degree, but she could do it, not only do it, but succeed during the worst of times. It is scary putting so much weight on one moment. Expectations always seem to ruin reality.
She woke at 4am to be able to get ready and down to Brighton in time. It was one of the first times she had been out the house in a month but was determined not to miss it. She sat at her desk and applied her makeup. She loosely curled her long dark hair which fell to frame her face. Taking one of Nannie's rings out her jewellery box, she placed it on her ring finger. Dressed in a long satin burgundy dress that tied at the back, being able to cinch her waist small. She made her train and before she knew, she was on her way down to Brighton, *home.*
As she stepped into the ceremony room, she gazed up at the walls of the Brighton centre which were lit with fairy lights, reaching the very top of the incredibly high ceilings. After finding their seats, she

LOVEY

sat with friends and waited for the students of Neuroscience to be called.

This is it.

It's here and she had survived.

A long four years has ended, and she had achieved something incredible.

Stood at the side of the large auditorium stage, between her two closest friends on her course, that by chance had surnames which alphabetically sandwiched her. She thought as she prepped herself not to trip and peeking out to the audience, she suddenly had an overwhelming view over, she thoughts of all the moments, big and small, that had brought her there. The hard work, terrible times she thought she'd never make it past the finish line.

Her close friends name was called. She watched him cross the stage. Next was her. The very moment she has clung too so many times.

"Olivia Farrow." beamed over the speaker.

The auditorium started clapping as she walked across the stage. She turned and looked at the huge crowd, thinking of where mum must be in the sea of people. She reached her hand out to thank the member from the university and walked down the stairs.

She was elated.

She sat and thought about how many small moments that had led her there, to that day.

   No… this moment was just as good as she had ever hoped. Nannie may not have been there and that hurt. But she would have been so proud and like Liv had said in her speech at her funeral, she was a part of those she still had around her, she was in her. *She was there.* Roe, or Elijah were not, on the other hand. When you're with a partner for a while, you imagine them at the big events. Observers of key milestones in your life. But they were never meant to be. That's not how the story was meant to go.

…And for the first time, in a really long time, that was really okay.

LOVEY

She left the Brighton centre, giving back in her cap and gown, feeling something really rare for herself. She was proud of herself. Proud of what she had achieved.
She left and went to have dinner with Flum and Grandad who she owed so much too. Unlike most, she didn't hang around. Towards early afternoon she headed back to London. She was still incredibly tired most of the time and today had drained her emotionally and physically. She couldn't help but remember Fred's delayed date for graduation was on the same day as hers.
"Means we can't be at each other's." he said after they both shared the dates of their ceremony's.
She always thought this was such a meaningful thing to say.
When she finally got back to her safe place she called home in London, after what felt like an incredibly long day, she changed from her long satin dress to her Sisters and Seekers oversized t-shirt. She sat on her bed and opened up her laptop. Most graduations live stream the ceremonies so she wanted to see if she could find Fred's moment. *She did.* She watched sat with her knees tucked up to her chest as his name was called, following his friend. She beamed at her screen as she watched his cheeky smile light up his face and as he tipped his cap.

She was so incredibly happy for him. Nothing less than what he deserved.

LOVEY

Chapter Sixteen

Lighter days were a chapter away

To you, the reader, things are good! Things have really changed. By this point I feel I can address you properly after we've been on this journey. So, the feeling in the air is different. The pain has passed. Depression has loosened its grip. Tides have turned. It feels new and it feels stable.

Liv found herself using her notes app a little less.

She was no longer on medication. She was able to leave the house. See her friends who had patiently waited for her to find her way back. She got the job. The job she needed. Working remotely where she would now take care of herself and earn some money, even on the days her depression liked to remind her she hadn't fully outran it. It gave her freedom and time. She would write and paint. She started to feel like her again. Her long black hair now reached her bum and she was starting to feel ever so slightly confident. She had moved on from Fred, he no longer lingered in her mind like before.

LOVEY

It felt strange. It felt like that month, the dark depression, was there to change things. Things she wouldn't have without it. It freed her in ways she never knew she was trapped. There is no magical prince charming rescuing her happiness, but she saved herself, with the help of friends and Flum of course. But this was down to her. The guy would come, she believed. But when he was meant to. She was done with men coming into her life to save her and instead, she was ready to find someone kind, loving and soft, when she didn't *need* them and that, *that is the greatest foundation of love,* she believed.

It's funny how it can feel everything was falling more and more a part, day after day, to everything falling effortlessly into place.

LOVEY

Don't worry, the right ones don't leave
or
they come back.

LOVEY

Look at Flimmie. The pair had been inseparable back in Brighton and Liv had left her and their friendship behind. She said goodbye to it and at any moment she wanted to hold it back in her hands, she quietly reminded herself she had made her bed and must lie in it.

But she came back... because the universe **will** guide you back to your people even if, for some reason in fate, you had to leave for a while.

Liv had done enough to permanently ruin their bond, but remember, *'You can't mess up something that is meant for you',* and these girls were. They were just each other's people. And now they are back. Back to sending voice notes over WhatsApp through the entire day, running around drunk after a bottomless brunch into an exhibition, cuddling up watching TikToks and barely saying a word, just being there, no matter what, for the second you need someone to be, for everything. For happy, sad, excited, good, and the bad times.

I could tell you thousands of stories as to why Immie was one those friends you don't want to live without. She loves *LOVE* just like Liv and she seeks the good in everyone she meets, whilst also being a strong, independent woman who she should be proud to be. Immie has often been the one that made life bearable, not just copiable but good. In lockdown, January 2021, they were unable to celebrate Liv's birthday so Immie threw her a surprise, decorating her entire flat with gold and black balloons and banners. She ordered them dinner and they had a party of two.

It was the perfect night.

"I knew you'd be back." Flimmie joking with Liv as they sat at their first proper dinner back together in London.
"I just had to take a minute, but I never stopped loving you Immie."
Liv said softly with tears in her eyes, knowing they had parted for a

LOVEY

reason. It was all meant to happen. But now, she has all the people and pieces in her life that make it healthy, happy and like *magic*. They say soulmates can come in many forms, that including relationships, friends, family, but regardless, Immie was a soulmate. She always felt different to Liv than her other friends.

It wasn't just Roe who was carrying Liv after the rape.

> Liv: Hey hun sorry I haven't been in contact
>
> Something happened on the date, I'll call you when your free but yeah haven't been very good
>
> Flimmie: I'm actually crying at these photos – you are amazing Fliv and you'll get through this I promise

Liv had sent three images of her body. The ones that had captured the layers of bruising, dark purple, pink, blue, green in colour over her legs and bum, red scratch marks laying on top of the bruises.

> Flimmie: Hey gorgeous, how's the rating today xxx
>
> Liv: 2
>
> I don't feel good today
>
> Flimmie: Okay that's fine, it's okay to feel not good, but every day is strength

Immie spent her days checking in on her, distracting her and coming round to sit with her.

*

"Hey hunny I know you're with the fam and Luke, but Dad just called me and I really needed to speak to someone…" Liv started to cry down the phone.

LOVEY

"Of course, hunny what is it?" Immie immediately incredibly concerned.
"Dad has cancer." she sobbed.

…So, to give a time frame to this, this came in amongst Nannie's cancer diagnosis, and a few weeks before the rape. He told her the night before her final exam of that term at uni.

You might wonder why I haven't mentioned her dad till now. She has always had a complicated relationship with her father. Grew up with conflicting feelings towards him. Without too much detail, he was an angry man sometimes, he mellowed out slightly as he got older but growing up was difficult and Liv's brother Jack, had it the worst. However, in the same hand of him being the angry, scary man, he was also very loving and affectionate. Couldn't go up to bed without a hug, bear hugs that he'd squeeze so tight as he counted down from ten. Maybe this is where her behaviour comes from of *one,* letting men treat her however they want, *two,* wanting someone soft, not intimidating, gentle, unlike him. She realised it was all manipulation. He was always very open about his own childhood and felt as though he'd had a hard upbringing and would use that to make her feel sorry for him, he'd continue to do this till this day. With certain people, including her dad, she always found it near impossible to hold a grudge. She'd felt bad, guilty.

Growing up Liv was physically bullied and abused, not by the hands of her dad though, unlike her brother. She was so used to fear, she'd often be taken by mum to the hospital for ongoing stomach pain since a very young, primary school age. Flum would rush her down as if it was appendicitis but nothing ever came back as wrong, yet still, huge pain. She'd later learn this was anxiety, panic attacks, but she could never remember a time without them or the pain.

LOVEY

*

Year 10

Liv loved school. She was good at it and can now acknowledge she put her worth on how she academically performed. Her 100% attendance was something that made her proud, but it never seemed to be an effort. School felt like a nice place to be. She enjoyed Maths and Science. She had good friends. Everything changed, however. In the summer holidays before starting year 10, Liv fell into her very first depression. She spent every single day in doors, in her bed, just wanting to sleep, all the time. It was strange, she didn't know why that's all she could cope with doing, but it was. School term rolled around and just like she had done for year seven, eight and nine, she got up, put on her skirt, shirt, tie, blazer and went to school. The first few days were okay, maybe a little off but it was good to be back, she thought.

> 6:30am.
> Hyperventilating.
> Crying.

She pleaded with mum to take her to school, *"not the bus."* she begged mum, telling herself she'd be fine if she drove her in. This stayed true for a while, maybe a couple of weeks. Flum would drop lavender essential oil on the cuffs of her school jumper and round her neck to smell if she felt unwell. "Take deep breaths" she'd say. It quickly turned and being driven in stopped working. Panic attacks in the car, outside the school gates, not being able to breathe, hysterically crying, it all started to consume the daily ritual. Eventually, after many mornings of the same ordeal and Flum watching how exhausted and mentally scarred Liv was becoming, Flum gave in. Liv dropped out of school.

For anyone who doesn't have panic attacks, they are so commonly spoken about now so they kind of lose their realism. But take it from

LOVEY

me, they are awful. They are the worst moment of your life. I will never be able to put into words what they feel like but please, they are terrifying. In some dark way, it is incredible how the mind can work and then how the body follows.

For those who have had them, *aren't they exhausting?* It takes Liv days to recover from one, properly, even now. But at this time, they were occurring daily, no time for her body or brain to rest or catch up. It was living hell.
Everyone bombarded her with…

> "Why?"
> "Why can't you go to school?"
> "Explain how you feel"
> "Are you being bullied?"

Everyone had a theory. Some were she was being bullied, she wasn't. But the truth is, Liv had no idea. No idea why all of a sudden, she couldn't go to school. Couldn't step foot in the building. But she did know it made her feel trapped. And she could not bear that feeling.

She started being home-schooled. She stopped seeing her dad from every other weekend to never.

"I'll come there and drag you to school." Liv's dad shouting down the phone to her whilst she sobbed.

She didn't want this… any of this. She used to love school, she thought. *How will I ever be a vet now.* In her mind, her life was ruined, before it had ever begun.

This is one of the reasons why Flum is so great. She listened to Liv. She knew her, she wasn't trying to get out of school because no kid likes school. She knew she was unwell and would only get better if she listened, heard what Liv needed.

LOVEY

She kept two friends from school. The ones she saw still saw while the others forgot her existence.

As the attempts to go in stopped, the panic attacks dramatically reduced but still occurred. It made day to day life start to become more bearable again. It allowed some time for her body and brain to heal.

There are a few requirements if you don't take your kids to school in the UK. She had to constantly prove the schoolwork she was doing, she had to start group therapy with other kids struggling like her. It's not the *easy* way out and actually sometimes it was worse in Liv's opinion. Kids hear *home-schooling* and think she had it made. She didn't and wished more than anything, to be a normal kid going school, like she had always been.

She got better slowly. A lot happened in that year but that's another story. She'd eventually go back to school for year eleven. Took all the courage she had left to walk back into that building after a year of being gone. Rumours start. Kids are mean. They all had a theory as to why Liv had dropped out but regardless, she walked in everyday to finish what she started, having gotten better enough to grin and bear it. It did however feel good to be back with her friends again. To be part of a group. Most welcomed her back with open arms.

After she went back for her last year, in her school bag she placed her beaten up copies of the poetry of Lang Leav. These words had the power to always sooth the tormented soul which motivated her to keep them with her always. They were unnecessary weight in her bag, but she found that surviving the last part of school would often see her sat in a cubicle toilet reading over and over her favourite poems, waiting for 3pm to come around. Lang Leav's poetry which seemed to ground the mind of someone who thought so much deeper than an average child. She'd tear pieces of paper she found

LOVEY

around her and bookmark the ones she loved the most. From the book 'Love & Misadventure' the poems *'Soul mates'*, *'Angels'*, *'A Dream'*, *'Dead Butterflies'*, *'Letting Him Go'* and *'Lost Things'* were ones she'd seem to revisit.

She left school with two GCSE's and would later re-do the rest of them at college to achieve A's, finally being able to do her A-levels and get to university.

It may have taken her longer, but she got there and did well. She also felt behind everyone else and it took her a while to truly believe you can't *'be behind'* on your own path. Panic attacks stayed a part of Liv's life forever, but she'd make it her life's mission to only keep people like Flum around her, people that are safe, soft and truly listen, even when it is difficult.

*

My hairs falling out

It started in school. The stress hormone, cortisol, is known in periods of stress to have a side effect of hair loss. This is because the cell signalling is disrupted and oxidative stress harms the normal processes of the hair cycle. During the time when panic attacks were every day, she started noticing her long thick darkest brown hair started to fall away. For a teen, it was the most distressing part. From then on, her hair never grew back to the same thickness.

She never really noticed till she was with Roe but during her panic attacks, she'd hold her head, grab her scalp, and pull at her hair. This is why, often, Roe would gently hold her hands as she endured an attack. You don't really notice what you're doing during. Unaware she was tugging at the hair she had left. So, I have not mentioned till now but Liv, from fourteen, has had extensions to overcome the ways in which her mental struggles presented so physically and resemble what she once naturally had.

LOVEY

Roe knew Liv never really liked people touching her hair. She was never one of those girls who wanted her hair stroked or played with. It was a part of her trauma. A part of her childhood abuse, but again, that's a story for another time.

*

Safe place

Liv couldn't tell you a time she didn't have to work ten times harder just to be normal. Trying to hide it, and making it seem effortless. But one trait of hers never wavered, she'd be the safe place you need. She'd be the safe place she never had. She'd always care because she knew what it felt like to feel so much, having no idea why or how to put into words. Because life truly is about the people you can sit in silence with, knowing you're safe and they understand, without you ever having to say a word.

*

Do you remember when Roe said,
"I'll see you in a year"

I told you the pair have an *'in'* with the universe. And this time it had put them in the same place, at the same time, almost a year later, to the day.

Looking towards the doorway, the view being blocked by the crowd of people that filled the sweaty club that was always busy, making it barely able to move on a Saturday night. *That looks like Roe,* she thought, looking at the tall curly haired man standing in the entrance.

It will be the very moment that you stop looking
for their face in a crowded room,
that they will appear.

LOVEY

Looking for one more second, she realised, that *is* Roe. All those scenarios she'd play in her mind as she'd lay in her bed, thinking of a moment where they'd bump into each other. Where they'd cross paths and stumble into one another's lives, it had happened. With her phone in one hand and a six-foot-two black haired guy she had hit it off with, being a friend of a friend, in the other, she continued to proceed to the door.
She grabbed the top of his arm softly.
"Hey!"
Both their hearts stopped.
His eyes lit up.
She watched the seconds of surprise behind his gaze.
"Hey." Roe still in shock at her presence.
The first thing that came into her mind and out her mouth was…
"How's Mollie?"
"Good." he replied with a small awkward laugh.
She continued to walk past him and out into the smoking area with the guy still in hand. She couldn't believe it. Same place, same time, no Mollie. Her thoughts ended there as she watched him leave the doorway and into the club. She had truly put him in such a secure box of, *he's happy and in a relationship, but how strange to see him.*

She entered back in, returning to her other friends dancing in the corner, finding he was standing nearby. All night they exchanged stares and passing nudges in the crowd, being ever so aware of each other's palpable presence. As Liv and the guy continued to break away from their friendship group to kiss in the corner, she often would emerge out of their embrace to Roe looking to then quickly whipping his head away from her direction. After a few more snogs with the handsome guy, he had to leave for an early flight to New York in the morning. He had made that known earlier in the evening when they all sat in the pub down the road but Liv managed to persuade him to extend the evening to the club. Before he left, they exchanged Instagram's and Liv walked him out, hugging and kissing goodbye. Walking back in alone, the pair the universe can't

LOVEY

quite separate, caught each other's eyes, *again.* Only this time the gaze felt different. Suddenly Roe turned his body around, now to face Liv closely, the closest he had been all night. Grabbing her waist and then lowering his hand to her bum which he gripped tightly, *and she knew,* she knew in that exact moment he wasn't happy, fulfilled. She also knew he was bad and was about to, if he hadn't already, cross the line. Their faces grew closer in the crowd of people, he moved his gaze down to her lips, then into her eyes, then back down at her lips. It was a matter of minutes until Roe took her hand and led her through the crowd and out to the entrance. Liv quickly let go and grabbed her friend to say she was leaving. Her friend proceeded to call it a night as well and followed. Stood outside the club, Roe waited to one side as she hugged her friend goodbye and left in the opposite direction.

"Come to mine." she says knowing *'his place'* now meant *'his and Mollie's place'.*

"No, no, let's go to mine." he insisted.

The pair crossed the busy road in the early hours whilst the high street still raged with people busy in the middle of their night out. They started walking, headed towards Clapham Common.

Look at his face. She couldn't believe she was looking at his face. She couldn't believe the universe had brought them back together. Crossed their paths on the rare occasion where everything that would need to fall into place, *did.*

They reached The Common where they had to walk through to get the Clapham Junction, where he had moved. As they made their way through the green, his impatience grew as Roe moved himself towards her, grabbing her face between his hands and kissed her passionately, like it couldn't wait a moment longer.

They hadn't kissed in so long.
They hadn't kissed in a year.

"I told you I'd see you in a year." Roe said confidently as they walked side by side. She looked up at him in surprise with her chocolate

LOVEY

brown eyes that had only held love for him, found his gaze, and looked back down at the pathway. They both knew how powerful that sentence was. That sentence said so much more than what left his lips.

He remembered, smiling to herself.

He made that promise a year ago. So much had happened since. So many things said and done, but no, he remembered, and it felt as though he had wished for his promise to come true, *just as she had.* She soon tucked this hope he left her with, the last time they saw each other, in the back of her mind after she saw he had moved on. She still couldn't believe it was him. *It felt meant to be.*

As they continued down the concrete footpath, surrounded by green either side, growing closer to his new home, he hung his head and confessed…

"This is bad isn't it." guilt suddenly casting over his heart, referring to his impending betrayal.

She took a moment and looked down at the path herself.

"It's us, it's different." she replied. Yes, even though she was incredibly drunk by the point they made the decision to go home with one another, there was a small part that believed it, he was still a good guy she could continue to trust, because it wasn't with someone *random,* someone who meant nothing, it was with *her.*

"Did you see I viewed your Instagram story the other day?"

"No! when?" her not understanding how she had missed that. She often found herself checking who had seen her story, at this point Fred's name moved from the top to being nearer the bottom after she unfollowed him.

"Yeah, I was going to message you." he continued as they strolled towards the end of The Common.

"Why didn't you?" expecting him to say, 'it wasn't the right thing to do', etc. But instead, he replied with the most unexpected sentence.

"I didn't want to change how you viewed me." he said softly, with his kind facial expression she knew all so well.

LOVEY

Strange, she thought. He seemingly cared more about how she viewed him, held him in her mind, than how it would destroy his girlfriend, or the life he had started to build.
After a mixture of serious, meaningful comments and banterous teasing, she was overcome with one question she had believed she'd never get to ask.
"Why her...?"
There it was.
The question that had plagued her mind for nearly a year.
She began to lighten the air up with, "I'm funnier, fitter, dress cooler." drunkenly messing around, teasing him knowing she had upped her league since they split, maybe there was an element of truth running through her curiosity. The pairs personalities were always so incredibly compatible, how could he find *more*? So why? They had *everything*? She really didn't understand what this girl had that was worth giving the exact life she had fought so hard for, over her.
He was silent for a moment but never lost eye contact. He bantered back with, "Oh confident, are we?" to which she laughed.
But his serious tone entered the conversation to answer the depth of her question.
"I don't know." he replied, seeming to genuinely be unable to find a better answer after he took a moment to search his mind.
I really think he didn't know. I honestly think if you ask Roe why he's not with Liv, he genuinely wouldn't know.

I think his love for her always scared him.

"You can't tell." he insisted what they were about to do wouldn't go any further than between them.
"When will you learn Roe?"
"...I'm your safe place,"
"...You know that."
She really meant it. She utterly believed she'd protect him ***forever.***

LOVEY

The pair eventually, after many stops to kiss and tease one another, made it near his home. Roe had complained throughout the journey that because of how hard he was, it was making it difficult and uncomfortable to walk. They finally reached the flat he now shared with his girlfriend. Stepping through the front door, into the hall facing the bathroom, then the kitchen to the right, bedroom and lounge to the left. Her New Balance trainers on the shoe rack. She couldn't process it. She had fought so hard, for so long, and he had given this girl everything she ever wanted, in less than a year. *It hurt.* Seeing it in the flesh was a new pain she had never felt. She went from room to room. Taking in the life he had built with her, yet, was still not satisfied by.

"Are you okay?" he asked as she tried to absorb the flat she had found herself in.

"You can go if you want." he added, as he read her conflicting mind. She took another look at their shared belongings, saw the large house plant Roe and her had gotten from the B&Q in Guildford when they were so genuinely happy, and *she couldn't.* Couldn't do it. Couldn't *not* care like she thought she could.

"Yeah, I think I should go." she said as she made her way down the two steps from the lounge, back to the front door.

He remained silent.

Reaching back to the entrance she went up and grabbed the latch to free herself from the home she should have never seen. As she was about to release the latch Roe immediately positioned himself to her side, reaching his hand up on the door…

"I don't want you to go." he said soft and quiet.

She froze, holding the handle. Internally a battle began to brew. After a moment of moving her eyes up and away from fixating on the closed door to then his eyes, she pulled her arm away slightly, bringing it to her side. He lowered his head to hers, her eyes staring at his lips. Their faces grew closer and finally, *they kissed.* Only this time meant more. It was slower, deeper. That was it. She recognised that was the moment that changed everything. She had given him every opportunity to choose her, to choose Mollie. But he didn't,

LOVEY

and for the first time, in a really long time, he chose Liv. As their kiss intensified, they backed into the kitchen whilst holding their intimacy. She dropped her thong from under her cream satin maxi skirt with a thigh high slit, to the tiled floor. Roe lifted her up, onto the kitchen counter, he undid his belt and trousers, and right before they do the very thing Liv thought would never happen again, he said under his breath...

"Is this okay?" – this is **the** most attractive comment to anyone who has been assaulted.

He can go a year and still want to check in, every time. It's the little things, that's what ran through her head. He wasn't too drunk. He was there. He was in the moment. He knew he was with Liv and was determined to not let this opportunity pass.

"Yeah." she quickly whispered with certainty.

The body she knew so well. The sex she knew so well and had missed. *There it was.*

Amongst their passionate intercourse, Liv's knee knocked a frame that was hung on the wall next to her. She would later walk into the kitchen and look at it the next morning and think, *Roe will put that frame straight and she'll never know.* Mollie would never know that the picture, which she probably picked out herself, was jolted out of place and off its hinges by the intense sex her partner, of a year, would initiate. "Let's go to your bed." she moaned after growing uncomfortable on the work top.

After using the kitchen counter, Roe picked her up and placed her back on the floor, and they moved to his bedroom. She laid down on the bed taking off the maxi skirt she had previous lifted up and yanked off her black boob tube. She now laid naked as he walked into the room. Roe looked over her as he took off the remainder of his clothes. His skin, his body, his arms. He leaned over her small frame and just before he resumed to put himself back inside, he said, "You haven't got anything, have you?

The pair never used protection due to believing each other were faithful and Liv had the non-hormonal contraceptive coil which he checked she still had as they grew just round the corner from his

LOVEY

new home. Liv passing an STI to him at this point would result in devastating consequences, but she did think it was already a little too late at this point of him asking as for what had just happened in the kitchen.

"No, no."

He continued to lower himself inside, standing off the side of the bed Liv later believed to be Mollie's. After a few minutes Roe switched to positioning himself to the centre of the bed, naked Liv followed his body and climbed over on top of him, leaning on her knees and lowered her mouth to his crouch.

"*Fuck*. I missed this. I forgot how you're so much better than anyone else at this." he moaned intensely after a few moments.

She laughed with her mouth full.

They continued their night, Roe moving her into different positions. Wanting to have her in every way he had most likely thought about for the few weeks prior, since he began to feel the desire to contact her. Suddenly this couple, again, find themselves laying there, back where they always end up, *together*.

Once more, she found herself stroking the soft brown ringlet curls she knew all too well. She took her hand from intertwining in his waves and grazed it down his back gently, reaching his lower spine which he met with an *"mmm."*

"Where are you living?"

"Elephant and Castle,"

"…A couple stops from Clapham North."

"I'll come see you in Elephant and Castle."

"Oh yeah?" she was surprised at how he was mentally planning for a reoccurrence.

"I was in Camden for a while… with my ex,"

"My ex hates you." Liv light-heartedly joked whilst stroking his back.

"Your ex?" Roe confused.

"Yeah, my ex since you."

"What's his name?"

"Elijah."

LOVEY

Roe turned his body inwards to face her. He looked into her eyes, taking his hand and grazed it up her leg and onto her body, stroking up to her waist. He took both hands around her figure and flipped her over onto her knees and *again...* they began to have sex. Suddenly, in the heat of the moment, Roe said something that caught tipsy Liv off guard.

"Who feels better, me or Elijah?" as he thrusts.

Liv took more than a couple of seconds to process quite an out of character comment, so he repeated.

"Me or Elijah?" wanting sexual gratification from her.

"You." she moaned as he continued with a new burst of energy.

    After the sex was done, Liv started to collect her belongings. She gathered her skirt and top from the bedroom floor and sat up to begin dressing herself.

"What you doing?" Roe leaning from across the bed, into her, seeming confused.

"Don't you need me to go?" looking down at his face, always assuming she'd be Uber-ing back to Elephant and Castle.

"No, stay." he insisted.

She settled back down, putting her rings on the bedside table and accidently spilling a glass of water he had got her, down the back of the side console, hoping it wouldn't affect the lamp placed on top. A few silent moments past while Liv was deep in thought.

"Where's Mollie, Roe?" having to understand how there was no possible chance she could walk in at any minute.

"In Wales." he said from the other side of the bed.

Liv knew Mollie was from Wales already as after they got together, she had watched a few reels she had put on Instagram, as the Welsh accent is a strong one, she put two and two together. Her Welsh friend confirmed the suspicion.

A few quiet moments past.

"Are you happy Roe?" laying there, not understanding why this had happened, knowing he couldn't be, *not truly.*

LOVEY

"I'm alright." he moaned, half asleep but still wanting to meet her questions with answers.
"Are you?" he added.
She was silent for a moment too long. Pondering his question.
He repeated again, "are you?"
"Yeah, I'm okay, I'm good."
If he had asked a few months before, her answer would have been a lie. But it wasn't. She was actually okay, she was good. Life was starting to get better, get to a good place.
"God, you drank so much, I swear you were constantly at the bar."
"Why do you think I drank so much?"
"…I saw you and I just…yeah, I just needed to keep drinking."
She laughed and then pondered over how she had such a powerful reaction on him. *Did I still mean that much?*
"Who were you with? I didn't recognise them." she questioned as she mostly knew all of Roe's friends.
"They're friends from school, I rarely see them."
"…I told them if they spoke to you, I'd knock them out."
She enjoyed his protectiveness. It had been a while since she felt that from him.

"Why not us?"

                                            …she *had* to ask.

Why wasn't this apartment, theirs? Why wasn't it Liv and Roe? Why had he handed Mollie everything she ever wanted?

He turned over inwards to face her.
"I think we'll always wonder that." he said softly.

She was a little surprised at his answer. She thought he'd say, "We weren't meant to be", "I do love Mollie", "We had our time." but instead he revealed that no matter how much he could settle into a new life, he still thought of her. *Had* thought of her. Had never really stopped and even come to terms with living with the wonder

LOVEY

of what life would have been if they had taken a different turn. He was right. The pair would forever speculate what life would have been had the universe paved a different path. A path where Roe was brave and became the man she deserved.

"Roll over." she said softly, knowing there was nothing else to say. Roe rolled back over and she resumed to stoke his hair till they both fell to sleep.

*

Roll over

Roll over. This was secret code. Okay, maybe not that far but it was special language to them. It meant something. I couldn't tell you the first time Liv said it, would have been very early into their relationship but it became a *'thing'* for them. An inside dialogue. They both grew to say it in their baby voices, the voices they'd mostly speak in to only ever came out of it then they were with company. *"Roll over"* Roe cosily commanding in his baby voice and immediately she'd turn her body to facing away from him as he nudged himself close into her back and wrapped his long arms around her, squeezing her in. *"Roll over"* from Liv's baby voice and he's automatically, like it was second nature, would turn onto his stomach and face the outside of the bed. She'd then lower herself down, slide one arm under his pillow, and use the other free hand to stroke his curls whilst slotting her leg in between his like a puzzle piece finding its perfect match. It became a way of saying *I love you.*

*

Roe: I'll keep you safe forever and ever

Roll over

*

Roe: I want a cuddle

Roll over

LOVEY

Liv: Roll over

*

Liv: Roll overrrrr

Roe: Roll overrrr

*

Roe: I love youuuuu

Roll over xx

Liv: Roll over

*

Cloud

Can I tell you a secret? There was a moment, laying in Roe's bed as they were drifting to asleep where a person cast into her mind like a cloud. Normally, every other single time she was with Roe, she would have never wished to be anywhere else, with anyone else, but this time she laid there in the quietness as she began to think of Fred. For the briefest moment she let herself miss him, then casting away the cloud in a passing breeze.

*

Leaving never felt so easy

The next morning felt strange. She woke extremely hungover. For the first time waking up next to Roe, she did not want to prolong it. She quickly placed her gold rings back on her fingers from the bedside table, gathered all her possessions, brushed her hair with a wide tooth comb she found in the bathroom, knowing that would be Roe's for his curls that he always deep conditioned and combed for them to lay right, and left before he was barely awake.

LOVEY

"See ya." she said half out the bedroom door, departing before they could speak anymore.

Leaving felt like the easiest thing in the world. Suddenly, she had her answers. All the things she had spent nearly a year wondering, all now solved. She left feeling free. She knew he missed her. Whether he'd ever be able to admit that or not, he now didn't need too. Knew things with Mollie were never as good as what Instagram made them out to be. She left thinking of every opportunity she gave him to not let last night happen. Walking home, *"This is bad isn't it"*, *"You can't tell anyone"* *"This can't go in the book"*, *"I don't want you to leave"*. But instead, there was no way in his mind he'd let Liv leave this time. Maybe it felt meant to be for him as well. Regardless, she decided to use the warm light of the Sunday morning to process what had just happened. She walked through the Common, where they had been, hours before, kissing and fooling around with each other. Yet this time, she walked through feeling so incredibly different.

*

Finally, she was done

It was the closure she never knew she needed or would get, but regardless, there it was, it had found its way to her.

> Liv: I think you've made a mistake by picking her. But I think I'm done being everything you could possibly want and you never being brave enough to choose. Maybe you'll never be fully honest with yourself. I really don't know what the universe needed to do, to show you. I'll always be your safe place and you don't have to worry about the other night, I'll always have your back but you can't pick me anymore. I'm taking myself out as an option, for good. Maybe you are happy or maybe guilt has thrown you back into things and you feel fulfilled again but maybe, one day, you'll get bored, unfulfilled and your mind, (that I know so well), will wonder because deep down you know it's not 'it' and it'll creep in again and you'll think of me, us and un-boring, and actually great could have been and were, 99% of the time, even

LOVEY

> under the circumstances. It may not sound like it, but I do truly want you to be happy. But I mean real happiness, the lasting kind. You're out of your mind for not picking us... I'll always think this, but we had our time, and you were right, life always had a strange way of bringing us back to each other, but I'm done with thinking about the life we could have had. Maybe you've made a mistake, maybe you haven't but either way you've run out of time figuring it out with me, I deserve better. I know this sounds so passive aggressive, but I really don't mean it like that
>
> Please be ok and safe (on your bike especially), like I've said before and I'll say it again, I'm routing for you, your happiness, always your ride or die x

There were the words. The words she was finally strong enough to say... *'I deserve better'*.

Along the way you needed to understand how Liv loved Roe. To then understand every action that has followed him. He was the first domino to fall. As we know by now, it was not the lack of difficult things happening prior to his entrance, quite the opposite, but he set in motion everything that has happened since. Liv and Roe were the very definition of best friends. The one you laugh with the most with. The one you never get tired of speaking too. The one you can never get enough of their presence. The one that feels like *home*. He was the one she wanted to share everything she had with.

They once had a beautiful moment and I have left till now to share it because the moment was simply perfect. It was the happiest she had ever felt, even to this day. Close your eyes and imagine it is late summer, in the evening where the sun has gone down, and the sky is about to darken. You are sat on a quite pebble beach with no one around. Roe had pitched the couples tent and layered duvets and blankets they had stuffed into the car, making sure to keep them warm. Roe dug a hole in the pebbles and placed his portable speaker inside, playing chilled RnB. The sky turned to black but was brightly

LOVEY

lit up by stars in the sky you could only see in this unpolluted seaside town. They laid their heads next to each other under the stars, with the quiet music filling the atmosphere combined with the soft crashing of the waves. Both had hands filled with hot chocolate that was made by the portable kettle Roe borrowed from his dad. I can't describe to you how perfect this night was. Roe always said, *"that night was one of the best nights of my life."* Cuddled up in the layers of sleeping bags and blankets, Roe re-emerged from the blackness after having a wee in the darkness and arrived back into the tent. He climbed across Liv and said in his sweet baby voice *"I love this."* It was radiating, *his happiness.* This night, these moments, reminded Liv in the times she convinced herself none of it was real for him, never felt the same as her. But he did. He loved her, and them, more than he ever anticipated. Do you want to know how I know? She could *feel* it. She could *see* it in this soft green eyes. You can't fake that type of love. That's the voice that called him back. When he'd wonder in his pain, in his own complex mind, but for the longest time, his love for her called him home. It whispered his name…

till it didn't.

*

Hangxiety

For any of those who experience '*hangxiety*' the next day after drinking too much and losing that ability to process your thoughts long enough to register what you are actually doing… *this one is for you.*

Liv is that annoying girl who drunk calls her entire phone book. She's always been like this, even in relationships like Elijah and Roe. She simply liked chatting rubbish when drunk. It loosened her reasoning of whether it was a good idea in reality and simplified it down to the pure desire to talk to who she was calling. As you can guess, it is one of her more annoying traits and how she'd feel the

LOVEY

next day was always awful. She'd have her usuals she'd call, Roe, Elijah, Fred, Harry, Flum.

So, for those who know the feeling of regret or embarrassment, then here are a few words…

> No one cares and anyone that does care you got a little too drunk and thought to call them, don't deserve your time.
>
> Give it a day, a week and most definitely a month and they and you would have 100% forgotten.
>
> Go outside. Go for a walk. The world can feel so small when you're living in your own head.
> We're on a floating rock, literally nothing matters, you are okay.
>
> The people that do matter, won't care and love you regardless.

After one particular night, it had been a few months since Fred and Liv had spoken or seen each other but she'd pop in with a drunk call now and then which she'd always be incredibly thankful he would never answer. Liv had unfollowed Fred a while back, but he stilled followed her, viewed her story. He had however, unfollowed her TikTok, art/clothing Instagram, but always kept her main account. After a bottomless brunch at Vagabond wine bar which was then followed up by attending an exhibition in their drunken states, which she remembers 0.2% of, she realised she had lost her keys. These would later be discovered in Immie's bag once she had gotten home, back in Brighton. This day was perfect, apart from the ending. But all in all, it was a day for the memory box.

She knew Fred would unfollow her eventually, no longer care at all about her at some point, but this day, turned out to be the day.

LOVEY

After eventually being able to get back into her house after frantically ringing the housemate she was closest with, she got back, put on her oversized bed t-shirt, and fell asleep. The next day hit her. The hangover yes, but so did a tornado of hangxiety which was causing mass destruction in her mind. She deleted her call history, barely being able to fully accept the vast group of people she had no recollection calling, including Roe, Fred, Elijah, and Eddie, Fred's best friend. She did have method to her madness, however. Once she had realised her keys were missing and Immie was on her late train home, she panicked. The only person who lived near her home in Elephant and Castle was Eddie. So, she thought, *'if I can just go to his, wait for someone in the house to reply and let me in, all will be well'*. She was already on her way to E&C and take it from me, it is not the safest place for a woman to be alone, intoxicated, late at night.

*

> Liv: Last night was a mess ahaha
>
> Sorry for calling
>
> Fred: Haha no worries I enjoyed it.

He replied the next morning

> Was a nice surprise this morning
>
> Liv: Least you know I was thinking of ya
>
> Fred: Exactly

It made Liv think of this conversation. It's hard to accept life had moved so far past the pair both feeling like this. This and another they had after they had stopped dating.

> Liv: No more drunk calls I promise
>
> Fred: Haha we'll see about that

LOVEY

Liv: Haha nah I won't, we have to stop talking at some point

Fred: No rush

*

"I just feel so stupid." Liv confiding in Flum.
"Everything I have felt, thought, was obviously just so much more than him... and then I drunk call him like an idiot. I didn't even want too. I want to rewrite everything with him..."
"Liv, this is *your* story, don't let someone else take away your voice, your words, your feelings, this is about you." Flum continued...
"Never apologise for how you have felt so deeply for someone, that's your *superpower*, you have always cared so much for people, there are not many others like you, and they were lucky you chose them, to care about."
She wanted to rewrite everything with everyone. A new plot where she didn't care, didn't feel so deeply, wasn't vulnerable with these people, but if we did that... say we did... okay, let's pretend everything you have read up till this point, didn't happen. And we rewrote it, but this time Liv was closed off, didn't care, didn't love, didn't feel, never allowed the vulnerable moments to exist, then, what would we be left with?

No magic.

None of those magical, star-exploding seconds where life felt like a movie, even for the briefest moment. It had to be like this and nor, she wouldn't change a thing. Every regret or embarrassing moment led to either a change in direction which was necessary or a new lesson that Liv could use to guide her next moment.
And Flum was right, Liv could apologise for being annoying, and weird, but never for caring and loving so much.

LOVEY

*

Meant nothing to

She absolutely knew she meant nothing to Fred. And most likely was a rebound from his long-term relationship. But nevertheless, he was the one she never liked revisiting in her mind. The others she found it easy to re-read texts and revisit memories, but with him it hurt and moreover, it hurt because she knew he didn't care or even think of her.

I think most people, if not all, have a person who we wished cared about us more than they did, do.

*

The puzzle pieces are starting to fit

It was only by chance that Liv viewed that particular Instagram story as she had promised herself, she'd stopped this detrimental habit but as she'd soon discover, it would give her all her answers.

Sketch, the restaurant.
Happy anniversary.
Wait, the beginning of September?
But hold on, what's the timeline of them?

Liv still holding her phone, she moved from Roe's Instagram to her camera roll, she scrolled back to august last year. There it was…19th of august 2021, in his bed. In his bed telling her they would always find their way back to each other. Last year, when Roe had come back into Liv's life, for that final season, they had been sleeping together on multiple occasions leading from July into the end of august. He sat there on that final night and made her promises about being magnets and confessing he just needed time and he wanted to come back together… *Wait, so all that time, he was with her? He had already met her? Was her boyfriend? Had cheated on her, so many times,*

LOVEY

with me? Was she the girl he was secretive of the night and next morning of the Euro Finals? Liv had been convinced Roe had met Mollie two months after their last encounter. So now he's truly, just a through and through, *a cheater.*

Let's replay something now, knowing what we know, let's re-live that last conversation.
"I wish I could read your mind."
"You basically can," Roe said quietly, hanging his head, standing in his bedroom in Clapham. "…You know me better than anyone." he added.
"I hate this Roe." Liv's quiet voice escaping her lips.
"I need time," He said softly, then paused.
"We want very similar things in life, and maybe we'll find our way back to each other, give me a year or two." he proceeded to promise. He continued… "I'll be twenty-six, twenty-seven, and thinking about settling down…"
"I know you're my person and I have to live with that." Liv confronting him, finally, with her heart.
A few silent moments past.
"Can I get a year in writing?" Liv quietly joked as they both exhaled with a small amount of laughter.
"I'll see you in a year." he added as final word.
Her eyes beamed a little and but then came back down as she knew she had to live a whole year without him.

*

The night before, cuddled up in bed, like they were no stranger too, and Liv in the only place she felt like she belonged, Roe's arms.
"We're like magnets." Roe protested trying to comfort her.
"We'll always come back."
"But if magnets are pulled too far apart, they won't come back." Liv added a rebuttal whilst nuzzled into his chest, slow, silent tears falling from your chocolate brown eyes.

LOVEY

"Ok, then we're like water, it's evaporates into the sky, goes away for a while and rains back down." Roe finding another one of his incredibly random analogies.
"But what if you rain back down in someone else's sea!" Liv met with worry.
He laughed softly and hugged her tightly into his chest.
"Please don't say all this if you don't mean it, just too…"
"… make you feel better." Roe finishing her sentence.
"I'm not," he continued, "I think we will find our way back."

Why Roe, why? I asked you, pleaded you, to not say it unless you meant it. Did you mean it? Did you not want to fully let me go? Did you still love me?

She remained silent for a minute.
"Even after everything? You think? Even after the…"
Liv paused for a moment. This entire time she had never said the word. She had said assault, or incident but she could never say…
"… after the rape. I was raped." she repeated almost more back to herself than him.
He looked at her, she could visibly see his heart break in his widening pupils. He couldn't say it either. He remained silent.
"I haven't said that out loud yet" she added quietly, still sitting more in front of him now, in his bed with red wine sitting on the bedside tables.
"I know you haven't." matching her quiet volume.
"Look, we'll figure it out." his more determined tone taking over.
"I can't right now, I think we have to live our own lives for a bit."

You can't right now because you have a girlfriend. Why were you planning our future and in turn, your new relationship's break up.

"Can we skip this bit? She said softly with heartbreak running through her voice.
"What, like a year? Roe asked.
"Yes." she replied, knowing what he'd say next.

LOVEY

"It doesn't work like that." he said sadly.

She knew this.

*

Reliving that morning

In the morning they knew it would be their last. He kept her close the entire time. When he started to work he moved his laptop over to her so she could sit with him, one leg over his. She put her face and rested it on the back of his neck, letting out a small cry at any moment of thinking that this was finally, *really, it.* He squeezed her tightly and moved her more over onto his lap. He later moved tummy down on his bed, taking a break from work to watch the Youtuber they both liked. He tucked her under his arm as she looked up at his with tears in her eyes. Besides the affection, he remained seemingly untouched by the impending goodbye.
"Why don't you care?" Liv annoyed the next day as she cried knowing she'd be leaving soon, to never return to that bedroom situated in Clapham North, ever again.
"Look if I think about it, I'll cry. So, I'm not going to. Trust me, this will hit me at 2 am on a random Wednesday."
"You'll be like Zimba." he said pulling the face Liv knew he had when he was trying not to cry.
"You'll be something I don't think about. Something I can't think about."
A few moments past, Roe wanted to do his best by breaking the silence with something slightly unrelated but light-hearted, she chuckled at his effort.
"Look see I can still make you laugh." he said quietly proud
"You'll always be able to make me laugh." Liv's comment adding to the tension that was pulsing around the room, both knowing how there was so much between them and knowing it was all about to be forgotten.

LOVEY

She knew Roe did he best to suppress how he felt but unfortunately, he wouldn't always be able to escape. This brought her no joy.
"You'll never see me again!"
"...How are you okay with that?" her voice began to quieten mid-sentence. He stood staring at her while being cemented to the carpet situated by his windows, the bed separating them. Suddenly, his feet became unglued from the floor, he walked over from across the room and was now mounted in front of her. He waited for less than a second and embraced her deeply. Hugging her so tight she could almost feel everything he couldn't bear to say. They did always have a power of communicating without having to say a word. She always felt she could read his mind like a book. Locked in their embrace, they both lowered themselves on the bed next to each other, sat looking intensely into each other's' eyes, then each other's lips, their faces yearned closer, they lingered over each other's lips for longer than you'd expect without touching, waiting for the other to make the last move. The moment was palpable. Then, almost simultaneously, they both met each other's lips with nothing but love, passion and heartbreak. Confusion cast into the air like a fog, but it also felt incredibly right. She said goodbye. She walked out his front door. She looked back once down the road and up into his bedroom. She dragged herself away from him for the last time. She cried all the way home.

Why Roe? I thought you were a good one. The image of you is ruined.

Isn't it all so different now?
Knowing what we know now?

LOVEY

*

Oh, no, so NOW she's done

Liv: This will be the last thing you will hear from me. Then I want you to totally forget I ever existed.

Okay I get it now. I couldn't for the longest time, work out why we didn't end up together and I now finally know.

I was never meant to end up with someone like you, an actual cheater. I mean too much. Worked too hard to be with someone like you. You have completely changed in my eyes.

As your anniversary is now, that means you cheated when we last saw each other last year and probably all the times after the assault. When you sat in bed and told me you just needed time and you wanted us to find our way back. "We're like magnets", and stupid water analogies but all with sentiments of it being us and you needing to figure things out, "I'll see you in a year".

After everything you have ever done, I have seen your biggest flaws, the worst sides of you and I've forgiven you, not only that but loved you, in spite of them all. And not because I lacked self-respect because I have an abundance of it now but because I truly believed you were a good guy, under it all and all you needed was someone to understand your mind and heart. I treated you with kindness and love, always

I actually thought I knew you. Better than anyone. I thought you were the sweetest soul and that regardless, I'd always love you, even from a far but I was wrong. I have no idea who you were or are.

As a heads up, it's in the book. It's all in the book because this is the moment, I need to put me before you, for the first time since we've known each other.

LOVEY

> Yes, you probably didn't need this message but again, I sent it for me. Finally, I'm done with you. And it's sad all our good bits are overshadowed now.

He read her WhatsApp message nine minutes after sending the text.

She never heard from Roe again.

*

Was any of it real?

Liv went over every detail, big and fleeting. Moment after moment her stomach would drop. So many times, she had been sure he had done something, but Roe was so amazing at making you believe his soul. He had a truly innocent demeanour. He was sweet, soft, goofy, quiet depending on who he was with, the exact opposite of what you'd expect from a cheater. Someone who found themselves only thinking of their selfish desires when tested. He was perfect till universe challenged him and let me tell you, he'll pick him, *every time*.

*

Istanbul

Girls know. Girls just know. They get a feeling. A sense. This was the first time Roe cheated on Liv. It was a month into their relationship, and it started with a lad's holiday to Istanbul.

He called every night, every night but one. She tried to think little of it, and she would rather be in denial than face whatever truth she'd find. Nannie always said, *'If you go looking for trouble, you'll find it'*. They had an argument after he was back over something unrelated and trivial. Whilst in the middle of the working day, she checked his Instagram following. It had gone up by one. Then an hour or so later, his followers also increased by one. This is back when Instagram followers were in order of most recent. She confronted him over the girl. After inspection, she lived in Istanbul,

LOVEY

where he had just been and didn't follow any of the other boys he went with, *only him.* She felt sick. She could have been sick. He made up lies of how it was the girl one of his mates got with.
"So why did you follow her?" a logical question from Liv and adding, "even the guy you say she got with, didn't."
"She followed me." Another lie as she knew he followed her first. He never, to this day, admitted what he did but look at his track record, his lies. He was truly obsessed with Liv and still, his ego, insecurity, complexity he has deep down, cannot be beaten by his love for others.

She pretended, even to herself, she didn't know he was lying, and they both moved on.

*

I just want to come home and cuddle you

After a night out in Guildford, he rang Liv incredibly drunk and very upset. He had gone out with one of his closest friends, who was known for cheating on his girlfriend.
"Ryan was trying to get me to chat with him to some girls" he slurred.
"I don't even know what's happening right now." Roe leaving a voicemail incredibly upset after Liv had stopped answering.
"I just want to come home and cuddle you." he preceded to plead.
This is guilt.
Being upset.
Scared he'll lose her if she knew.
So easy to spot once you know.
Guilt seeped through his pores.

…but Liv believed him, *always.* Every time till she couldn't. Till he gave her chlamydia because he had put his dick in another girl. Who knows how many. He had always prided himself on being different

LOVEY

to his mates. Would never do that to Liv. But he did and could continue to.

*

Elijah, you were right

Elijah was right. He had always been puzzled which quickly led to frustration over why she still saw Roe as a misunderstood angel rather than a man who had repeatedly shown no love or respect and hurt her to no end, knowing she'd never do the same. Liv was always incredibly protective of Roe. Shame it took a year to truly be released from his innocent demeanour which cursed her judgement. She felt so incredibly sad that she had wasted any moment with Elijah, thinking of Roe.

Elijah I'm sorry. I'm sorry I tried so hard to defend his character. You were right. I wish I could tell you.

Liv: You were right about everything… if only you knew

She typed out in their WhatsApp chat to which she back spaced every letter, knowing they had their time, and it was over.

*

Was her life jacket actually what was drowning her?

All this time Roe was what saved Liv. So she believed. But could it have been, he was a part of what was dragging her to the bottom of the ocean…all this time? What was holding her back. Her love for him blinded her.

She truly needed to unlove him, to love herself.

Being his safe place meant she couldn't be her own

…and well, that was unacceptable.

LOVEY

If you ever wondered throughout this book or doubted if Roe ever did really love Liv, as she questioned many times, I can't explain it, but *she knew*, he did. He really did. Maybe too much but he truly loved and adored her. You may say if you love someone you wouldn't treat them in the ways we have witnessed but my stance is yes, maybe that's true, but Liv had hurt people she truly loved, so maybe Roe had too. *The way he looked at her. The way they constantly laughed together.* There were so many moments that couldn't have been fuelled by anything other than love and that's how she knew. He was complicated and selfish, *yes,* but that didn't change the fact he loved her *and always maybe would.*

After getting this far in the book, could you ever imagine a world where Liv told Roe to forget her, forget she existed, because she didn't. Once she was free from him… fully… she could finally live the life she was meant too. She would forgive him but never forget. Because forgiving doesn't mean it's okay, that you'd see them in the street and smile but instead it releases you from what they've done and sets you free. She was done trying to understand, done protecting him, putting him first when it had been so long, maybe never, since he had done the same. *He had fully lost someone truly special.* That will forever be on him, not her.

*

Hi Mollie, I'm really sorry to have to send this

It had been a month since Roe and Liv had slept together, and the spell and emotional hold Roe had created over Liv was starting to disappear. I think he honestly believed Liv would never betray his trust, loved him *too* much. He always knew he was her weak point. Little did he know who Liv had become in his absence. *Strong.* She needed to give Mollie the choice she was never given. She needed to stop doing what Roe wanted her to do, and instead, do the right thing.

LOVEY

> Liv: Hi Mollie, I'm really sorry I have to send this, but I truly think you deserve to know. Me and Roe slept together while you were in Wales about a month ago. I promise it as well was instigated by him. He told me he had viewed my story the week before and was going to message me. Also judging by your anniversary, he cheated last year with me as well. He's done the same to me in the past. I'm so sorry and if you want to talk anymore, I'm here.

Ten minutes into Liv's weekly Zoom therapy session with Sarah, Mollie replied. Mid explaining the situation to her therapist, she looked down at her phone screen which lit up beside her laptop. "She's replied."

> Mollie: Can I call you?

Sarah suggested she take the phone call and turn her mic and camera off and she'll be there for when the conversation was done. In one sense, it was perfect timing. Liv felt like she had some support, she wasn't alone.

Her heart pounding, Mollie's number lit up her phone.

Mollie began the conversation by asking what exactly had *supposedly* happened. Liv knew she had nothing to convince her of and simply began awkwardly relaying that night's events. She began to explain their interactions last summer as well, explaining the overlap she had recently discovered.
"I'm not sure what you know but something happened last summer…"
"Oh, Roe's already told me." Mollie interrupted.

What. *He told her?* She wasn't expecting her to know. He had USED the worst thing to happen to her as a justification as to why he still had saw her in that time. But it doesn't, *does it?* Justify anything.

LOVEY

Flum was the one that told Roe, yes. But he had a choice. So, again, yes, he wanted to be there for her once he knew, that's fair, but no one, including Liv, asked for what it soon became again. At this point Roe had turned the conversations from post-it notes too…

> Liv: Saturday, house party in Balham
>
> Roe: Ahh nice I think I'm out
>
> Liv: Ahh nice yeah think we're going out after
>
> Roe: Ahhh well not sure where I'm going so maybe could link up
>
> Am quite horny
>
> I think you should come up tomorrow… I'm in Crawley for work so can meet and have an evening no?
>
> Liv: Yeah sounds good
>
> Roe: I'll text you when I'm leaving work, hop on a train to London?
>
> And then I fuck you all night

Liv could guess that this would be how he deflected the blame to the girl he had recently made his girlfriend at the time. "She had been raped, I had to be there for her." But that's not how it went… *was it, Roe?* He crossed the line. She needed his help, *yes.* She needed his safety and support. But he chose to blur the lines once again after a little time had passed. He knew Liv loved him. Had never really stopped.

Why Roe? Is there nothing that's just between us anymore?

"Well, um," Liv taken back, "that really wasn't Roe's place to tell." her tone immediately becoming more protective of yourself.

LOVEY

Someone had to protect her, she thought, and she knew by this point and more, it was not, and was never, Roe.

Liv was hurt. It is the most intimate detail someone can know about her. You don't tell people. It's not your story to tell. You say, *"something not nice happened"*, or *"she was really mentally unwell and I had to be there for her"* blah blah, but you don't take anyway the most vulnerable knowledge and just give it away, like it was nothing, to your new girlfriend.
The conversation continued.
It was quite obvious early on that Liv was the enemy, not Roe.
"I've heard *a lot* about you." Mollie making sure to emphasize the 'a lot'.
Liv went silent.

What could he have possibly said? What did I ever do but love him? Make him laugh? Forgive him? Try and save him? I wasn't perfect but I tried.

…Roe, what did I ever do to you?

Coming back out of her own thoughts of what Roe could have possibly said which would had been so incredibly negative for Mollie to be able to use against her, Liv continued to explain accurate details of their encounter, their shared flat, and then explained that he had done the same to her in the past, trying to emphasise this was not out of character behaviour anymore, something Liv always believed till recently.
"If you know how it feels, why would you do it to someone else?" Mollie growing in anger.
Of course, that question was valid, and Liv knew what it felt like to be so incredibly protective of Roe. Mollie was trying her absolute hardest to spin that Liv was either lying or the reason it happened. It's so easy to believe his sweetness, she had spent three years making every excuse under the sun for him. She didn't blame Mollie.

LOVEY

"I thought because I was his first girlfriend, he would make mistakes." Liv trying to explain what he had done to her whilst also justifying why she forgave him for so much.
"That's not acceptable though." she interrupted again. Goodness, if only it was that easy, Liv thought at Mollie's cut and dry approach to Liv's love.

After an emotional phone call between the two girls which Roe had successfully broken both their hearts, upon request, Liv explained their flat they shared, the bedroom, where the kitchen was, *it was awful*. Liv sent through the screenshots from summer last year which proved Roe had cheated at the beginning as well, the last message Liv had sent Roe and pictures of sexting, proof that Roe had on multiple occasions, betrayed Mollie, actually, both on them.
After Mollie received the evidence, she sent Liv a final message.

> Mollie: I hope you realise what your actions have done, you've literally ruined my life – now please stay out of it.

> Liv: I take full responsibility for my part. I hope you realise at some point it was Roe that ruined your life, his actions

I will say, Mollie would now have just **some** of the facts and have her own decisions to make but if she watched it, play out, as if she was invisible and she could stand back and watch that night over, hear the words he said, the way he said them, how he was so incredibly aware of what he was doing and was even more determined to not let the opportunity pass… she would have gone home from work that day, packed her belongings and never spoke to him again.

Mollie was right in most of the things she said and had every reason to hate Liv. Liv wanted her to hate her. But what Liv would never be able to explain to this unfamiliar girl, would be how it feels to go through everything Liv and Roe had, all the moments, the love, heartbreak, the promises, and most importantly, every moment Roe

LOVEY

could never fully let go of her, because… *that's all she needed…* but he kept her on a string, in the background on purpose and to then see each other almost a year to the day, just like he said they would. He had a choice that day, a year ago, when he had started also seeing Mollie, he could have said "No Liv, I don't love you, we both need to move on" and finally let her go, but no, he couldn't, he has, to this day, never been able to say that to her and instead it was "We'll always come back together", "I promise I wouldn't say this if I didn't mean it", "I'll see you in a year."

After everything, all these pages you've read, I hope you see there was so much more that went into that night than Liv carelessly sleeping with someone who had promised his heart to someone else.

So much more.

*

Was it because it was me?

"It's good you're so visual Liv, I'd forget all the details." Immie said in a voice note, after Liv divulged Mollie had tried her absolute best to not believe her till intimate details proved it was indisputable.
"She needed to know… before she built a life with him, she deserves to know who he really is or who he can be."
"Liv, you absolutely, 100%, did the right thing."
"It's not my job to make sure he doesn't fuck up his relationship, that's on him."
"If it wasn't you, it would have been someone else, eventually."

Maybe Immie was right, maybe she wasn't. Did he cheat because he still couldn't fully let Liv go? *Maybe.* That was the story Liv also wanted to believe. But he did also cheat on Liv, betrayed her multiple times, gave her an STI, and they didn't matter. Those people had no meaning. So, maybe, just maybe, this is who he is… that fact *broke* Liv's heart, but also set her *free*.

LOVEY

Liv would always understand Mollie's reasoning. That moment you say to yourself 'If I forget this moment, heartbreak, betrayal, in exchange, I get the life I wanted, I get to keep my best friend'. Liv had done this with Roe many times before. You convince yourself that, time will move you both on and it was a mistake and he'll be so remorseful he'd never hurt me like that again. Unfortunately, it does not work like this. It took years to realise how truly powerful someone's actions were over their pretty, pleading, scared, words. Mollie would most likely tell herself it was Liv's fault. Roe would probably lie and tell a version of the story where Liv instigated the night, and he drunkenly went along with it. And even know it's frustrating when you feel your truth is being twisted, she didn't feel the need to convince Mollie or anyone for that matter. She could go about each day and the rest of her life, knowing exactly what truly happened, could swear on baby Bud and Flum that it did, and knowing how Roe really felt about her, and what he'd spend his life pretending doesn't exist within him. Again, the only reason Liv told Mollie was to give her a choice which was only given to her when it was too late and to prove to herself, she was completely done with Roe.

Please Roe, prove me wrong. Prove that Mollie did the right thing by staying and that I did not waste years of my life just to learn lessons from someone who I loved so much. Don't just be a painful lesson again to someone else like you were to me.

You adored it didn't you? That I held you so highly. You let me though. Even though you knew you had a devil on your shoulder.

A part of her was proud of herself because she knew, she never would have told Mollie, would have protected Roe her whole life, kept his secrets, if she had even the tiniest amount of love left for him. *It was all gone.*

LOVEY

*

In that moment

In that moment she realised something quite remarkable. He had been *him* all along. This man. He hadn't suddenly changed, or the depression didn't destroy his loyal side. Steal his sweetness. She realised for the first time all these 'out of character' actions were all *in* character and in reality, the only part that didn't align was what she had built him to be in her mind. She built him to be someone soft and safe and loyal and she used little pieces of his personality to convince herself she was right. Used his best moments as evidence. She believed he could have been that person but wasn't. He wanted to be but couldn't. Couldn't not hurt those who grew to love him most.

*

Villains

You may by now have opinions. Opinions of Liv or of the men that have touched her life. You may see these men for their flaws. But there is only one man in this story which was a villain and he remained without a name.

Yes, each one hurt her. But it is so easy to forget what is happening behind their actions. But also, yes, there is a fine line between understanding and excuses.

Liv does not want you to see them as villains in her story. They each were important in different ways. Liv is most likely a villain in Mollie's story but that's it, you'll play different roles in different people's lives. We are all the villain in someone's tale. But in others you'll be the hero, the friend, the main character in your own.

We all have an internal battle. We all make mistakes. Our feelings lead to actions. Actions maybe we are not always proud of, but we

LOVEY

do. Growing is realising life isn't black and white but every shade of grey.

We are human.

But it is how you use it to move forward and become better, and that's where the understanding stops. The excuses and understanding halts when lessons are not learnt. Habits are formed and disrespect and selfishness replaces love and loyalty.

Regardless of all,

To love Liv, you have to love Roe.
Even a tiny amount.
Because, without him,
she simply would not be here.

*

One last scenario

She imagined a last conversation. In her mind it would be one where she knocked on his door, he now shared. The door she should have never seen. She'd knock and his unexpecting face would answer. She'd stand before the door frame and hand him this book.
"I'll be the girl you'll forever think about and never stop loving." she'd say. She'd lift her hand and gently hold one side of his face.
"I know you Roe. Like you always said. Truly know you. I know the devil that lives within you but it's okay, it's okay now because I'm no longer the one he hurts."
She'd hold his eyes in her gaze then drop her soft hand from his face and turns and walks away.

He'd never see her again.

LOVEY

*

10th September 2022

A year ago today Liv was sat, cuddled up on a mattress on the floor of Elijah's living room, with bed sheets hanging from the TV to the back of the sofa, creating a den. Elijah lit candles and they snuggled into each other to an episode of Black Mirror, one of Liv's favourites. Now, sat on a train platform, she reflected on how much had truly changed in one year and if only she had known what laid ahead. Liv was lucky, she was never plagued with thoughts of regret, she truly believed things happened how they were meant to. Even though it was hard seeing the Instagram stories of *'a year ago today'* of her new relationship with Elijah and how happy she was at that time, she wouldn't go back, she liked her present and for the first time in a while, she stopped looking back at the people who had been in her life and instead started looking forward to who she was yet to meet. There will be a day where, without expecting it, she'll meet someone, and it will be the beginning of something.

LOVEY

Chapter Seventeen

I know it's a cliché, but I can't tell you how much Liv had changed over this year. As you've seen, we have journeyed back further than just a year ago to the rape, whilst also witnessing other key moments which had their influence. But mostly we have stayed with the grips of summer 2021 too summer 2022. What made Roe so special was, for so long, he made the terribleness worth it. Just because it led to him. It always gave her a sense of peace, she searched so hard for. She felt normal with him, like she didn't have to be that broken person she decided her past made her to be.

But she had finally found that feeling again… but this time, for the first time, it was from herself. She was okay, maybe even glad in a dark beautiful way, that all of it happened. The assault. Roe and his betrayal. Being with Elijah. Meeting Fred. Because it got her here, and here is really fucking good.

Maybe I was better for it all.

I'd like to reassure you, the reader of something. She was finally okay. Liv would redo Edinburgh. She booked a solo trip for the

LOVEY

week running up to Christmas 2022. Being able to revisit the Christmassy magic. She would go to Paris for her birthday at the end of January 2023 with Flimmie.

This year was the hardest yet most defining of her life. And she had finally come out of it, being someone, *she had only dreamed of being.* Of course, she would have loved for Nannie to be here, to talk to her, see her, show her everything she had done, achieved. But she carried her with her, *always.*

The darkness wasn't so cold anymore.

She became content. She no longer felt the desperate need to escape to Australia. She needed plans and deadlines to tug her through times that felt the present needed to be worth a future, but she no longer yearned as her present was now a comfortable place to be.

Her mind now, who she is, how she thinks, how truly strong she feels, how she sincerely makes decisions for her, it felt like a blessing. Maybe Flannie Puff was looking down, holding baby Bud as she wriggled, being so incredibly proud.

LOVEY

Her mind was finally stronger
than her feelings.

LOVEY

Life had tested her, over and over and she had won, she was starting to win. It was overwhelming. She felt she was growing up. No longer at the mercy of life and her mind.

You have suffered enough

                                              It is time you finally won

LOVEY

1. The universe truly, wholeheartedly,
   works in the most weird, wonderful,
   purposeful, magical way… even in the
   moments you think nothing is happening…
   everything is happening, you just can't see it,
   but you will.

   I promise.

Nothing is chance and life is working it out for *you*.

LOVEY

2. Timing is *everything*.

LOVEY

3. One day, you'll be so glad
   you didn't end up with what
   you yearned so deeply
   to have.

I promise.

LOVEY

4. The things you're scared of
   will change your whole life.

LOVEY

5. Everything is temporary,
and sometimes that fact is
really great.

LOVEY

6. Forgiving doesn't mean it's okay
what happened, but it does mean permission to

let go.

LOVEY

7. There will be people, people you feel so naturally, magnetically drawn too and you'll sense with every fibre of your body, that their meant to play a powerful part in your life and you'll probably be right, but it sometimes powerful doesn't mean lasting.
But once you realise this fact,

Let.
    Them.
        Leave.

            Or even better…

                You.
                  Leave.
                    First.

LOVEY

8. I keep a battered small corner of paper
in the back of my phone case, it is the thing I live by,
and it has freed me…

You can't mess up something that is meant for *you.*

LOVEY

9. It's okay to be hurting as much as you are.

It won't always be this way.

One day it will feel better

and you will look back

at how it was always

meant to be

this way

LOVEY

10. No one cares – in the best way.

Just do what makes you happy.

LOVEY

11. Thoughts are not facts

LOVEY

12. Choose people who choose you

LOVEY

13. *Stay soft*

Try to not let the hard ways the world can work steal the softness you hold within you.

LOVEY

14. You will always be able to feel when it is time to start a new chapter,

                      all you have to do is

                                          listen.

LOVEY

15. you need not worry. your people will find you. if you are meant, you'll find a way, maybe even a way back, if you have once crossed paths before.

LOVEY

16. and in love, be with someone kind.

> I think there is no better feeling
> in this world than to
> care about someone,
> love someone,
> and have them
> love and care for you too.

LOVEY

It's interesting losing someone you loved so intensely. You always hold out a tiny piece of hope they'll come back. Even though a part of you may hate them, love them, miss them, wouldn't ever be with them again, would take them back in a heartbeat and all these emotions exist in the same moment, and fully letting go feels like the ultimate loss, *what if you're meant to be?* You'll think.

>...But you're actually *free. You're finally free.*

>Remember, you can't mess up something that is meant for you.

>I promise the universe will reward you for choosing you.

I'd rather be alone, than be any less than I deserve

LOVEY

*

She stayed

You might wonder what Mollie did after Liv told her what her boyfriend had done. Judging by Instagram they stayed together. We of course do not know what goes on behind closest doors, but they remained together. Liv felt relieved. She knew Mollie was never going to leave Roe. She was older than Liv and Roe and had in her mind just started to build a life with him. She had forgiven him, made excuses for him so she knew Mollie would too. The most important thing for Liv was to give her a **choice** that she was never given so the rest was up to her. She no longer wanted to live with the feeling of '*If only she knew.*' She had now made a conscious decision to be with someone who she knew had betrayed her, at the beginning and a year into their relationship. And if he'd do it after a few of weeks of moving in together, a time you'd imagine to be happy and exciting, there would never be a time he wouldn't. But she decided to stay, and Liv truly hoped Roe would never break either of their hearts again.

LOVEY

*

I feel everything

Being a feeler can feel like a curse. I'd define a feeler maybe similar to an empath. You feel *everything*. Good and bad but times a million. Your stomach will drop. Your heart will pound. It's easy to hate this trait, feeling so deeply as it can easily make you feel different, *out of sync with others*. Why do I care more? You'll ask yourself. Why do I love deeper? Feel sadder? Fall harder?

…But it means you *feel*. It connects you to the world in a way others will never get to experience. Whilst they stroll upon the surface, living their ordinary life, feeling ordinary things, you'll glow, you'll cry, you will create magic. Because that's what the good moments feel like, *they feel like magic,* and that, well that creates a life of meaning that you should never want to throw away.

LOVEY

*

What if I asked you?

What if I asked you… would you take back the hardest moments of your life?

> So they never happened.

Take a moment to think of what that would really mean

Had a minute?

Okay, I believe most wouldn't. Not really. Because it is those precise moments that have made you who you are. They define us. Not just those moments but everything we do after. It teaches us lessons we need. Makes us feel things we needed to feel.

What happens **to** us… doesn't define us.

> …but what we decide to do with it, does.

LOVEY

*

The ways we're bound by our spirit

No two souls find each other by accident.

I did a lot of reading of *'Twin flames'* as I often felt Roe and I were bonded a way that was deeper, more meaningful than what could be easily described. I felt it when we met. I learnt the many different ways we commonly speak of different connections, finding three to be the main.

The twin flames

Some say twin flames share the same soul. Others say they share the same energy frequency. I like to believe our souls are all our own but energy, *yes*. The connection you feel is beyond any other. It is filled with ways you are the same. It's all the parts about yourself suddenly being in front of you in the form of another being. This connection is viewed as the most intense. They are seen to be the catalyst to immense spiritual growth which mirror your deepest desires and fears. They show you the best and worst parts of you.

They say that down the line of this type of connection there is a 'spiritual awakening'. This is in the form of a period of separation. During this period, it is said there is a *'chaser'* and a *'runner'*. Then once parties have gone through this process there is often a reunion. But it is what the two souls do in this time that is important. If one undergoes tremendous growth and other does not, it will not work.

They say you don't always end up with your twin flame. Sometimes you aren't better together.

LOVEY

Soul mates

Ah, soul mates… you feel you've known this person before. They feel familiar. Like home, almost instantly. If you're lucky, they are often the ones you share a life with. They teach you what it means to love yourself and not just another being. Soulmates can come in many forms but in the romantic sense they are believed to be your perfect fit. I don't believe you are not *whole* without the elusive soul mate we are told to find but I do believe there is a special type of feeling, magic, that belongs between two people that cannot be replicated.

And a **Karmic partner**

Now this is the one I knew of the least. Karmic relationships are known to not be easy. They are believed to be there to teach you something you are yet to learn. They say with a karmic partner that it presents as an all-consuming passion but is difficult to keep. Many say these connections are turbulent, filled with passionate arguments, red flags, you fall extremely quickly, you feel co-dependent, and there is, all in all, a lot of drama. These connections are looked at and believed to be the ones to teach you valuable lessons.

I truly believed Roe was my twin flame. I thought what we found was something *real.* The type of love you search for. Twin flame was the only way I could describe the feeling of our bond and the way we always found our way back to one another. This or soul mate. If it wasn't for the ways the universe parted us I would have called him a soul mate. Maybe he was… and maybe we simply weren't destined to end up with one another.

> I view us a little differently than that now.

LOVEY

Being his first love battered me
but it also gave the rest of my life meaning

he'd forever think of her
always wonder what life would have been,
if only he had chosen her
if he had been brave enough to become the man she deserved
but he knew,
he knew he couldn't,
become the man she deserved,
so, he left, said goodbye,
lovingly released the girl he knew no one would compare too
he would one day,
regret loosening his grip of her heart

LOVEY

why was i not enough?

lovely, just because he chose someone that was not you
does not mean he loves them more
sometimes,
they rather pick easy,
someone who requires less of them

roe knew liv required him to be a better,
a stronger man
stronger than he was prepared to become
so he decided to find less so, he could, in turn,
remain less

I know you loved him
more than you wanted to breathe sometimes
but life,
the universe,
gave you hell
so you could later
walk through heaven

LOVEY

*

There will be people in your life that will change everything

Sat in a pub in Clapham on a Sunday not long before this book had to be finished. She looked across at her two beautiful friends. Liv took a moment as she watched her two friends laugh with one another in the heat of a funny remark. She realised something. She was *home.* She had searched high and low for that feeling. She tried to find it within her family, only having it with Flum and Flannie, she tried to find it in men who never treated her with the love she gave and now she realised she had become good at finding it within small moments with the ones she loved. And that meant she had found it within herself.

Georgie once said something interesting but in the most ordinary way. Just as it was a passing comment to her, it was the biggest compliment to Liv.
"There's people you meet that you think, they *would* have been great had they not had bad things happen to them, but you're not, you're amazing *because of it*, and that makes you incredible."
Liv looked at her and thought how many times she'd been terrified she'd end up one of those people who were broken before they could even begin. She smiled across the table at her best friend who had no idea how much of what she had just said, had meant to her.

I truly believe we meet those who we are meant too, along our way. Emily and Georgie were those people. They were the effortless type of love that felt like fate. Liv had met both through her work, but they quickly became the closest people in Liv's life, as well as her other friends she was blessed to have. They became family.

Sometimes, the people who are your *family*, the people you weather the storm with, the ones who make you feel safe and seen and protect and love you. They are not always the ones linked to you by blood. For some they are, but for the ones who find family in the

LOVEY

friends they keep, my goodness, Liv's friends had taught her she was loveable and worth protecting. They knew the deepest depths of her mind and sat with her with through it all.

Sat above her desk is a picture she had printed. It says...

'I promise you can still make a beautiful life for yourself even if you lost many years of it to abuse, mental illness, or trauma'.

...she was starting to make a beautiful life for herself, despite it all.

*

Can I tell you something?

By now you know Liv very well, but she still might not know you, depending on who's reading this. I wonder about you. Who you might be? Where you are or how you've felt. Nevertheless, I'd like to tell you something regardless of who are you or what *you* think of *you*.

It has taken the hardest journey for Liv to have finally found a place in the world where she could trust herself and her mind. Where she could feel safe and powerful whilst also remaining soft and warm, but a lot of the way it has felt easy to slip back into a place of self-destruction, a place where that little voice, who knows all your weaknesses and flaws likes to sit on your shoulder and whisper the ways you aren't good enough.

LOVEY

So, I'd like to tell you something, the same thing I'd tell Liv.

What if I said you aren't too far gone?

>You *are* a good person
>You *are* deserving of love
>You *are* not broken
>You *are* not a burden
>You *are* beautifully irreplaceable

LOVEY

Chapter Eighteen

It is time to end but there are a few last words that must be said. A letter to each of those who meant the most... *a final word.*

Dear *Fred*,

I am so grateful we met. You probably have no idea how big your impact was. I think it surprised us both how easily we fell into each other's personalities. You made me laugh, *a lot*, and I did you. You made me feel like the person I used to be, the person I liked, before anything bad had happened. You were my Yellow by Coldplay, that or, First Class by Jack Harlow, for the fact you loved that song. The invisible cage that had been built by another person last summer, didn't exist with you. You had the key, just by being you and I knew you were special from the moment we met.

Our fate was not to fall in love and share any more than a brief couple of months together but thank you for showing me I wasn't broken, *am* not broken and I can be who I used to be and maybe *more*.

LOVEY

So, *Fred*, you were brief but your presence in my life was powerful and nothing short of what I needed, to finally piece myself back together.

Liv x

*

Dear my *Prince, Slug, Elijah*,

I want to start my letter to you with an apology. I met you one week after saying goodbye to Roe and so soon after the rape. I had no idea who I was, what anything meant anymore and how to love again. I'm sorry I didn't appreciate the big and small moments that you tried to fill with love for me, because yes, we both made mistakes, both did things we probably regret but I'll always be sorry there was a cloud over you that only lifted months after our breakup. I can now finally see you, see the moments I couldn't before. My days in Camden cuddled on the sofa or sitting on the kitchen top with red wine in both our hands as I watched you cook our dinner, listening to music and laughing together, *it was a dream.* You gave me a place to heal, to be protected. You fully gave yourself to me, and you loved me when I was truly unlovable and for that, I thank you. I remember you once said, *"I love you for who you are now, not who you once were or could be."* It breaks my heart to think of this because, only someone truly special could have loved me through that time. I did it though. I finally found my way back to the person I promised I'd be again. I know you'd be so proud of me. I know I loved you and I tried so hard, but I think I couldn't love you how you deserved while I was healing from so much, I'm sorry this message comes so late.

I'm sorry we had the entire world working against us… I wish we had met at a time like now where I'm softer and more healed because I believe so much could have been different, but we met when we were meant too and I'm grateful for everything we were. The lessons we learnt and the small perfect moments we shared. We

LOVEY

had so much, you and me. That's why we held on like we did, even in the toughest times. But life has moved us both on and we had our time.

All the happiness in the world, you deserve it

p.s. no one makes me laugh like you do

Your misses, your bun girl.

*

And of course,

Dear *Roe*,

You and I were pure love. We had all the makings of a beautiful life and in another multiverse, we would have grown old together, with our children, having built a magical existence with one another, having travelled, and experienced all life's milestones. We had the laughs, love, and everything in-between. We taught one another so much and unfortunately that involved pain too, however, *you saved me*, and *I saved you*. We were both bright beaming lights which drew us out our darkness.

I thought for the longest time you were the one, I now know, you were *'one of the ones'*, but not *'The One'* because, you would have picked me. You would have shouted my name from outside my window. You would have rode down to Brighton on your motorbike and told me you couldn't and wouldn't live without me. You would have never let me leave that day, and I know you fought so hard for us, so many times, but you never stop for the one you love, and that's how I know. I'm glad I finally found a way to leave you in the past like a beautiful sunset I once saw but disappeared into the horizon, nevertheless. Your happiness will always be mine.

LOVEY

…you'll always feel a little like *home* to me.

So, *bub, floe, my life jacket, the reason I've not floated up to heaven so many times,* thank you for giving me millions of beautiful memories that only you and I will know and get to relive in our minds.

Be brave and go have the best life.

All my love, *always*,

Your bubba bear, lil sausage, ride or die, Liv

> Now, this would have been my letter to Roe,
> had the spell not been broken,
> done everything he has done.

So, this is now my last word…

Dear Roe,

Did I ever really know you? Do you know you? Do you know how you find the ability to hurt those who, you know, with every fibre of their being, would never do the same to you. I'm sorry by the end I truly didn't recognise the boy I fell in love with, all those years ago, I'm sorry it took so long to have no love or care left for you.

If I don't know who you are, does anyone?

I haven't loved anyone like you, before or since. But I think that's a good thing. I think you get one person you love so much you let them destroy you, your good nature, your heart that is only yearning for love, all just one time. You were that. I lost everything loving you.

LOVEY

But that won't mean who I do fall in love with, in the future, I love less, I'll love them in a new way, where they let me love myself as well as them. I couldn't love myself when I loved you. Because if I had, I would never have stayed, never had taken you back all those times, never tolerated the ways we both know you let me down, in fact, our relationship would have probably never existed. But it did. And now I finally know what it means to love myself, more than I love you.

I'm sorry I couldn't protect you any longer, from your own worst flaws. For the longest time I thought I could save you, save you from yourself, by the sheer amount that I loved you. Maybe I have, not in the way I always believed I would but in telling your girlfriend what you had done, capable of, you now, for the first time, maybe had to face real, physical consequences of your actions. I always wanted to protect you because I believed you deserved it, I now am free and realise you don't, and haven't in a really long time. I spent so long being scared of the mental weakness I knew you had. The people who love you need you to be better. I hope you figure out the insecurity, complexity, of your mind before you hurt any more good people.

It will always be a shame that our relationship, your first love, turned into being nothing to me. *Nothing but a painful lesson.* I will probably carry you with me *always*. But not in the way I always thought I would. Now, you'll be a symbol to remind myself if I can love you like I did, lose you like I did, be hurt by you like I was, and say goodbye to you like I have and love myself more than you, I can truly do *anything*.

It's funny Roe,
the end of us,
the *true* end of us,
was the beginning of me.

LOVEY

Regards,

Liv

*

And finally,

A letter to Liv, *Myself,*

I know this year and beyond has been the hardest. I know you've not wanted to exist and felt as though you were looking at a stranger when looking in the mirror. I know you have wanted to crawl out of your body as it hasn't felt like your own and someone else lived inside. I know there are things and moments that have happened that you are not proud of but…it got you here. You are a completely different person and in the best ways. And along the journey, you've managed to pick up and keep the best parts that had previously shattered on the floor. The way you love, care, your humour, softness, but now, you are stronger, your world is fuller. So, there's a few things I hope for you. I hope you always love yourself more, even just 1% more than you love others. I hope you never stop being vulnerable and scared in the moments that need your bravery. I hope the people you meet in your life light up parts of you that make you glow. I hope you make all your dreams come true. And… I hope you find that love, the one you've dreamt about.

Please remember, this was all *you.*

No one else, you did it. You pieced yourself back together. Yes, people helped, certain players had their part, but you picked yourself up off your bedroom floor so many times whilst surrounded by means of no longer existing. *You* left that day, leaving Fred's, knowing you didn't want to but knew it was the right thing to do. *You* finally found the strength to tell Roe you deserve better and left him in the past. *You* got yourself a Neuroscience degree. *You* got

LOVEY

yourself a job you enjoy and feel good at. *You* are the one your friends and family adore.

You are the one who took the most awful moments and have turned them into this book, into nothing but strength. It takes a special person to take the worst things that happened to them in life and use them as a power, rather than the reason they sink. Because, we know, sinking is easy, drowning is comfortable but no, you refused to let that be how the story ended.

So, go create the best life possible and never let anything or anyone take anyway the sparkle you have spent so much time building.

And also, *Liv*, take your time but never ignore the fire that's in you to achieve your dreams – *Everything meaningful takes time*

Love,

The person you've spent years and tears becoming and younger you would be so proud to be.

LOVEY

*

Only a chapter

The irony is, I thought Roe was my book. I thought every chapter of my life would have him in it. I thought each dozen pages would reveal a new adventure or obstacle we'd face, but no. He was a chapter. And in fact, my life, the story of my life, has just begun only now I am equipped with so much more.

This book will act as only a chapter of my life too. As I draw to a close all that you have relived with me, I aim to leave it all here, in these pages.

One day, hopefully, when I'm older, maybe having a love and family of my own, I will sit in my cosy home, taking a moment to myself and open back up these pages and relive from such a different place.

I'll look back in how I managed, somehow, to turn pain, into purpose.

LOVEY

Chapter Nineteen

I vow to stay *soft*.
I vow to still *feel*.
I vow to be *brave*.

LOVEY

*

Flannie's magic, she's here

**The most incredible
thing happened.**

In the days leading up to this book finally being done, completed and put into print, the most miraculous, magical thing happened.

Remember when Liv lost all her voicemails from Flannie? How her previous phone provider told her they were deleted and lost in the world of tech as she switched over. Well, a few days ago Liv dropped her iPhone 8 plus she'd had since 2018. This time dropping it, not being the first, it smashed her screen and decided it was finally time for a new phone.

Upon transferring her data over and setting up her new iPhone 13, a notification popped up. Five voicemails. She clicked on the tab along from *'Recents', 'Contacts'* and *there they were.*

She instantly started crying in disbelief.

All of the voicemails, spanning back to 2015, her voice, her soft voice calling her *Lovey.*

It was the most magical sign.

She was here.

She couldn't believe it.

"It's a sign." Flum said with certainty.

…And suddenly, *by magic,* they were there. And just in time to tell you.

LOVEY

Liv took it as a sign that she was in the right place, at the right time. Doing the right thing.

Her Flannie had come back and was in fact, never far away.

Some moments feel like magic.

For the first time, in a long time, happy tears fell from her eyes.

*

I think that's where she got it from. The sheer amount Liv loved. *Cherry Perry, Flannie Puff*, always was a true hopeless romantic. It was one her favourite things, to sit and listen to Nannie's stories, about the men she'd crossed paths with, the tales of lost love, *the one that got away.* She spoke of how different they had been. How she had felt to have them and also lose them. It was quite special how she could look back so fondly, so positively, with only love in her eyes.

After she passed, Flum and Fliv took the diaries she kept. In them were lots of little notes, dates, plans and also poems. I'd like to leave one here for you, *I know she'd love me to.*

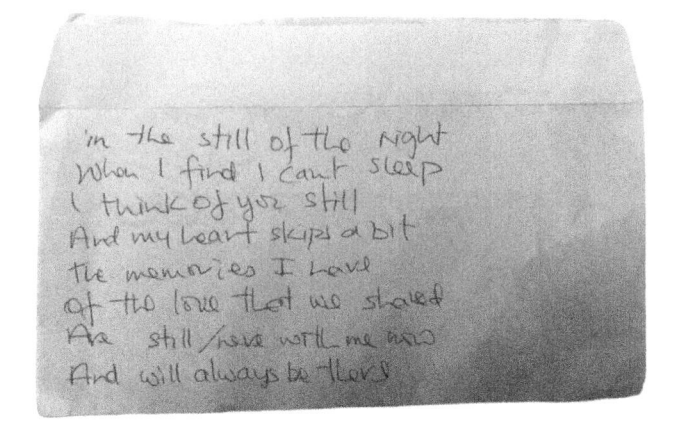

> In the still of the night
> When I find I can't sleep
> I think of you still
> And my heart skips a bit
> The memories I have
> Of the love that we shared
> Are still here with me now
> And will always be there

LOVEY

She shared her heart with Flannie Puff, that's why it was unique. The love letters she'd write, poems, the way she loved, all her. *All them.* She was also incredibly strong. Always had been. Independent. Ambitious. She had an edge which gave her the perfect balance of soft, safe, strong, resilient, and loving. She was everything Liv wanted to be. Her softness never comprised her strength.

She was special.

Flannie Puff, I love you with all I am, I miss you more than any words I could write. I know you are with me always.

LOVEY

*

A note from Flum

07/11/22

Fliv,

As you finish up the last bits of the book, I just wanted to write to you with some thoughts. I know it has all been such an emotional journey as even re-reading one of your favourite books is bittersweet, this must be such an incredibly poignant time.

I don't know where this past year has gone. In just twenty days' time it will be a year since we lost our wonderful Flannie and I know she is with us and is so proud of you. She was always a tower of strength and guiding light for us both and somehow, we have survived without her being here, our worst nightmare losing her, and look at what you have achieved. I remember when in the literal depths of despair, you rose up, MacBook in hand and started writing and writing and with your sheer strength and passion, despite all the events of this year, you never faltered, in fact, the book was your lifeline and you never let go.

This is what you must remember, you took a bad situation and turned it into something that helped save you from the darkest of times. It will always be a testament of your strength, your determination and the person who rises up from the lowest times and turns it into magnificence.

Never doubt yourself Fliv, you have the fight and drive of Flannie in your heart and you will always be fine. I'm so glad too that by the end of this book, I am happy. You need not worry about me anymore. I have been given my own second chance.

We know that in life there will always be sadness and happy times too and the spaces in between where we think about what we have lost or been through, but we will always survive with Flannie's love in our hearts.

I love you Fliv Puff, so very proud of you

Flum

LOVEY

T he Last Chapter

So, if you're reading this, Liv is now an author before turning twenty-five, a Neuroscience graduate, artist, clothing designer, sexual assault survivor, and despite it all, still a hopeless romantic that believes in love and better yet… she's only just begun.

I'll tell you a secret as to why I've kept writing. As I'm sure you can tell, it's been a bumpy ride, *a Harry Potter reference for you there,* but I have done my best to explain all the moments, big and small, the best I could.

Simply, it's been my lifeline, it's the reason. I vowed to only finish it when things got truly better, when there wasn't a happily ever after, but when life was just simply, good. Something to maybe give hope to someone who needed it, like I did, so many times. I started writing two days after the rape. Lying in bed, needing to put distance between me and it. Hence mostly being written in third person. To make sense of it. The events. How I got here. Who I was then and now. To tell you a secret, originally when I opened up a new Microsoft word document on my laptop and propped myself up enough in bed to hold it on my lap, I had full intentions of writing my goodbye note. All the reasons I couldn't bear to exist any longer. To explain how now it had become too agonizing to continue. However, instead of this document, titled 'Second-hand suicide', becoming nothing more than a few pages explaining how much pain I was in, it then slowly became the very thing that has allowed me to keep going. It became a place I'd come to process things, as they all happened. You see, there has to be a reason. A reason why this all happened. Something good has to come of it. Lynn once said after the assault, *"You'd make a great counsellor you know, for people who have suffered like you,"* she took a pause, *"you have a way about*

LOVEY

you, the way you say things, how you make others feel.". Maybe this book is that...me helping someone who needs it. That safe place. Shed the ego and be raw and vulnerable. As Nannie said when things were tough, *"Everything leads to something."* I knew what she meant by this. And I, me, me being Liv, am determined to create a reason that isn't about pain and blackness but about strength in vulnerability so maybe someone feels *something*.

You now know the deepest parts of my life and mind, I hope you'll be gentle with it and gentle with others. Gentle with the girls who have suffered. Gentle with those who have lost love. Gentle with men who are trapped in their own mind. Maybe gentle with strangers you see on the tube. I hope you're slower to judge other people. I hope I created an escape, maybe not the happy and light one I wished I could but something you could connect too, nevertheless.

LOVEY

Acknowledgments

I would like to thank *Nannie, Flannie puff, Cherry Perry*, who isn't here to see this become a reality but for always bringing the light when there seemingly wasn't any and for always making me believe in love.

I would like to thank all my therapists, Sarah, Lynn, and Tara who have had a unique yet tremendous effect on my ongoing recovery and for making the world a little more bearable in the moments I needed it most.

I would like to thank my friends, who truly know me, who know my heart, who love me, who *see* me and make me feel I'm worth protecting. Thank you for being my family.

I would like to thank *Harry,* for always, *no matter what,* being there for me. I know you'd do anything for me, and I thank you for being vulnerable in this book. Your note served to something I could never do.

I would like to thank the men who have shown me that I can feel safe, love exists, and magic is possible.

And finally, I would like to thank Flum. Thank you for being weird, wonderful, brave, my best friend, biggest supporter and for showing me life can be whatever I want it to be and to never stop being a hopeless romantic.

LOVEY

The only power I have in this world is to use what I've been through to help at least one other person – *Liv Amber Rose*

𝕷𝕬𝕽

Printed in Great Britain
by Amazon